GOVERNMENT IN THE PALMETTO STATE
Volume II
Perspectives and Issues

DISCARD

Edited by
Charlie B. Tyer
and
S. Jane Massey

Bureau of Governmental Research and Service
University of South Carolina
Columbia, South Carolina 29208

i

Aiken County Public Library

Aiken-Bamberg-Barnwell-Edgefield
Regional Library System

Copyright 1988
Bureau of Governmental Research and Service
University of South Carolina
All Rights Reserved

ISBN 0-917069-06-4

Preface

The first volume of the *Government in South Carolina Series* appeared in 1983 and was titled *Government in the Palmetto State*, edited by Luther F. Carter and David S. Mann. This was followed by two volumes on local government in South Carolina in 1984 edited by C. Blease Graham and myself. Next came a five module series of publications aimed at our secondary schools on the South Carolina governor, legislature, political parties and elections, city and county government. With this volume, *Government in the Palmetto State: Perspectives and Issues*, the series is complete. Altogether it has taken five years to prepare four books and five modules on South Carolina government. The intent has been to prepare materials which would be useful to college and public school classrooms, as well as to anyone interested in learning more of the governmental institutions and processes in our system of government in the Palmetto State.

The many contributors and editors of the material in the series have provided a valuable service to the people of South Carolina and deserve a special thank you. In addition, one person has over the last three years devoted a great deal of time to this project and provided invaluable assistance in assuring its completion — Ms. Pinkie Whitfield. To her a special thank you. All those involved with this effort hope that this will lead to further research and publications on South Carolina government.

June 1988

Charlie B. Tyer
Series Editor

CONTENTS

1

Government in the Palmetto State: Perspectives and Issues

S. Jane Massey and Charlie B. Tyer

Introduction

As the 1980s draw to a close and we prepare to enter a new century, it is appropriate that we pause and consider the "state of the state." South Carolina has undergone dramatic changes during this century in its economy and its governmental institutions. Indeed, someone returning to the state after a lengthy absence would find significant changes.

In 1983, the Bureau of Governmental Research and Service began an effort to document the governmental system of our state and the issues confronted by it. *Government in the Palmetto State* was published in 1983 and primarily examined the politics and institutions of state government in South Carolina. This was followed in 1984 by *Local Government in South Carolina*, a two-volume set of books that explored local government politics and institutions, as well as the significant policy issues affecting local governments. With this second volume of *Government in the Palmetto State*, the effort to document the mechanics and condition of state and local government in South Carolina is completed. This volume will explore policy issues which affect the state as a whole by focusing on issues which primarily require state action for resolution.

For the purpose of discussion, we have grouped the issues to be addressed in this volume into five categories: environmental and natural resource issues, social policy issues, public opinion and political attitudes, financial and human resource management issues, and the economy and economic devel-

S. Jane Massey is associate director for research at the Bureau of Governmental Research and Service, University of South Carolina. Charlie B. Tyer is a faculty member in the Department of Government and International Studies and former director of the Bureau of Governmental Research and Service at the University of South Carolina.

opment. These categories are merely for purposes of organization, for one will quickly see that the issues they represent overlap and interweave. Indeed, complexity is a significant feature of most of our problems today. To begin to understand these issues, we believe that it is necessary to first identify and isolate them. Then, they must be placed in the context in which they relate to other issues. It is our hope that this volume will be a starting point for consideration of these issues in that context.

Environmental and Natural Resource Issues

Issues involving our environment and the use of our natural resources have become a serious area of debate for South Carolinians in recent years. This debate has centered on questions such as how to encourage economic growth and accommodate technological change without sacrificing environmental quality; how to balance private property interests against the public interest; and how to allocate natural resources among competing interests. The issues of hazardous waste management, radioactive wastes, water policy, and coastal zone management embody these dilemma.

Kearney and Sinha write that hazardous waste management may be called the *environmental issue of the 1980s*. Millions of tons of hazardous wastes are generated in the United States each year. These wastes may threaten groundwater supplies or pose other health hazards by contributing to birth defects, blood disease and cancer. South Carolina is a major producer of hazardous wastes and is the site of one of the largest waste dumps in the United States. Thus, this issue has attracted the attention of our state legislature, governor and congressional delegation on more than one occasion. Kearney and Sinha give us an analysis of the legal issues relating to hazardous wastes and the technologies that have developed to dispose of these wastes. They also focus on what has been done in South Carolina to grapple with this problem. From their chapter, we see that issues like this are not unique to South Carolina, or even to the United States. Moreover, we find that the problem of hazardous waste is a by-product of our drive for economic development and a higher standard of living, thereby raising other concerns than just health and environmental impacts.

A related issue is that of radioactive wastes. Kearney discusses the palmetto state perspective in the following chapter. Again we find that South Carolina has played a pivotal role in nuclear waste policy in the United States as a result of the construction of the Savannah River Plant and the Chem-Nuclear facility in Barnwell for storage of low-level nuclear waste. A high percentage of the waste produced in the United States is stored in our state, a fact that has caused much concern among our political leaders. Efforts to deal with this issue have involved the U.S. Congress and other states through attempts to form interstate compacts to share the burdens and risks of managing these highly dangerous wastes. This issue is a part of much larger concerns than where such wastes will be buried, or whether they will be produced at all. Nuclear wastes are a product of our national defense, industry, health care system and many more facets of modern life that we have come to take for granted. Thus, complexity and trade-offs again seem an integral part of this issue.

Another important aspect of the environmental debate in South Carolina is how to protect and allocate out natural resources. In chapter three, Hite discusses how water policy in the state has evolved and why concerns have arisen during the past thirty years over water. Historically, South Carolina has had an abundance of water. Beginning with a drought in the 1950s, however, we began to realize that water is a resource that may be scarce at times and in some parts of the state. Hite discusses the potential adverse impacts if water policy is not taken seriously, such as groundwater contamination which in turn could force limits to be placed on coastal development. An additional concern he raises is with the fragmented manner in which water is distributed in our state and the necessity for assuring that the multitude of providers pay adequate attention to maintaining their infrastructure in order to meet the needs of tomorrow's citizens and businesses. Thus, while water is not a serious issue now, Hite identifies it as an issue which will become more important as time passes. Timely action and planning in the balance of this century can assure adequate water resources for future South Carolinians.

Another natural resource issue which has received attention only relatively recently is coastal zone management. The South Carolina coast is a major economic resource for the state, bringing in millions of dollars in tourist spending annually. With the growth of retirement communities, the coastal areas are experiencing increases in its year-round population. Pomeroy describes the coast's unique features and traces its historical development. He points out that our perceptions of the coast are changing. We are beginning to become aware of the consequences of unmanaged growth, and that the coastal region is a rich resource which cannot be replaced once depleted. As we try to balance the need for growth and jobs with our desire to maintain a natural resource, tensions will be created which will require thoughtful decisions. Government will play a large role in these decisions through permitting activities and land-use regulations. How the State handles this responsibility will be one of the major concerns in the coming century.

Social Policy Issues

While there are certainly many social policy concerns which vitally affect the lives of the citizens of South Carolina, three have been selected for discussion

3

here. They are education, indigent health care and prison overcrowding. Each of these issues has received substantial attention in the recent past and will likely continue to be important in the future.

Education is the subject of the chapter by Kearney and Peterson. They focus on the passage of the *Education Improvement Act* in 1984. This interesting perspective on this landmark legislation gives us an appreciation of the political nature of education policy and how the Riley Administration went about developing its strategy to assure the passage of this act.

Health care for people who do not qualify for government health plans (e.g., Medicaid or Medicare) and who also do not have employment based or other private insurance received a great deal of attention by the public in the 1980s. News stories of hospitals turning away uninsured patients also focused gubernatorial and legislative attention on the medically indigent. In her chapter, Massey describes who the medically indigent are and why the traditional solution of shifting the cost of their health care to paying patients is no longer adequate. South Carolina's response to the problem of medical indigence is discussed, as well as the challenges which still face the State in providing health care to those who could not otherwise afford it.

Finally, South Carolina is widely known as a state that sends a lot of its citizens to jail. In part this has been due to increasing crime rates, but this does not totally explain our high rate of incarceration. Jos and Tompkins give us an illuminating discussion of prison overcrowding in South Carolina. They describe the growth in crime, the changing public attitudes, and the consequences for corrections officials. The legislative response and the role that the courts have played in forcing this issue on the public agenda is analyzed. They conclude with a discussion of the options and choices we face. Should trends continue, this issue too will be with us in the new century.

Political Attitudes

While issue areas like hazardous wastes or indigent care may not have been salient public policy issues until relatively recently, political attitudes have been a constant environmental variable of governmental activity. In his chapter, Maggiotto discusses the changing nature of South Carolinians' political attitudes in the context of the south generally and South Carolina specifically. Using the results of several statewide polls, he reviews public opinion on such issues as education, crime and punishment, the economy, social welfare and moral issues. Finally, he discusses the changing nature of partisan identification in South Carolina and documents an unmistakable trend toward the Republican party. While the state may not be categorized as a strong Republican state, he argues that two party competition is emerging as a regular part of political life in South Carolina. Thus, in terms of politics, the state certainly does not resemble itself at the turn of the century.

4

Moreover, the changed nature of political competition may condition the way we respond to issues in the future, such as those discussed in this volume. Hence, the attitudes of our citizens are important to our understanding of the challenges and promises of the future.

Financial and Human Resource Management Issues

One of the most important changes which has occurred in South Carolina this century is the creation and institutionalization of its executive branch of government. Yet, this has occurred outside of the public consciousness so that very few citizens are aware of this development.

The executive power in South Carolina state government is split between the governor and an entity called the Budget and Control Board. While most citizens might think the governor is the chief executive of the state, that is true in title only. The real center of executive power in South Carolina is the Budget and Control Board. Graham, in his chapter on the evolving executive in South Carolina, describes the evolution of the Board and how it came to its present form. The existence of this board makes South Carolina unique among the other states, and makes our governmental system much more difficult to understand. Yet, this unusual system shows signs of enduring and perhaps becoming even stronger. Thus, we have created a new institution for the citizens of the next century to use to confront the issues of the 21st century.

One facet of the Budget and Control Board's primary duties is budget preparation. Budgeting has received a great deal of attention during this century as a result of several study commissions or groups. Grose describes the evolution of budgeting in South Carolina and efforts to modernize the state budget. This discussion helps us see how the Budget and Control Board operates and also how change has occurred in one policy arena: public budgeting.

Another important facet of the Budget and Control Board's responsibilities is personnel management. Hays and Thomas describe for us efforts to modernize the work force of the state. We see how great strides have been made during the previous decades to upgrade the administrative structure and policies of state government. Again, this has occurred under the rubric of the Budget and Control Board. With this structure, state agencies will confront the problems and issues discussed here.

The Economy and Economic Development

The final section of this volume contains three chapters that focus on our economy and economic development. The economic health and future of our state is closely tied to the social issues discussed in this volume. Economic

5

development is also at the heart of the controversy surrounding the environmental issues described earlier. Thus, this section on the state's economy includes many elements touched on in earlier chapters.

Ellson's chapter begins this discussion of the state's economy by tracing the way our state's economy has changed this century. From agricultural and textile dominance, we have moved to a manufacturing and service economy. Some feel that we are in the midst of another economic transition. Ellson's discussion helps us understand where we have come from, where we are, and where we may be headed. It also points up some fundamental challenges we will face in the future. One of these is the growing discrepancy between regions of the state. The gap between the prospering, primarily urban, areas of the state and the static, primarily rural, areas will complicate other concerns such as education, natural resource policy, and health care.

The problem of rural South Carolina is given closer attention in a chapter by Henry and McMullin. In this chapter, the rural counties of the state are analyzed as three distinct areas which share some problems but which also have unique characteristics. Henry and McMullin describe the characteristics of these rural areas and present some recommendation for state action to facilitate rural economic growth.

The final chapter by Birch deals with the growth and development of our state and the implications of that growth. In this chapter, several of the factors which influence growth are described. Many of the issues treated in the earlier chapters resurface here. Birch's chapter provides a good illustration of the interrelated nature of the many issues facing the state in the next century.

It is our hope that after reading this second volume of *Government in the Palmetto State*, the reader will have a greater appreciation of the complexity of the problems facing the state. At the same time, we believe that each of the authors helps to demonstrate that none of these problems are insurmountable. The challenge for the State and its people as we enter a new century is to confront these issues and build on them for a better South Carolina.

2

South Carolina and Hazardous Waste Policy: Managing Toxic Substances from Cradle to Grave

Richard C. Kearney and Chandan Sinha

Introduction

Hazardous waste management has been called "the environmental issue of the eighties" for good reason. The U. S. Office of Technology Assessment estimates that in the U. S. alone some 275 million metric tons of hazardous wastes are being generated each year. This is a conservative figure that includes only those hazardous wastes that are subject to federal and state regulation. According to the U. S. Environmental Protection Agency (EPA), at least 80,263 hazardous waste sites in this country have contaminated surface impoundments; ninety percent of them pose a risk of contaminating the groundwater. Once groundwater is breached by toxic materials, it takes centuries to clean itself out sufficiently so that it can be safely consumed by human beings.

The future costs of coping with the hazardous waste problem are astronomical. The Office of Technology Assessment in 1985 estimated a total cleanup price, just for sites that are presently identified, of approximately $100 billion. It is expected that annual hazardous waste cleanup costs may rise to $12 billion per year by 1990 as a mere fraction of known, uncontrolled sites are treated. Meanwhile, from 100,000 to 250,000 road and rail shipments per day threaten the health and safety of hundreds of thousands of citizens.

Richard C. Kearney is an associate professor in the Department of Government and International Studies at the University of South Carolina. Chandan Sinha is a 1987 graduate of the Master's in Public Administration Program at the University of South Carolina. He is presently pursuing graduate studies in political science in Delhi, India.

Although limited data exist regarding the short and long term human health and environmental effects of exposure to hazardous wastes, more than 200 types have been found to cause concern; many more are suspected carcinogens. They may also contribute to birth defects, blood disease, and respiratory problems. Hazardous wastes are literally everywhere. They are found in the obvious locations like solid waste landfills and hazardous waste dump sites. They are present in mines, industry, waste dump sites and in the form of chemical residues in agricultural fields. And they lurk in our homes, schools, automobiles, and places of work (See Figures 1 and 2).

Figure 1
Sources of Hazardous Waste in the United States

Chemicals and Allied Products	71%
Transportation Equipment	10%
Primary Metals, Petroleum, Refining, Fabricated Metals	8%
Machinery	7%
Electrical, Gas, Sanitary Services and Others	4%

Source: U. S. Office of Technology Assessment

Figure 2
Examples of Toxic Chemicals Found In and Around the Home

Paneling and Insulation (Formaldehyde)	Medicine
Ammonia-based Cleaners	Floor Wax
Spot Removers	Furniture Polish
Drain Cleaners	Old Paint
Wood Preservatives	Paint Thinner
Antifreeze	Gasoline
Car Wax and Polish	Rust Preventive
Swimming Pool Chemicals	Weed Killers

There are four kinds of hazardous wastes: ignitable, corrosive, reactive, and toxic. Ignitable wastes are those that burn readily and cause fires and the spread of toxic particles. Corrosive substances destroy living tissue on contact and even decay metals. Special containers are required for their storage. Reactive materials react spontaneously with air or water creating heat or poisonous gas. Toxic wastes are those that if ingested, absorbed or inhaled by humans or animals can cause substantial and irreparable damage to their health.

What the federal, state, and local governments decide to do about this seemingly overwhelming problem represents a true test of the mettle of elected officials and public servants. It also represents a challenge to all firms and citizens, who must take responsibility for the hazardous wastes that they produce and utilize. If the challenge is not met successfully, the result could be the despoilment and poisoning of our beautiful and productive land and water resources.

This chapter will examine the policy environment of hazardous waste management, including the legal setting and treatment technologies. Then we shall explore the hazardous waste problem in South Carolina. We shall see that despite considerable progress during the past several years, much remains to be done if our children are to live in a safe and healthy world.

The Policy Environment

Hazardous wastes are the byproducts of industrial production. As they accumulate, they must be disposed of or made harmless through some sort of treatment. Until about 1970, the storage, treatment, and disposal of hazardous waste was not regulated by government. Producers did as they saw fit. Some disposed of waste on-site in lagoons, ponds, or burial pits. Others paid to have their wastes hauled away to solid waste landfills or similar facilities. Not uncommonly, storage and disposal practices were careless and unsafe. The potential danger to health and safety was dramatically brought to the attention of the American public by incidents such as Love Canal, where a Niagara Falls, New York, community was dissolved in the 1970s through evacuation of over 200 families who were threatened by dozens of dangerous chemicals seeping into nearby surface water, school property, and basements. In 1978, President Jimmy Carter declared Love Canal the first human-made environmental disaster area in the United States.

Love Canal and situations like it led environmental groups (which had been effective in promoting congressional passage of such far reaching environmental laws as the National Environmental Protection Act of 1969, the Clean Air Act of 1970, and the Water Pollution Control Act of 1972), citizens, and public officials to call for government regulation of hazardous waste management and disposal. The federal government responded with three important

9

pieces of legislation: the Toxic Substances Control Act (TSCA), the Resource Conservation and Recovery Act (RCRA), and the Comprehensive Environmental Response, Compensation, and Liability Act (Superfund).

The *TSCA* provided for the federal Environmental Protection Agency (EPA) to develop a data base on the health and environmental effects of chemicals. Producers of the chemicals were required to furnish needed information. The EPA was authorized to oversee the testing of potentially dangerous chemicals before they became available in the marketplace. If EPA judged a substance to pose an imminent hazard to public health or to the environment, it could delay marketing of the chemical or, in some cases, ban it altogether. Although the intent of TSCA was laudable, the dimensions of the chemical problem have overwhelmed EPA's capacity to cope with it, since some 65,000 chemicals are presently in use in the United States with more being developed every day.

RCRA defines hazardous wastes as ignitable, corrosive, reactive, and/or toxic. It establishes a "cradle to grave" tracking system to account for hazardous wastes from the day of their creation to the day they are disposed of. Facilities involved in the generation, storage, treatment, disposal, or transport of hazardous waste are required to keep accurate and timely records and make certain reports. Firms dealing with hazardous wastes in virtually any manner must secure an operating permit from EPA or an authorized state agency.

RCRA designates EPA as the lead federal agency in implementing the law. However, once EPA is satisfied that a state's hazardous waste program is equivalent to and consistent with RCRA standards and guidelines, it may authorize the state to manage its own program. If individual states are unable or unwilling to assume responsibility for the regulation of hazardous waste, EPA retains operational authority within that state's boundaries. While states upgrade their own programs to meet RCRA standards they may receive interim authorization by EPA. Full, or final, authorization is granted when a state can show that its program is equivalent and consistent with the federal requirements and that it is able to provide for adequate enforcement of its program. As of 1986, 26 states had received final authorization (Figure 3), including South Carolina. As we shall see later, it was only after much conflict and some ill will that South Carolina won final EPA authorization.

Passed in 1976, RCRA mandated EPA to develop a federal regulatory framework for hazardous waste within 18 months. However, it took EPA more than four years to complete it. Court-ordered deadlines, a suit by environmental groups, and other pressures finally forced EPA action. The slow implementation of EPA regulations undoubtedly resulted in a good bit of last minute dumping in questionable locations. Moreover, it soon became apparent that RCRA suffered from serious defects. The three most important

Figure 3
Status of State Programs under RCRA, (7/1/85)

No Authorization	Interim Authorization		Final Authorization	
Alaska	Alabama	New York	Arkansas	New Hampshire
Hawaii	Arizona	Ohio	Colorado	New Jersey
Idaho	California	Oregon	Delaware	New Mexico
Michigan	Connecticut	Pennsylvania	Florida	North Carolina
Wyoming	Illinois	Rhode Island	Georgia	North Dakota
	Indiana	Washington	Kentucky	Oklahoma
	Iowa	West Virginia	Louisiana	South Carolina
	Kansas	Wisconsin	Maryland	South Dakota
	Maine		Massachusetts	Tennessee
	Missouri		Minnesota	Texas
	Nevada		Mississippi	Utah
			Montana	Vermont
			Nebraska	Virginia

11

defects were that RCRA ignored abandoned sites, that it was not inclusive enough in defining and regulating hazardous wastes, and that it relied almost exclusively on the dangerous technology of land disposal.

Congress amended and reauthorized RCRA in 1984 to respond to these and other shortcomings. The amendments expanded RCRA coverage of hazardous wastes, extending EPA jurisdiction to construction firms, dry cleaners, machine shops, and other small waste generators producing 100 to 1000 kilograms monthly (the earlier limit was 1000 kilograms). The amendments prohibited the disposal of bulk or non-containerized hazardous wastes in landfills and, generally, called on the EPA to minimize industry usage of land disposal. The 1984 amendments also strengthened disposal, monitoring and liability insurance requirements for firms operating disposal facilities.

The problem of abandoned waste sites was addressed through separate legislation enacted by Congress in 1980. The Comprehensive Environmental Response, Compensation, and Liability Act, better known as Superfund, set aside $1.6 billion for cleanup operations over a five year period. Most of the money (86%) would come from a tax on individual generators of hazardous waste, supplemented by federal budgetary allocations. States would have to contribute 50% of the cost of cleaning up sites situated on land owned by state or local government and 10% of the expense for sites located on private property. Following cleanup, federal and state governments could pursue legal action to recover cleanup costs from the parties responsible for the site's contents and storage or disposal problems.

In order to determine which locations to clean up first, EPA asked each state for a list of uncontrolled sites along with data on type and quantity of wastes. Based on this information, EPA ranked the sites for emergency cleanup, waste destruction, containment, or other actions. Several South Carolina locations ranked high on the list, including Carolawn in northeast Chester County and Bluff Road in Columbia (See Figure 4).

As in the case of RCRA, implementation of Superfund was mismanaged by EPA. Under former EPA Director Anne Gorsuch Burford, prioritizing of cleanup sites was politicized, with first consideration given to states whose congressional representatives were "friends" of President Reagan. Reflecting the Reagan administration's lack of commitment to environmental regulation, EPA administrators sought to cut spending on Superfund and implemented cleanup actions very slowly. After the first 5½ years of Superfund (1980-1985), EPA had completed cleanup activities on only 15 of the 888 sites identified as priority areas. In early 1986, the $1.6 billion had been spent. Cleanup activities ground to a halt across the country. In South Carolina, work was stopped at ten high priority sites. Superfund finally was renewed by Congress in October, 1986, in spite of a threatened veto by President Reagan. The new program allocates $9 billion to cleanup activities and requires EPA

Figure 4
South Carolina Sites Approved for
Federal Superfund, September 1987

Carolawn, Inc., Fort Lawn (Chester County). Groundwater contamination by volatile organics and other substances.

Geiger/C&M Oil, Rantowles (Charleston County). Localized contamination by waste oil and industrial solvents.

Independent Nail Co., Lobeco (Beaufort County). Extensive groundwater contamination by heavy metals, including cyanide, lead, and zinc.

Kalama Specialty Chemicals, Lobeco (Beaufort County). Suspected groundwater contamination by industrial wastes.

Koppers Company, Inc., Florence (Florence County). Groundwater contamination by creosote.

Leonard Chemical Co., Rock Hill (York County). Groundwater contamination by chemical wastes.

Golden Strip Septic Tank Service, Inc., Simpsonville. Groundwater contamination by industrial solvents

Palmetto Wood Preserving, Dixiana (Lexington County). Suspected groundwater contam nation by wood-preserving chemicals.

SCR&D, Dixiana (Lexington County). Groundwater contamination by industrial solvents, acids, and paints.

SCR&D, Bluff Road (Richland County). Groundwater contamination by industrial and chemical wastes.

WamChem, Inc., Lobeco (Beaufor County). Groundwater and surface water contamination by industrial solvents and other wastes, including toluene and benzene.

Medley site, Gaffney (Cherokee County). Groundwater contamination by industrial and chemical wastes.

Rochester site, Travelers Rest (Greenville County). Groundwater contamination by volatile organics and other substances.

Sangamo-Weston Inc., Twelve Mile Creek - Lake Hartwell site.

Palmetto Recycling, Inc., Columbia (Richland County). Groundwater contamination by lead.

to improve the pace and scope of Superfund. The expanded program will be financed through increased taxes on industrial chemicals and on large corporations. A special tax on petroleum will be used to pay for the cleanup of leaking underground gasoline tanks across the United States.

Strategies for the Treatment of Hazardous Waste

One of the best strategies for hazardous waste management is to reduce its volume. This may be done at the source of production through changes in generation processes, substitution of ingredients, segregation of waste types, and recovery and recycling of reusable materials. The volume and danger of hazardous waste may also be reduced by physical, chemical, and biological treatments (See Figure 5). Examples include evaporation, dialysis, filtration, incineration, biodegradation, and absorption of contaminants from aqueous (water) streams into carbon or resin. The EPA estimates that industries are capable of reducing their hazardous waste by 15 to 30%. Much experimentation is taking place today as the economic incentives for volume reduction increase.

The storage of hazardous waste usually is meant to be an intermediate step between generation and storage, although temporary storage sometimes becomes *de facto* disposal when waste remains at a site indefinitely. In some cases it may actually be preferable to store especially dangerous, non-reusable wastes in monitored, above ground concrete mausoleums until new disposal technologies emerge. About 38% of the hazardous wastes in the United States are placed in surface storage.

One of the most controversial aspects of hazardous waste management is disposal. EPA estimates that 57% of hazardous wastes are disposed of through underground injection (mostly in the oil and gas industry) where wastes are pumped into highly porous rock formations below the earth's surface. Injection wells are now prohibited in South Carolina for waste disposal but there were 122 known wells drilled before this technique was banned. Only around 3% of the nation's hazardous wastes are *landfilled* (dumped into excavated pits), although this type of disposal has created the most public furor. All landfills eventually leak, in spite of continuing efforts to construct secure facilities that will protect ground and surface water from pollution. Even though new landfills are situated in thick deposits of clay, double lined with plastic, and carefully monitored for leakage, problems are inevitable, most of them the result of rain percolating through a landfill and into the water table. A new but relatively untested disposal strategy is *ocean incineration* of hazardous wastes aboard specially designed ships. It is argued that no significant pollution will result from burning the wastes, but the possibility of accidents in port or at sea has caused the EPA to question the viability of this approach.

Figure 5
Description of Treatment Technologies

Technology	Description
1. Incineration	Waste are burned at high temperatures to destroy the hazardous constituents.
2. Stabilization/ Solidification/ Fixation	Wastes are mixed with a hardening or binding agent, called a fixative, to reduce the mobility of the wastes or to solidify them.
3. Soil flushing	Water is drawn through soil to remove the wastes and then the water is treated to remove the contaminants.
4. Soil aeration	Contaminated soil is exposed to air through tilling or with a submerged pump. The air reacts with the waste to detoxify or decontaminate it.
5. Biological treatment*	Microorganisms, particularly bacteria and fungi, are used to breakdown or remove contaminants from wastes, especially in wastewaters such as in sewage treatment plants. More recently, biological treatment is being used to detoxify or decompose the hazardous constituents in soil. This is known as landfarming.
6. Chemical treatment*	Contaminants in wastes are destroyed or rendered less toxic by using chemical reactions.
7. Physical treatment*	Hazardous constituents in wastes are not destroyed, but instead are separated and two waste streams are produced. One is a concentrated volume of hazardous material and a second is a nonhazardous soil or liquid.

* Hazardous wastes can be chemically, biologically, or physically treated in place. This is known as *in situ.*

Though incineration is commonly offered as an alternative to landfills, its use does not cause the hazardous waste problem to vanish in thin air. Indeed, little has been determined about its effects on the environment and animal life. Since the incineration process involves transportation, offloading, and blending, the risk of potential releases should also be taken into account. Moreover, not all hazardous substances can be incinerated, especially those that are non-liquid, of low BTU value or a high metal content.

The search for new hazardous waste disposal technologies is in its infancy. However, most experts agree that industry must reduce its reliance on injection and landfilling.

15

The Politics of Hazardous Waste Management

A plethora of policy interests contend in the arena of hazardous waste politics. Only 20 years ago hazardous waste disposal occurred through unregulated actions by generators, shippers, and disposers. Then the federal government, through congress, the president, EPA, DOT, and the courts, entered the arena with legislation, directives, regulations, and court decisions. Today, state and local governments and citizens groups have joined the fray in this contentious policy arena. Citizen organizations have been particularly visible during the past ten years as they seek and provide hazardous waste information, inspect waste facilities, and organize and lobby for political action.

Local citizens are guaranteed access to hazardous waste policy making through Section 7004 of the RCRA. This section requires EPA and the states to promote public participation in the development, implementation, and enforcement of RCRA provisions. Most citizen participation is negative in character, aimed at disrupting the siting of proposed waste facilities through expression of the NIMBY (Not In My Backyard) Syndrome. Rarely do citizens' groups offer support for siting proposals.

Each major interest seems to hold a profoundly different view of hazardous waste policy issues, as a variety of intergovernmental tensions and conflicts pervades the national, state, and local government policy arenas. Bureaucratic actors tend to favor technological solutions for the hazardous waste dilemma, preferring to reserve decision-making for "the experts." Politicians are buffeted by the conflicting needs to provide for waste disposal facilities in *someone's* backyard while satisfying the demands of citizens opposed to facility siting. Federal officials are often in disagreement with state officials, and neither tends to see eye to eye with industry representatives. The struggle to discover a common ground for policy agreement is extraordinarily difficult. Even in the face of an aroused citizenry, the industrial interest groups are highly influential and frequently superior to citizen organizations in financial resources and political skills.

To facilitate implementation of RCRA requirements DHEC has developed a computer tracking system and reporting procedures. The generators, transporters, treatment, and storage and disposal establishments connected with hazardous wastes are required by law to notify DHEC and the EPA about their activities. DHEC and EPA issue them identification numbers. In 1984 the Hazardous Waste Tracking System (HWTS) was created in response to the need for a comprehensive data management and monitoring system for hazardous waste. The HWTS enables the Bureau of Solid and Hazardous Waste Management to follow the movement and fate of hazardous waste from the time it is generated to the time it is disposed. The System stores data on the flow and amounts of waste created, lists of transporters, and the destination of waste from each industry. Important information such as data on licensure status of transporters and insurance coverage are compiled by HWTS. Authorization and contingency fund information is also stored in the system. Compliance by generators and disposers can be determined by comparing their files. Computerized quarterly report forms, designed by the bureau, are completed and submitted every three months by industries.

Slowly, federal, state, and local authority is being sorted out in hazardous waste policy. Under RCRA and Superfund, minimum standards of waste control have been implemented nationwide. Operational responsibility, however, is gradually being exercised by state and local governments. Eventually, the national role is to recede to oversight and inspection of the state programs, mediation of interstate disputes, and perhaps funding of research and development programs.

Generally speaking, the states have done well in taking over the responsibility for hazardous waste management activities. Although some states continue to be laggards, most have confronted the key issues legislatively and administratively. Revenue shortages have constrained the actions of some states. Others, like South Carolina, assess fees on the production, treatment, and disposal of hazardous wastes to pay for state regulatory activities and related matters such as technical assistance, planning, and emergency cleanups. Such an approach seems to make good sense: those who generate, transport, store, treat, and dispose of hazardous wastes ought to pay the price for regulation.

Occasionally state and local conflicts occur, often involving siting issues. Local governments reflect the opinion of their citizens in opposing the placement of hazardous waste facilities in their jurisdiction. Some states permit the expression of local views, then make a siting decision preemptively. A handful of states allow local governments to veto siting decisions. Others utilize mediation and arbitration procedures to settle siting disputes. All states confront a similar dilemma: balancing the relative weight of public opinion alongside technical considerations, administrative recommendations, and industry preferences. Citizen voices must be heard, but facility siting decisions ultimately must be made by responsible state governments.

Hazardous Waste Policy in South Carolina

In many ways, South Carolina is a prototypical state in the hazardous waste policy field. Its industries make the state a major producer of hazardous waste, it is the site of one of the largest waste dumps in the United States, and it has served as a battleground for many conflicting voices in hazardous waste policy making.

In South Carolina more than 10 billion pounds of hazardous waste (including hazardous waste water) were generated in 1985 by 505 generators spread all across the State. The three counties with the highest number of generators are Greenville (73 generators), Spartanburg (66 generators), and Richland (39 generators). In the same year the State received a total of 302,312,814 pounds of hazardous wastes from 823 generators located in 30 states and the Commonwealth of Puerto Rico. North Carolina (7,914,218 lbs.), Florida (5,613,317 lbs.), and Georgia (4,195,686 lbs.) were the highest contributors. (See Map 1 and Figures 6 and 7 for further details).

South Carolina policy parallels that of the national government in many respects. The state statutory framework is established under the South Carolina Hazardous Waste Management Act of 1978 (HWMA) and an extensive body of regulations, developed by DHEC, that implement the act. The HWMA and its implementing regulations have been amended on several occasions. Under HWMA, hazardous wastes are classified by type and tracked from cradle to grave. All classified wastes are subject to a manifest and quarterly reporting systems so that they may be followed from point of origin to ultimate disposal. Standards are set forth which must be honored by generators, transporters, disposers, and firms that store or treat hazardous wastes. Standards which cover record keeping, facility design and construction, operational requirements, permitting procedures, and financial responsibility are enforced by DHEC through a permitting process and by monitoring firms' compliance. DHEC's monitoring and enforcement staff include chemists, engineers, geologists, and other classifications of employees located in Columbia and throughout the state.

In South Carolina, an occasionally bitter struggle between DHEC officials and EPA representatives has set the tone for intergovernmental conflict. Problems began in 1983 when the General Assembly passed a law banning out-of-state hazardous waste from states which prohibited burial of that same type of waste in their own jurisdiction. EPA officials, seemingly assuming the role of the U. S. Supreme Court, informed DHEC that the South Carolina law was in violation of the Interstate Commerce clause of the U. S. Constitution. Unless the law was changed, EPA would refuse to grant final operational authority to South Carolina's state hazardous waste management program.

The ban was dropped from the legislation. However, EPA continued to withhold final authorization for DHEC for more than two years because of three "problems in performance." First, EPA insisted that DHEC must issue an order to comply more quickly when it found a facility to be out of compliance with a regulation. Second, DHEC would have to cease issuing "openended" compliance orders that did not specify a date for compliance. Finally, DHEC would be required to assess higher fines for violations of rules and regulations. DHEC insisted that within the context of South Carolina its

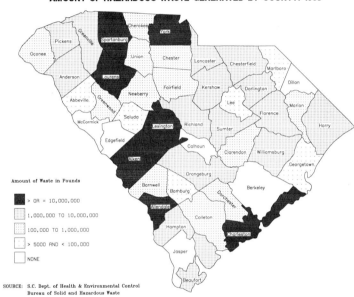

MAP 1
AMOUNT OF HAZARDOUS WASTE GENERATED BY COUNTY: 1985

Amount of Waste in Pounds

> OR = 10,000,000

1,000,000 TO 10,000,000

100,000 TO 1,000,000

> 5000 AND < 100,000

NONE

SOURCE: S.C. Dept. of Health & Environmental Control
        Bureau of Solid and Hazardous Waste

19

Figure 6
Number of Generators and Facilities by County, 1985

County	Generators	On-Site Facilities	Off-Site Facilities	Companies
Abbeville	2	0	0	2
Aiken	17	3	1	17
Allendale	2	1	0	2
Anderson	23	3	0	23
Bamberg	3	0	0	3
Barnwell	4	0	0	4
Beaufort	6	1	0	6
Berkeley	11	2	0	11
Charleston	27	7	2	28
Cherokee	10	0	0	10
Chester	7	2	0	7
Chesterfield	7	0	0	7
Clarendon	2	0	0	2
Colleton	3	1	0	3
Darlington	10	0	1	11
Dorchester	5	2	1	5
Edgefield	2	0	0	2
Fairfield	2	0	0	2
Florence	14	3	1	14
Georgetown	3	0	0	3
Greenville	73	6	2	73
Greenwood	18	8	0	18
Hampton	1	1	0	1
Horry	8	2	0	8
Kershaw	5	2	0	5
Lancaster	6	0	0	6
Laurens	16	2	0	16
Lee	1	0	0	1
Lexington	22	4	1	22
Marion	4	0	0	4
Marlboro	5	1	0	5
Newberry	2	1	0	2
Oconee	12	0	0	12
Orangeburg	10	2	1	10
Pickens	12	2	0	12
Richland	39	4	0	39
Saluda	1	0	0	1
Spartanburg	66	8	8	67
Sumter	18	6	4	18
Union	5	0	0	5
Williamsburg	4	1	0	4
York	17	2	1	17
STATE TOTALS	505	77	23	508

Source: South Carolina Department of Health and Environmental Control
Bureau of Solid and Hazardous Waste

Figure 7
Amount of Waste Received From Out-Of-State Generators For 1985 (Thousands of pounds)

State	Generators	Treated	Stored	Disposed	Recovered	Total
Alabama	12	122	288	1,586	2,278	4,273
California	1	17	0	0	0	17
Colorado	1	0	0	221	0	221
Connecticut	11	5,512	0	3,487	0	9,002
District of Columbia	1	4	0	0	0	4
Delaware	9	44	0	3,914	0	3,958
Florida	110	5,530	847	11,123	5,613	23,113
Georgia	89	948	474	28,680	4,196	34,298
Illinois	7	5,205	0	182	0	5,387
Indiana	2	183	0	28	0	210
Kentucky	6	20	34	1,459	75	1,587
Louisiana	2	72	158	0	71	301
Massachusetts	25	772	0	13,127	0	13,899
Maryland	28	284	0	5,878	0	6,163
Michigan	4	756	0	13	0	769
Minnesota	2	16	0	0	0	16

Montana	1	0	0	518	0	518
North Carolina	300	6,897	2,455	91,835	7,014	109,100
New Hampshire	4	47	0	118	0	165
New Jersey	46	2,490	0	28,723	0	31,213
New York	12	353	0	498	0	851
Ohio	8	792	0	48	56	895
Pennsylvania	15	2,185	0	1,492	52	3,729
Puerto Rico	2	610	0	43	0	653
Rhode Island	1	0	0	783	0	783
Tennessee	35	4,517	136	1,138	822	16,855
Texas	1	586	0	0	0	586
Virginia	71	5,204	192	11,558	1,779	18,733
Vermont	1	0	0	2,985	0	2,985
Wisconsin	1	4	0	0	0	4
West Virginia	15	1,998	24	9,932	70	12,024
TOTAL	823	45,170	4,607	229,610	22,926	302,313

Source: South Carolina Department of Health and Environmental Control
Bureau of Solid and Hazardous Waste

22

own policies were preferable to those mandated by EPA. Essentially, DHEC believed that it was more productive to utilize a less formal method in convincing firms to correct hazardous waste problems. EPA was accused of having "a report card mentality" by DHEC. Once these remaining issues were resolved to EPA's satisfaction, final authorization was granted for South Carolina to operate its own program in November 1985. Since then amendments in the State regulations have been made in concordance with those in the Federal regulations.

South Carolina also has created its own version of Superfund. The State's Hazardous Waste Contingency Fund, which receives revenues from fees assessed on hazardous wastes taken to the Pinewood facility, is used to clean up troublesome sites that are too small to qualify for priority listing by the U. S. Superfund. By 1986, approximately $5 million had been collected in the fund. Authorized by the General Assembly in 1983, the State Superfund was first used to clean up pesticides at the Black River Hardwood site in 1985. Since then, ten additional sites have been approved for cleanup (Figure 8). GSX Services of Reidsville, North Carolina, has a contract with DHEC for cleanup activities.

Figure 8
Sites Approved by DHEC for Cleanup with State Superfund

Name & Location	Type Waste	Status
Black River Hardwood Site, Kingstree (2)	Pesticides	Completed
Rutledge Property, York County		Completed
Atkins/McAbee, Cherokee County		Completed
Elmore/Spires, Spartanburg County		Completed
Stokes, Greenville County		Completed
Carolina Chemicals, Lexington County	Pesticides	Underway
Wayside Farms, Bishopville (2)	Pesticides	Underway
Nichols Air Strip, Marion County	Uncertain	Underway
Love Springs, Cherokee County	Uncertain	Underway

Once a problem site is identified, DHEC seeks to convince the responsible parties to pay for required cleanup activities. If necessary, DHEC may bring suit to recover its cleanup costs from recalcitrant parties and, in addition, damages up to three times the actual expenses. DHEC has added several new positions to implement the State Superfund, including a "special investigator" to track down violators for the prosecution of criminal cases.

Several significant hazardous waste facilities are situated in South Carolina.

There are two commercial incinerators (GSX in Roebuck, and Stablex in Rock Hill), used mostly to evaporate liquid wastes. Other commercial facilities are located in Sumter (CP Chemicals, Inc.) and in Ravenel (Stoller-Mii). As of 1983, there were some 1015 regulated generators of hazardous waste in South Carolina.

The Pinewood Facility. One facility dwarfs the others in size, controversy, and potential danger. That is the Pinewood site located in Sumter County. What started in 1977 as a Fuller's earth mine for the production of kitty litter has grown into one of the largest hazardous waste disposal facilities in the United States, and one of only two EPA-approved "secure" commercial chemical waste landfills in the eastern United States (the other is in Emelle, Alabama). Once owned by Bennett Mineral Company and SCA Services, Inc., the facility is presently owned and operated by GSX Corporation (a subsidiary of Genstar Corporation, a Canadian firm).

Spread over 280 acres, the Pinewood site is only 1200 feet distant from the Lake Marion wetlands. It contains at least 153 types of hazardous waste. Between commencement of waste operations in October 1980 and December 1984, 462,879 tons of hazardous wastes were buried there. That figure does not include substantial amounts of unreported wastes buried during the 1977 to 1980 period, before EPA and DHEC monitoring requirements went into effect. The Pinewood site is used by over 800 chemical waste generators across the country; only about 200 of them are situated in South Carolina. North Carolina was the largest contributor of Pinewood waste in 1984 with a total of 59,541,095 pounds. Other large users were Georgia, Florida, Virginia, Tennessee, and West Virginia. Even though these six states accounted for more than 82% of the out-of-state wastes received by Pinewood in 1984, none of them has a commercial hazardous waste landfill within its own borders. All told, approximately 70% of all waste being buried at Pinewood originates outside of South Carolina.

Aside from the question of fairness, the major issue involving Pinewood is water. If hazardous waste migrates into Lake Marion, at risk would be the water quality; plant, animal, and fish life; and recreational and tourism contributions of the entire Santee-Cooper lake system. Moreover, the landfill sits over three aquifer zones that provide drinking water for many citizens in South Carolina and neighboring states.

The geological characteristics of the Pinewood site are ideal, since the Fuller's earth is highly absorbent and a natural barrier to waste migration. The design of the site is intended to divert any accidental spills into a collection pond. Special barriers are utilized, such as plastic liners in the underground trenches. GSX management seeks to employ the latest technology to contain wastes on site. They also prohibit some especially troublesome substances such as PCBs and dioxin. Further precautions are taken through extensive monitoring activities by GSX, DHEC, and EPA. Yet, all hazardous waste landfills eventually leak, and Pinewood is no exception.

Already hazardous wastes have been discovered in groundwater on the site. An EPA report in March 1986 cited evidence of nickel in groundwater samples. The EPA report also criticized GSX for numerous maintenance and monitoring violations. The federal agency stated that too few monitoring wells were on site even though GSX had increased the number from nine to thirty-three after paying EPA a fine of $14,500 as a result of an earlier EPA study. More recently, monitoring by DHEC and GSX uncovered seven petroleum-based pollutants in the Black Creek aquifer — the shallowest of the three subterranean bodies of water on the site. Since the Black Creek aquifer lies above the Fuller's earth, drinking water has not yet been affected. GSX has been ordered by DHEC to devise a plan to remove the chemicals, even though the contamination probably is the result of an earlier owner spraying a petroleum compound on the roads at the site during operations to mine Fuller's earth in the 1970s.

It is critical that the GSX facility be thoroughly monitored. If hazardous waste migrates into groundwater used for drinking purposes, the human and monetary costs could be enormous. About 60% of South Carolina's population uses groundwater for drinking; 96% of the public water systems in the state utilize groundwater. Should the Santee-Cooper system and its aquifers become contaminated, cleanup operations, if undertaken, could bankrupt both Santee-Cooper and the State. DHEC has estimated the expense of excavating, loading, shipping, and redisposal of the Pinewood wastes at $1,070,532,000 (if the Pinewood dump were filled to permitted capacity). Less comprehensive actions would cost hundreds of millions of dollars.

During a licensing proceeding in 1985, DHEC sought to convince GSX to raise its insurance coverage for Pinewood cleanups and accidents. GSX's existing policy provided "umbrella" coverage for 14 GSX facilities, but no specific coverage for Pinewood. A DHEC report recommended that the company be required to provide a $100 million corporate guarantee for on and off-site protection and, generally, broaden its insurance coverage of the Pinewood facility. In January 1987, DHEC ordered GSX to carry at least $30 million of insurance for the next three years. The adequacy of GSX coverage for accidents and cleanups at Pinewood is still the subject of controversy.

The Savannah River Plant. The second most threatening site with regard to groundwater contamination is the Savannah River Plant (SRP). SRP is a sprawling, (300 square mile) federally owned facility that is involved in various hazardous and radioactive waste activities related to the production of atomic warheads. Eight major hazardous waste sites are situated at SRP; there are at least 164 "waste management units" as well. Its special status as a federal defense facility, the very large volume of wastes produced, and the mingling of hazardous and radioactive wastes, make SRP a highly complex situation. Although the U. S. Department of Energy (DOE) claimed that SRP was exempt from RCRA requirements, a lawsuit by the Natural Resources Defense Council resulted in a judicial decision in 1984 that RCRA did, indeed, apply to DOE facilities. Today, DHEC is responsible for regulating and monitoring hazardous and mixed wastes on the site.

In 1983 high levels of toxic solvents were found in the important Tuscaloosa aquifer at SRP. This, and other leaks, have led DHEC to call SRP "the most significant ground water contamination" known in South Carolina. Most of the contamination comes from 160 seepage basins that were used beginning in the 1950s for the disposal of a wide variety of hazardous wastes, including dangerous chemicals, pesticides, and heavy metals.

The State wants SRP to clean up its problem sites and improve its monitoring activities. So far, hazardous wastes have not migrated in ground or surface water outside of SRP boundaries, although the likelihood of such migration is thought to be high. Meanwhile, several lawsuits that would force DOE to abide by federal and state hazardous waste laws at SRP are awaiting action.

The Bluff Road Hazardous Waste Site. One of South Carolina's worst hazardous waste problems was the Bluff Road location, operated as a "storage" facility by South Carolina Recycling and Disposal, Inc. (SCRDI). Actually a dump, it contained numerous kinds of hazardous waste, left unlabeled in more than 7,000 rusting 55 gallon drums. Following a storm in July 1977, leaking chemicals reacted with rainwater to form a cloud of hydrochloric acid that resulted in 50 people receiving hospital treatment. Efforts by DHEC to convince SCRDI to clean up the dangerous mess were to no avail. EPA testing in July 1980 discovered extensive chemical contamination of soil and groundwater, leading to a federal lawsuit against SCRDI demanding the chemicals be inventoried, repackaged, and properly disposed of within 60 days. EPA also fined the company $25,000.

When SCRDI did not comply with the order (the firm filed for bankruptcy), federal Superfund money was applied for. Eventually, 12 of the original waste generators agreed to pay $1.95 million for removal of 75% of the waste; the remainder was to be cleaned up using Superfund money. Five nonparticipating generators were taken to court. By mid-1983, all drums had been removed. Remedial work (testing of soil and groundwater) continues.

Intergovernmental Policy Issues

Notwithstanding RCRA's devolution of hazardous waste management authority to the states, South Carolina's policy decisions in the future will largely depend upon what the national government decides to do or not to do. RCRA amendments aimed at curtailing the landfilling of hazardous wastes through incineration and other treatments could mean that Pinewood will be used as no more than a repository for treatment residues by the early 1990s. Thus, both volume and toxicity of wastes might be reduced at that facility.

However, there are countervailing forces that could conspire to keep incoming waste volume at or near the present legislatively-imposed limit of 150,000 tons per year. As State Superfund cleanup proceeds in South Carolina, the burial limit might be waived in order to provide disposal space for waste removed from leaking sites. Also, the national Superfund program requires landfill space and only Pinewood and the Emelle, Alabama facilities qualify in the Southeastern region for some types of waste disposal. Critics have questioned the sagacity of digging up hazardous waste from one hole only to put it in another, but continued landfilling of Superfund waste will continue for at least the next few years. Finally, RCRA amendments that mandate increased monitoring systems and financial resources for disposal facilities are causing many of them to close down operations. This, too, is placing additional demands on the Pinewood facility, as will new RCRA requirements mandating that all land disposal facilities utilize double trench liners and expensive leak detection systems by November 1988.

Ideally, of course, each state should be responsible for providing treatment and disposal facilities for hazardous waste produced within its borders, just as they are for radioactive waste under national legislation and interstate compacts. But citizen opposition to siting hazardous waste facilities is very intense. Elected officials who are not responsive to citizen pressure in this policy field are quite likely to sacrifice their office in the next election. There is a great need to construct additional treatment, incineration, and disposal facilities across the country and that need will grow in coming years. Yet many recent efforts have been stifled by the hostile climate of public opinion, including an attempt by one waste management firm to build a 500 acre landfill east of Charlotte, North Carolina, and an effort by GSX to site a waste incinerator in Laurinburg, North Carolina; either would have relieved pressure on Pinewood from the Tarheel State.

Other siting efforts remain at a near standstill throughout the nation. If future siting of waste facilities is to be successful, strong leadership and hard decisions will be necessary at the state level. In some cases, local public opposition may have to be overridden by the state, although an appropriate level of citizen participation in siting decisions should be maintained. South Carolina could encourage action by neighboring states through making the Pinewood facility increasingly expensive to use. The General Assembly has raised disposal fees at Pinewood several times and has maintained a differential fee for South Carolina wastes and those produced out-of-state. Further fee increases, along with tightened restrictions on volume, could help reduce the high percentage of hazardous wastes coming from out-of-state. Before leaving office, Governor Dick Riley proposed lowering the volume at the GSX site and increasing the state tax on waste. Such an approach could encourage other states to reconsider the construction of landfills and promote careful consideration of less expensive alternatives to land disposal in South Carolina. It would also supply additional resources for the State Superfund. But, so long as burial at Pinewood remains cheaper than the alternatives (the alternatives presently cost two to ten times more), the waste will continue to pour in.

Clearly, more thought must be given to creating incentives for states to assume responsibility for hazardous waste produced in their own jurisdictions. Higher disposal costs at Pinewood certainly would provide strong economic incentives. However, care must be taken to preclude a challenge to the out-of-state fee differential under the Interstate Commerce clause, as is presently being threatened by a coalition of 60 firms in the hazardous waste industry. A fee differential appears to be supportable, so long as it remains relatively modest. (Presently, out-of-state waste is taxed at $18 per ton, in-state waste at $13 per ton). A huge gap in fees would invite legal action from other states or their waste generators.

A controversy has been created by the movement towards new treatment facilities and the desire in South Carolina to control their proliferation. In November, 1986 the Executive Director of the Washington, D.C. based Hazardous Waste Treatment Council complained to EPA about South Carolina's policies in this regard. The Council felt that the fee structure for hazardous waste in this state discriminated against out-of-state waste generators, and the permitting process was aimed at delaying or preempting the expansion of treatment facilities. DHEC insists it is guilty of neither charges and contends that both the fee structure and the permitting process have been approved by EPA. It further points out that adequate risk assessment of treatment facilities and processes is necessary before new facilities can be permitted. Higher fees could increase the risks of illegal hazardous waste disposal through "midnight dumping" or other unsafe methods. Thus, DHEC must follow fee hikes with stepped up enforcement activities. Of late DHEC has tightened its grip on regulation by taking firm actions ranging from violation notice, as in the case of Ethyl Corporation of Orangeburg, to severe financial raps on the knuckles. Fines of waste violators by DHEC climbed from $228,596 in 1984 to $650,035 in 1985, indicating increased DHEC oversight. For the first time, DHEC also shut down a violator, Suffolk Chemical Company in Chapin. The authority of DHEC to take this strong action is important. The General Assembly may need to consider strengthening DHEC's regulatory power further, since violation of the State's hazardous waste laws constitute only a misdemeanor at present.

In addition to economic incentives in implementing regulatory programs and siting decisions, political incentives are needed as well. The key element is the replacement of intensely adversarial relationships between hazardous waste policy actors with more cooperative strategies. Progress is being made through government-industry-citizen information sharing and dissemination, federal-state agreements under RCRA and Superfund, and interstate cooperation through sharing information on hazardous waste activities. A promising, yet somewhat limited approach is the waste materials exchange, where efforts are made by state governments, private corporations, or other entities to seek out buyers and sellers of hazardous wastes. Often a waste produced by one company serves as a raw material for another company. By exchanging wastes, buyers and sellers reap economic benefits, while the volume of wastes requiring treatment or disposal is cut down. In early 1986 some 35 exchange programs were operating in the United States, including the Piedmont Waste Exchange which covers South Carolina and North Carolina.

DHEC has been accused of having no clearly conceived and wideranging policy framework that would allow the development of an effective program in South Carolina. Other states like Tennessee and North Carolina have not only developed such a broad based policy agenda but they have also linked it with economic development. Considering the fact that South Carolina is already a critical state in terms of hazardous waste disposal facilities, the need for a comprehensive hazardous waste management plan that charts future directions is imperative. The plan should consider various options concerning the Pinewood facility, alternatives to landfilling, waste minimization strategies, risk assessment, the range of state regulatory activities, and the proper role of local government and public opinion in siting decisions. The plan should also deal with the issue of whether or not a state takeover of the GSX operations in Pinewood is feasible, and if any future landfills should be built on state-owned land.

In this regard, an initial step was taken by DHEC in November, 1986 with the announcement of the creation of a Hazardous Waste Policy Task Force to devise a comprehensive hazardous waste plan. The Task Force is broadly based, including representatives from DHEC, public interest groups, the General Assembly, governor's office, and industry groups. The members are appointed for two year terms, and the general chairman is elected by the DHEC Board from among the members. The committee is divided into subcommittees of 8-10 members to work on specific areas of interest. The Task Force is expected to submit quarterly written reports and recommendations to the DHEC Board. The committee receives support from DHEC which provides it with technical information and clerical assistance. DHEC has proposed an agenda for the hazardous waste management program consisting of ten items. They are: adequacy of regulatory standards; proper risk management evaluation; siting criteria; number and types of facilities needed to manage hazardous waste; exploration of an alternative technology philosophy; hazardous waste management alternatives; waste minimization alternatives; transportation of hazardous waste; public education; and, financial responsibility. To what extent the Task Force will be able to incorporate all these issues in the overall hazardous waste management policy, only time can tell.

It is important to future generations of South Carolinians that we take charge of our hazardous waste problems and deal with them openly and wisely. If we do not, the problems may well overcome our capacities to react effectively and result in a permanently poisoned, and ultimately uninhabitable, environment.

References

Bowman, Ann O'M. (1985). "Hazardous Waste Management: An Emerging Policy Area Within An Emerging Federalism." *Publius* 15 (Winter): 131-144.

Bowman, Ann O'M. (1984). "Hazardous Waste and South Carolina." *Public Affairs Bulletin.* University of South Carolina, Bureau of Governmental Research and Service. No. 27 (November).

Epstein, Samuel S., Lester O. Brown and Carl Pope (1982). *Hazardous Waste in America.* San Francisco: Sierra Club.

Lester, James P. and Ann O'M. Bowman (1983) (eds.). *The Politics of Hazardous Waste Management.* Durham, N. C.: Duke University Press.

3
Radioactive Waste Policy: The Palmetto Perspective

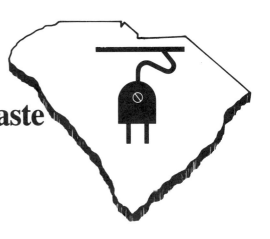

Richard C. Kearney

Introduction

Radioactive (nuclear) waste policy is characterized by emotionalism, extraordinary complexity, and a multiplicity of mutually distrustful policy actors at the national, state, and local levels. It is a policy badlands that must be traversed, although most elected officials dread passage through its hazardous political landscape. This chapter will describe the key role that South Carolina plays in radioactive waste policy, focusing on the intergovernmental policy actors, the legal environment within which they operate, and the policies that have emerged since the first atom was split some forty-five years ago in the hurried efforts by the United States to develop atomic weaponry.

The Policy Actors

During the late 1940s and the 1950s, nuclear technology and programs were the sole responsibility of the federal government under the Atomic Energy Act of 1946. The Atomic Energy Commission (AEC) monopolized the development and regulation of all matters related to atomic energy. Amendments to the Atomic Energy Act in 1954 permitted private parties such as utilities to use nuclear energy and materials for the generation of commercial electricity. The AEC retained its regulatory role under the amendments, and was granted authority to license commercial enterprises and to manage radioactive waste. States were first permitted to assume responsibility for certain facilities and activities characterized by low levels of radioactivity in 1959 with Congressional passage of an "Agreement States" provision.

Richard C. Kearney is an associate professor in the Department of Government and International Studies at the University of South Carolina.

Twenty-six states have chosen to enter into such formal arrangements, including South Carolina.

The Energy Reorganization Act of 1974 abolished the AEC. Its activities to promote the development of commercial nuclear energy were transferred to the Energy Research and Development Administration (ERDA), and then to the new U. S. Department of Energy (DOE) upon its creation in 1977. The regulatory functions of the AEC were placed in the Nuclear Regulatory Commission (NRC), where they remain today.

Congress first "intergovernmentalized" nuclear waste storage and disposal in 1980 with enactment of the Low Level Radioactive Waste Policy Act, which authorized states to form interstate compacts for the management of low level radioactive waste. Then, in 1982, Congress passed the Nuclear Waste Policy Act for the storage and disposal of high-level nuclear waste.

Figure 1
Types of Radioactive Waste

Low-Level (LLW): A nuclear waste with low levels of radioactivity and a short half-life. Most break down to safe levels of radioactivity within a year; some, however, remain dangerous for up to 300 years. About 60% are produced by nuclear power reactors, and the remainder by medical and research institutions and nuclear-related industries. Examples of low-level waste include contaminated tools, laboratory clothes, animal carcasses, pharmaceutical by-products, and bulk wastes (wood, dirt, concrete, steel, etc.).

High-Level (HLW): Extremely toxic for up to hundreds of thousands of years, this waste consists of spent fuel rods and assemblies from the approximately 90 operating commercial nuclear power plants in the U.S. and several foreign facilities. Substantial amounts of high-level waste are also produced in the manufacture of nuclear weapons.

Transuranic: Liquid high-level waste that has a long half-life, produced in the fabrication of plutonium for nuclear weapons and in the reprocessing of spent nuclear fuel.

Mixed Waste: Substances composed of mixed hazardous and radioactive waste. In mid-1987 this type of waste was placed in the regulatory authority of states hosting defense facilities, under the federal Resource Recovery and Conservation Act (RCRA). The status of mixed waste remains an issue for commercial facilities.

The complexity of radioactive waste policy is evident in the number of policy actors and in the legal environment. Federal actors include the Nuclear Regulatory Commission and U. S. Department of Energy, as well as the Environmental Protection Agency (EPA), which sets radiological criteria and standards that are intended to protect the environment; the Department of Transportation (DOT), which develops and enforces regulations for transporting radioactive waste; and the U. S. Department of Defense (DOD), which regulates defense related radioactive waste. The twenty-six Agreement States, which regulate low-level institutional and industrial waste, and other state and local governments are concerned with protecting the health and safety of their citizens within the context of shipping and disposing of nuclear waste. Important private actors include the utilities with nuclear power plants, firms and medical facilities that produce and dispose of radioactive waste, and interest groups representing a wide variety of nuclear-related concerns.

Figure 2
Policy Actors in Radioactive Waste Management

Federal	State	Local
NRC	Agreement States	Municipalities; counties
DOE	Other States	and special districts
DOD	Governors	concerned with generation,
EPA	Legislatures	transport, or disposal operations
Congress	Courts	within their jurisdiction.
President		Courts
Courts		

Interest groups representing the nuclear power industry, disposal industry, medical and research institutions, and environmental interests; other entities involved in the generation, transport, and storage of radioactive waste.

Influential private interests in South Carolina radioactive waste policy-making include the utility companies that operate nuclear reactors (SCE&G, Duke Power, Carolina Power and Light), firms that produce nuclear waste (e.g., Westinghouse Nuclear Fuels near Columbia), and Chem-Nuclear Services.

Chem-Nuclear Services has held the state contract to operate the Barnwell Low-Level Waste (LLW) facility since it opened in 1971. It has sought to have the state authorize higher volume limits for LLW and brought pressure upon legislators to extend the operating life of the facility beyond its scheduled closure date of 1992. The firm is owned by Waste Management, Inc., a large multinational corporation. Chem-Nuclear Services has a well-connected team of lobbyists including a former chief lobbyist for the South Carolina Chamber of Commerce, a former chairman of the State Democratic Party, and a former top aid to Governor Riley.

The legal environment of radioactive waste policy is composed of the Atomic Energy Act and its amendments, the Low-Level Radioactive Waste Policy Act of 1980, Hazardous Materials Transportation Act of 1974, the National Environmental Policy Act of 1969, the Nuclear Waste Policy Act of 1982, and a host of federal regulations and state and local legislation and regulations.

Figure 3
Legislation Related to Radioactive Waste Policy

Atomic Energy Act of 1954, as amended – Makes federal government the predominant policy actor in all phases of the nuclear fuel cycle, from mining uranium to disposal of waste. Amendments permit limited state "agreements" to manage certain LLW, but DOE (formerly AEC) maintains sole regulatory authority over siting and operation of nuclear reactors and HLW.

Low-Level Radioactive Waste Policy Act of 1980 – Makes each state responsible for providing for the disposal of LLW generated within its borders (except for defense waste). States may dispose of LLW within their own borders or enter into interstate compacts for disposal out-of-state.

Hazardous Materials Transportation Act of 1974, as amended – DOT is responsible for vehicle, driver, and packaging regulations for transporting hazardous materials, including radioactive waste.

National Environmental Policy Act of 1969, as amended – Requires that federal agencies prepare an environmental impact statement for major activities that significantly affect the environment (e.g., radioactive waste disposal sites).

Nuclear Waste Policy Act of 1982 – Sets forth procedure for selection of two or more burial sites for spent nuclear fuel. Procedure is to include regular consultation with relevant states and a limited state veto of a selected site, subject to Congressional override.

State and Local Legislation – Various statutes and ordinances to enter into Interstate Compacts, and generally, to oversee, regulate, restrict, set conditions for, and prohibit the transportation of nuclear waste and/or the establishment of nuclear waste facilities within legal jurisdictions of state and local governments.

Nuclear Waste and South Carolina

Although the national government has dominated radioactive waste policy, the states have become increasingly important actors in the field. No other state, with the possible exception of Washington, has played a more salient role than South Carolina. South Carolina's leadership in nuclear waste policy comes naturally by virtue of the tremendous presence of nuclear activities. The state has been destined to play a pivotal role in nuclear waste decisions since the early 1950s when the massive Savannah River Plant (SRP) was constructed by the federal government to produce weapons grade plutonium and tritium for the nation's nuclear armaments stockpile.

Today, SRP operates four nuclear reactors under the authority of the Department of Energy (DuPont, Co., is the private contractor). Some 25-30 million gallons of liquid HLW (transuranic) are stored in tanks in underground "canyons." At some undetermined future date, the waste is to be solidified into concrete and shipped off to an as yet unidentified, permanent disposal site. Commercial HLW (spent fuel assemblies) are stored on-site at the six commercial nuclear power plants in South Carolina, while awaiting a final solution for the HLW problem. Approximately 45% of the LLW produced in the U. S. is being sent to Barnwell for burial at the Chem-Nuclear facility. The commercial power plants, the Westinghouse fuel fabrication plant near Columbia, and numerous other LLW-generating industries and institutions make South Carolina rank among the top five LLW producing states in the nation.

In mid-1987 South Carolina acquired the authority to regulate and monitor hazardous waste and "mixed waste" generated at SRP. (Previously this was the responsibility of the Department of Energy (DOE).) DOE had a very poor record of managing wastes at SRP. A draft Environmental Impact Statement estimated costs of up to $3.1 billion to clean up waste from eight seepage basins contaminated by DOE operations. Removing all hazardous waste from SRP could cost as much as $12 billion. In the future, the South Carolina Department of Health and Environmental Control will insure that DOE works on cleaning up the waste and puts into place an extensive system of wells to monitor any movement of hazardous substances from the waste sites.

Perhaps the best way to try to make sense of South Carolina's high profile in radioactive waste policy is to divide the policy field into defense waste, commercial HLW, and LLW.

Defense Waste

In terms of policymaking, this is the simplest type of waste to understand. Put plainly, the U. S. Department of Defense and Department of Energy enjoy a virtual monopoly in the policy field, operating under the veil of "national security." Defense waste is treated separately from non-defense waste, whether it is high-level or low-level. Most of the HLW is in a liquid sludge form stored at federal facilities in South Carolina (SRP), Washington (Hanford), and Idaho (National Reactor Testing Station). Defense LLW is disposed of at these and other locations. Spent fuel from foreign power reactors is also stored in the U. S. (mostly at SRP) as part of the "Atoms for Peace" program.

South Carolina's role regarding defense waste is restricted, even though great quantities of it are located within its borders and the human health and safety risks are substantial. SRP's four operating reactors, like those in the Chernobyl disaster in the Soviet Union, do not have containment domes to capture radioactivity released during an accident. Rumors, charges, and reports of an alleged release of large quantities of radioactive materials into the atmosphere in March 1955 have surfaced, although the SRP and DOE have denied that such an event occurred at SRP. (High radioactivity readings in March, 1955 in South Carolina have been attributed to a release two days earlier in Nevada). However, there have been several documented cases of contamination of the atmosphere (tritium) and groundwater attributable to activities at the SRP. Critics also worry about the location of transuranic waste storage tanks in an earthquake-prone area, and the accumulation of explosive gases in the tanks unless they are vented regularly.

The DOE has been considering construction of a modern, safer, more efficient "New Production Reactor" for the weapons program which might eventually permit some or all of SRP's reactors to be shut down. The new facility could be built at SRP or another federal site (Washington or Idaho). South Carolina officials, while highly critical of SRP's track record in managing radioactive and other hazardous waste, recognize the importance of that facility to the Barnwell area economy. More than 14,000 jobs are directly attributable to SRP activities. During 1985, the issue of the new reactor became highly politicized as Secretary of Energy Donald Hodel suggested building one or more new reactors outside of South Carolina, even though an internal government study favored SRP. As of late 1987, however, tentative plans called for starting construction of the reactor at SRP in 1990, with completion estimated for the year 2000.

Commercial High-Level Waste

Each year, one-third of the highly radioactive fuel assemblies in the core of each of the operating nuclear power reactors in the U. S. must be removed and replaced with new, more efficient assemblies that yield the thermal heat necessary to drive the generators that produce electricity. Today, spent fuel remains the legal responsibility of the utility companies that produce it. Most of it is kept at the reactor site in cooling ponds. Originally, the spent fuel rods were to be "reprocessed" to recover reusable uranium and plutonium, but President Jimmy Carter deferred reprocessing in 1977 for reasons related to nuclear nonproliferation and the fear of terrorists acquiring weapons grade plutonium. President Reagan reopened the possibilities for reprocessing in 1981, but the economic benefits were too meager to attract the levels of private investment necessary to develop a suitable program. Meanwhile, more than 60 tons of spent fuel are being produced annually. As cooling ponds begin filling to capacity, some utilities have resorted to shipping fuel assemblies to newer reactor sites with available space, a technique that critics refer to as "musical fuel pools."

Under the *Nuclear Waste Policy Act of 1982,* Congress established complex procedures for the eventual selection of two or more disposal sites for commercial HLW. The search has focused on identifying sites in salt, basalt, tuff, and granite formations throughout the country. The location of the initial facility has been narrowed to three prospects: Deaf Smith County, Texas; the Yucca Mountains in Nevada; and Hanford, Washington. The search for a second site in a granite formation within one of seven eastern states was cancelled in 1986, due to vociferous public opposition within all the potential host states and a DOE estimate that the first repository will not be filled until 2020. Construction of the proposed huge, underground facility remains doubtful even for the first group of prospective sites because of objections from elected officials and citizens. The 1998 projected opening date has been delayed until 2003, but even that appears optimistic.

South Carolina has granite formations that DOE initially considered for siting the second commercial HLW facility, but strong protests from Governor Riley and the congressional delegation persuaded DOE to drop South Carolina from the eligibility list. The principal argument was that South Carolina has done its part in serving as host for LLW and for the thousands of gallons of transuranic waste at SRP; other states should have to share the burden.

While South Carolina appears to be out of consideration as a commercial HLW site for the time being, the state remains near the top of the list of potential "temporary" spent fuel storage locations. When spent fuel reprocessing was considered a viable option, a consortium of multinational corporations formed Allied General Nuclear Services (AGNS) and purchased land from SRP, near Barnwell, to construct a spent fuel reprocessing facility. AGNS never commenced reprocessing operations in spite of an investment of greater than $500 million. Efforts to resume construction have failed, as have attempts by AGNS to sell the facility to the federal government or to a private firm.

At the AGNS site, however, is a large, and completed, fuel receiving and storage station originally designed to hold spent fuel while it awaited

37

reprocessing. This station could be utilized as a cooling pond to house spent fuel rods temporarily until a permanent HLW facility is finally built and operational. This approach is permitted under the language of the Nuclear Waste Policy Act, which provides for Monitored Retrievable Storage (MRS) of spent fuel awaiting final disposition some time after 1998. DOE has agreed to assume responsibility for all spent reactor fuel in 1998 and must make arrangements to put it somewhere. Because timely construction and licensing of a permanent facility is increasingly unlikely, the MRS option will probably be taken.

The DOE's first choice for a MRS is a location near Oak Ridge, Tennessee, close to the abandoned Clinch River Breeder Reactor project. All told, eleven potential MRS locations are being considered, three of them in South Carolina. The AGNS site would probably have been first choice had it not been for the state's adamant opposition to hosting any sort of additional radioactive waste facility. Moreover, Governor Riley and several members of the state's congressional delegation have long been vocal opponents of a "temporary" HLW facility. Their arguments and testimony before Washington policymakers have, interestingly, created an anti-nuclear perception of the Palmetto state in Washington, quite a change from the open-arms posture of South Carolina just a decade ago towards anything related to the nuclear industry.

Still, there remains the possibility that the MRS facility may be sited in South Carolina. The state of Tennessee filed suit against DOE, asking that it be removed from consideration as host for the facility. It appears that DOE will lose the suit. Presumably it will ask Congress for permission to select another state. In that event, AGNS, or South Carolina's two other possible sites (Savannah River Plant and the Cherokee Nuclear Station) will receive a close look.

Perhaps the most frustrating aspect of defense and HLW policymaking, from the perspective of South Carolina, is that the state influence is so limited. Defense radioactive waste management at SRP is beyond state jurisdiction except for monitoring mixed waste and releases of radioactivity. Similarly, commercial HLW management has been dominated by the federal government even though the Nuclear Waste Policy Act formally calls for regular consultation with state officials regarding site selection and related issues. DOE has never been sensitive to state concerns and is unlikely to change its posture in the foreseeable future. Thus, what we are left with is a policy field with a single dominant actor (the federal government). The state role is essentially that of monitoring federal actions and utilizing the office of the governor and the members of the congressional delegation to express the state viewpoint. National policymakers may or may not listen responsively.

Fortunately, the state policymaking role has been greatly expanded in the final category of radioactive waste that we will explore.

Low-Level Waste

Low-level waste is produced in all 50 states. It is packaged and shipped for burial at Barnwell; Beatty, Nevada; or Hartford, Washington. Several other LLW burial facilities operated elsewhere during the 1960s and 1970s, but were closed down between 1971 and 1978 because of leaks, technological problems, and used up storage space.

South Carolina has played a major role in the formulation of national LLW policy. Governor Riley's dissatisfaction with the inequitable burden imposed on South Carolina, which included the shipment of 80-90 percent of the nation's LLW to Barnwell during 1978-1979, prompted him to impose a volume limitation and to increase disposal fees. Today, the Chem-Nuclear Services facility receives around 45 percent of the nation's LLW.

Based in large part upon the recommendations of the governors of South Carolina and the other two LLW host states, Congress in 1980 passed the Low-Level Radioactive Waste Policy Act. The governors, responding to growing citizen and legislative opposition to their states serving as radioactive waste garbage dumps, developed a strategy for a national LLW policy in which other states would share the burden. During 1979 and 1980 the three states took actions to regulate more closely the packaging, transportation, and burial of waste at their respective sites. Then, acting almost in unison, the governors provoked a national crisis.

South Carolina announced a further increase in disposal fees and a substantial reduction in the volume of waste to be permitted entry into the Barnwell facility. The governor of Nevada implemented a series of temporary closures of the Beatty site because of packaging and shipping violations. Washington also intensified state regulatory activities, and its citizens approved an initiative banning out-of-state LLW except from those states agreeing to develop their own burial sites.

Faced with the impending closure of medical and research facilities with limited on-site storage capacity and mounting pressure from the threatened nuclear power industry, the federal government finally responded in 1980 by enacting the Low-Level Radioactive Waste Policy Act. The Act set forth two basic principles: (1) that each state should be responsible for LLW generated within its own borders; and (2) that the states should carry out their LLW responsibilities through formation of interstate compacts. Regional arrangements among the states would constitute national policy on LLW and insure that the states would retain their constitutional responsibilities for protecting the public health and safety and for controlling and regulating land use.

Interstate compacts have been used throughout the history of the U. S. to resolve disputes and common problems. Interstate compacts are provided for in the U. S. Constitution. They have the full force and effect of federal law, state law, and contract law. Any party failing to meet its obligations under an interstate compact is subject to a variety of judicial proceedings.

Around 123 compacts are in effect today, dealing with issues ranging from water pollution and pest control to taxation and crime. The process of compacting is usually long and tedious, taking an average of about five years from the beginning of negotiations to the final stage of implementation. Four processes are required:

1. The *negotiation* of a draft compact by delegates from each interested state.
2. *Ratification* of the terms of the compact by the legislatures of the states wishing to become parties to the agreement.
3. *Congressional consent* through incorporation of the compact language in a national statute. (Consent may be implied in some cases and thus not require formal Congressional action).
4. *Implementation* of the terms of the compact by the party states, usually through a compact commission composed of representatives from each state.

In essence, responsibility for initiating, negotiating, and implementing interstate compacts rests with the states. The compact has proven to be a useful and highly flexible means of settling interstate disputes and coordinating programs and activities. The approach seemed well suited to the complex policy issue of radioactive waste management and certainly, in the eyes of three governors, a vast improvement over the *status quo.*

The federal government was rather happy to turn over to the states full responsibility for the management of this troublesome radioactive garbage. All interested parties were hopeful that through interstate compacts the states could formulate acceptable regional solutions to the LLW disposal dilemma.

Within months, compact discussions were initiated. Rapid progress in negotiating the compacts was made by some states. By late 1985, 39 states had ratified a regional compact. One state, Texas, decided to establish a disposal site for in-state usage only. Seven compacts have been ratified by Congress, a necessary step in LLW compacting because the LLW agreements would constitute enhancement of state political power within a policy field formerly dominated by the federal government. Figure 4 displays recent data on the composition and status of LLW compacts.

A serious problem arose during the congressional consent stage that nearly killed the compacting process. A provision in the LLW Policy Act permitted compact regions with operating burial facilities to exclude out-of-region waste after January 1, 1986. This was made part of the Act to encourage action by siteless regions to promptly identify host states for new facilities and to proceed with licensing and construction. Site selection and development take three to five years so expeditious action was necessary following passage of the LLW Policy Act in 1980.

Figure 4
Compact Groupings as of August 1, 1987

Midwest*
Wisconsin
Indiana
Iowa
Ohio
Michigan-H1
Minnesota
Missouri

Northwest*
Idaho
Washington-H
Oregon
Utah
Alaska
Hawaii
Montana

Central States*
Kansas
Oklahoma
Nebraska
Arkansas
Louisiana

Rocky Mountain*
Colorado
Nevada-H
New Mexico
Wyoming

Southeast*
South Carolina-H
Georgia
Florida
Tennessee
Alabama
North Carolina-H1
Mississippi
Virginia

Appalachian*
Pennsylvania-H
Delaware
Maryland
West Virginia

Central Midwest*
Illinois-H
Kentucky

Nonaligned
Texas
Puerto Rico
District of Columbia
Rhode Island
Vermont
New Hampshire
Maine
New York
Massachussetts
Connecticut
New Jersey

*–Ratified by the U. S. Congress
H –Designated Host State
H1–Designated but has not consented

41

Three of the compact regions had operating burial facilities — the existing ones in Barnwell, Beatty, and Hanford. Pennsylvania later volunteered to serve as LLW host for the Appalachian Compact, Illinois for the Central Midwest Compact,and California for the Southwest Compact. However, several states producing high levels of LLW had not joined a compact (e.g., Massachusetts, New York), while others (e.g., Michigan, Ohio) were in compacts that were encountering difficulties in designating host states. Therefore, representatives from siteless regions and non-compact states felt it necessary to bottle up the compacts in various Congressional committees. From 1983 to 1985, the compacting process was frozen in Congress.

The position of the states in siteless regions was that they did not have sufficient time to locate, license, and build LLW burial facilities by 1986. Compact negotiations were said to be more difficult for some regions such as the Northeast, where the heavily populated states did not wish to locate a dump site near population centers, while the rural states generated small amounts of LLW — not sufficient quantities, they believed, to justify serving as trash receptacles for their big volume neighbors. These states sought to push back the 1986 deadline so that their nuclear waste generating facilities could continue to operate and not be threatened with closure.

The position of states in regions with operating LLW burial facilities was that the states in siteless regions had wasted four years, failing to demonstrate significant progress in identifying a host state or in formulating a compact. Why should they be permitted additional time? Furthermore, representatives of the three sited regions claimed that new above-ground storage technology would insure that waste generators would merely be inconvenienced, not closed down, while new host states were identified and facilities were licensed and built.

It was here that South Carolina once again proved to be a major participant in national policymaking. Under Governor Riley's leadership, a national crisis was provoked by the three states with operating disposal facilities. Also playing important roles in supporting South Carolina's efforts to pry compact consent legislation out of Congress were Senator Strom Thurmond and Representative Butler Derrick.

In January 1985, Governor Riley stated emphatically to the other governors, to members of the South Carolina Congressional delegation, and to Congressional committees that he would close down the Barnwell dump to out of state waste, or perhaps altogether, on January 1, 1986 unless Congress approved the Southeast Compact. Although the legality of such a move is subject to U. S. Supreme Court interpretation there was little doubt that Riley meant what he said. The South Carolina House of Representatives supported the Governor by approving legislation that would close the Barnwell dump, in the absence of congressional consent, on January 1, 1986.

During March 1985, Riley testified before House and Senate committees in Congress, reaffirming his threat, but also indicating a willingness to compromise. Riley, joined by the governors of Nevada and Washington, engaged in intense negotiations with congressional members over the next three months. Finally, an agreement was struck. Access to the operating LLW sites would be permitted until 1992. In return, a series of deadlines would be imposed on states without disposal arrangements, with substantial financial penalties for lack of progress. LLW volume would be limited at the three operating burial sites and surcharges on LLW entering those sites would be more than tripled over several years.

Although the compromise legislation was acceptable to the majority in Congress, individual members were unhappy about certain aspects of the agreement. The bill was tied up over the summer and through the fall of 1985. Just as Congress was about to adjourn on the final day of the session, the legislation was passed by voice votes of the House and Senate. The potential crisis had been averted once again. Congressional consent to five interstate compacts had been won.

While most compacts have been wrestling with the designation of an initial host state and the licensing and construction of the first facility, the compacts with operating dumps must select a host for their second LLW facility as the Barnwell, Beatty, and Hanford sites wind down operations. The first test of this aspect of the compacts has come in the Southeast Compact. Under its terms, Barnwell will be shut down at the end of 1992. Another state must either volunteer or be designated by compact representatives as the second host state.

In October 1985, prior to congressional consent, representatives of the Southeast Compact Commission met and approved a preliminary plan for a LLW dump to replace Barnwell. The second site would open in 1991 and operate for twenty years. If no state volunteered to serve, one would be designated by the commissioners based on a set of criteria including volume and type of waste generated, transportation distances and systems, weather, and population density. The commission hired a New York engineering consulting firm, Dames and Moore, to collect requisite data and help with the selection.

In the absence of a volunteer, the Commission in September, 1986, designated North Carolina as the second host state. The designation followed a bitter argument by North Carolina that if updated figures on population density, waste volume, and other variables had been used, it would have dropped to number three in the rankings, behind Alabama and Virginia. North Carolina's legislature has introduced a bill to withdraw from the compact. If this is passed, North Carolina will have to dispose of its own large quantities of LLW, for it will be an outcast from the other interstate compacts. North Carolina would possibly be required to dispose of other states' LLW as well, since it would not be protected from the Interstate Commerce Clause of the U. S. Constitution.

If North Carolina withdraws, the commission would designate the second choice, then the third, and so on. Alternatively, the Southeast Compact could break up, in which case South Carolina would be expected to continue to operate the Barnwell facility for South Carolina generated LLW only. All former compact members would be left to their own devices. At the time this paper was written, it appeared likely that North Carolina would remain a member of the compact and begin searching for a disposal location.

Disposal costs represent an important future issue because of a declining volume of LLW requiring disposal. Once projected to reach 5 million cubic feet per year, the total LLW volume fell to 1.8 million cubic feet in 1986. Utilities with nuclear power plants have drastically reduced their volume of LLW through compaction, incineration, and minimization of the amount of materials exposed to radiation. Slightly declining or stable LLW volume is projected into the 1990s. Additional, regional "supercompactors" will come on-line to join those already operating in Oak Ridge, Tennessee, Channahon, Illinois, and several other sites, and higher quantities of LLW will be incinerated. Meanwhile, no new nuclear power plant construction plans have been announced for a decade.

Interstate compacting will reduce significantly the volume of LLW disposed of at regional facilities as new host states begin accepting waste. According to industry spokespersons, this will substantially drive up waste disposal costs. Certainly, an important question that must be addressed is whether or not multiple, small compacts can be economically viable as waste volumes diminish or stabilize. If the answer is no, then the consolidation of compacts may be expected during the next few years.

Conclusion

In the extraordinarily complex policy field of radioactive waste management there is a plethora of salient policy actors. Federal, state, and local governments, in addition to special interests in radioactive waste management, vie for power and influence. A highly varied and complex legal environment makes this policy field even more difficult to understand and predict.

Nuclear waste policymaking is very important for a number of reasons. First, it is directly related to the health and safety of the population. Second, the waste problems are growing as the volume of all types of nuclear waste continue to build up each year. Third, it presents a critical test in intergovernmental relations and problem-solving.

The management of radioactive waste represents a special challenge in intergovernmental problem-solving because, unlike most policy choices, it involves the concentration of costs and the diffusion of benefits. Only a few states will be burdened with the responsibility of radioactive waste storage and disposal, while the remaining majority benefit from the sacrifices of the few. Moreover, radioactive waste is a highly emotional policy issue, loaded with negative symbolism and syntax. No jurisdiction seems to want to carry around its neck the albatross of nuclear waste.

South Carolina has played a pivotal role in low-level radioactive waste policymaking. Our policy options and influence are highly restricted in high-level waste management and quite limited in defense-related waste. For the latter two types of nuclear waste, cajoling and jawboning the Congress and the President is sometimes the best we can do, other than continuing to monitor HLW and Defense facilities and their surroundings for leakages and releases of radioactive materials.

In the case of LLW the policy position of South Carolina is much stronger. We have been the leading state actor in developing a solution to the LLW disposal problem — a role that is certain to continue as the Southeast Compact struggles with the difficult issue of designating an unwilling host state and convincing the designee to assume its proper responsibilities.

Radioactive waste policy in South Carolina has experienced a remarkable turnaround since the mid-1970s. An open arms posture towards all things nuclear has become a closed arms stance as the state and its political leaders have insisted on fairness and equity in sharing the burdens and risks of managing radioactive waste. Our challenge in future years is to continue our struggle to win acceptance by all policy actors of the principle that those who produce radioactive waste have the responsibility for disposing of it. Nothing less is acceptable.

References

Colglazier, E. William (ed.) (1982). *The Politics of Nuclear Waste*. New York: Pergamon Books.

Kearney, Richard C. and Robert B. Garey (1983). "American Federalism and the Management of Radioactive Wastes." *Public Administration Review* 42 (January/February): 14-24.

Kearney, Richard C. and John J. Stucker (1985). "Interstate Compacts and the Management of Low-Level Radioactive Waste." *Public Administration Review* 45 (January/February): 210-220.

Kearney, Richard C. (1986). "The Southeast Low-Level Radioactive Waste Compact: Is It Working?" *Public Affairs Bulletin*. Bureau of Governmental Research and Service, University of South Carolina, No. 34 (November).

Kearney, Richard C. (1981). "Nuclear Fuel Reprocessing and the Barnwell Nuclear Fuels Plant." *Public Affairs Bulletin*. Bureau of Governmental Research and Service, University of South Carolina, No. 11 (April).

4

Water Policy Issues in South Carolina

James C. Hite

Introduction

South Carolina has an abundant supply of water. In an average year, South Carolina's streams pour about 33 billion gallons of fresh water into the Atlantic Ocean each day. Beneath the ground of the Coastal Plain are great aquifers holding still more water in amounts that no one has yet been able to measure.

So great are the state's water resources that there has been little need until recently to worry much about water resource policy. Until the middle of the twentieth century, South Carolina remained largely a rural state with an agriculture-based economy. Severe droughts occasionally caused problems for farmers, and the development of manufacturing in some places resulted in pollution of streams. Yet compared to the problems of poverty, race and illiteracy that historically plagued the state, water problems were of little significance.

The industrialization and urbanization that have come in the second half of the twentieth century have changed many things in South Carolina. Pollution spread in our streams, lakes, and coastal estuaries. Increased pumping from wells along the coast to provide water for growing cities, tourists, and retirement communities pulled salt water into the aquifer, contaminating the water supply. Some growing cities in the Piedmont found that local streams were not large enough to supply all the water needed by their expanding populations. Leakages of poisons from waste disposal sites seeped through the ground and contaminated the wells in some communities. South Carolinians began to discover that water could no longer be taken for granted.

Water problems seldom are confined to individuals. When they occur, they affect whole communities or cities or regions. Solutions to those problems require actions by government. So problems of water quality and quantity almost inevitably end up in the political arena, and the management of water resources becomes a governmental function. Since these problems are

James C. Hite is professor of agricultural economics in the Department of Agricultural Economics and Rural Sociology at Clemson University.

relatively new in South Carolina, governments in this state are still struggling to find the best way to manage the state's water resources.

In this chapter, we will examine the struggle in South Carolina to develop a state water policy. We will review the state's water law, the efforts of South Carolina to deal with problems of water pollution, and some new concerns, such as groundwater contamination, water supply, and water conservation. Like all struggles, this one has taken place within a historical context, and so we will begin our examination by viewing the history of water policy in South Carolina.

Evolution of South Carolina Water Law

Common Law Doctrines. Because South Carolina first achieved a political identity as a colony of Great Britain, the water law of South Carolina is rooted in British law and custom. There are two kinds of law in the British system — statutory law, which is the law passed by legislative bodies like Parliament, and common law, which is based on custom, tradition, and precedent (as reflected in past court decisions). The common law dates far back into the early history of Britain, and it was that common law that was transferred to all the British colonies in North America.

In general, the British common law treated water in streams as Crown property, meaning it belonged to the monarch who held it in trust for the benefit of the people. The monarch could, and often did, grant special rights to use streams to various individuals or groups. More often, individuals and groups simply used streams in the everyday course of going about their business. If that use continued over the generations and became a custom and tradition, it was recognized by the common law. The courts might step in and prevent new uses of the stream if they interfered with uses that were sanctioned by longstanding custom and tradition.

In early South Carolina, the settlers made use of the streams every day. Navigation was one of the most important uses since the waterways were by far the easiest way to travel about and to move goods from place to place. The development of rice production in coastal South Carolina introduced a new use of streams. The rice planters diked off fields, installed sluice gates in the dikes, and dug canals, using the rise and fall of the tidal streams to either flood or drain the fields as required.

Not until the early settlement of the backcountry did serious conflicts over the use of streams begin to arise. The terrain of the Coastal Plain meant that there were few opportunities to use the flow of the stream to power a water wheel. But in the Piedmont, some settlers put dams across streams and built sluices to power water wheels for mills. The dams blocked navigation, and so the first major conflicts over use of streams developed.

Since the building of a mill dam represented a substantial capital investment, wisdom required that the dam not be built until the right to obstruct the
stream was firmly established. So most mill owners petitioned the General
Assembly for a special grant for use of the stream, similar to those that had
historically been granted to various individuals or groups by the British
monarchs across the ocean in England.

Until 1790, the South Carolina General Assembly routinely issued grants
on request, arguing that failure to do so would hamper settlement. But as the
countryside filled with people, the number of petitions for grants coming to
the legislature began to increase. People began to object to mill dams that
blocked navigation, or that prevented fish from moving in the stream (Steirer
and Hite, 1983: 3). For example, in 1812, the General Assembly was asked
to force all mill dams to remain open because:

It is the just right of every citizen to receive what blessing divine
providence did intend them to receive from fish having a free passage
up said Tyger River . . . (Petition to General Assembly, 1812: 1812-03-
0087).

Conditions were changing. The legislature became increasingly reluctant
to issue grants for use of streams. But how was it to be decided what uses of
the streams should be permitted and what uses prohibited?

The 1820s were a period of intense interest in improvements in navigation
in the United States, and especially in the South. South Carolina appropriated
$1.5 million dollars (an enormous sum in those days) to support building of
canals and locks and general improvements in navigation. A state board was
established, and then when it seemed to be floundering, a superintendent of
the navigation improvement effort was named. Some canals were built and
some streams were cleared of snags and other obstructions.

Yet, large as the appropriation was, it was insufficient for the task. The
introduction of the steam locomotive and the development of railroads rapidly
made the navigation efforts less urgent. By the late 1820s, many South
Carolinians were becoming disgusted with the General Assembly's misman-
agement of water resource policy. Indeed, even the General Assembly, itself,
seemed to be looking for a graceful way to shed the responsibility for
managing the state's water resources (Steirer and Hite, 1983: 4-5).

In a landmark court case, *Toomer v. Barksdale*, handed down in 1826, the
South Carolina courts provided the General Assembly with the escape it had
been looking for. The case was decided using what has come to be known as
the riparian doctrine of water law, and the South Carolina courts were the first
state courts in the United States to embrace that doctrine (Steirer and Hite,
1983: 5). The doctrine was simply a re-interpretation of the common law. It
held that all landowners along a stream had a right to the reasonable beneficial

use of the flow of that stream so long as the use did not interfere with the co-equal rights of all other riparian landowners. By 1835, the Committee on Internal Improvement of the South Carolina House of Representatives was rejecting all petitions for special rights or for adjudication of conflicts over use of streams, referring petitioners to the "riparian remedy" available in the courts (Report of House Committee on Internal Improvements, 1835).

A few other cases decided by the courts during the 1800s served to refine the riparian doctrine. But, in fact, few people bothered to incur the expense of litigation and the number of cases reaching the courts was small. The meaning of "reasonable use," for instance, still remains unclear in South Carolina, that being a question of fact determined by a jury. Pollution and detention of water for power production have been held in several cases to represent unreasonable uses. The few cases that have been adjudicated also seem to lean toward preserving natural flow, suggesting that any use that tends to disrupt the natural flow of a stream might not be allowable. Yet almost no cases have been decided since 1920, and legal scholars are unsure about many aspects of the legal rights to use water in South Carolina streams (*South Carolina State Water Assessment*, 1983: 27-28).

The riparian doctrine applies only to water in watercourses or lakes, not to groundwater or to what is referred to in law as "standing surface water," — or water on the surface that is not in a watercourse or lake. A watercourse must have a definite channel with banks and it must discharge into another stream or a body of water. The South Carolina law regarding both groundwater and standing surface water is also common law.

The South Carolina courts have followed the "common enemy doctrine" with regard to standing surface water. Under that doctrine, every landowner has the right to take whatever measures are necessary to protect his or her property from damage, even if in doing so he or she backs water up on neighboring land owned by others. That doctrine has been modified, however, in South Carolina to specify that a landowner cannot deal with surface water so as to cause a nuisance. The question of whether the backing up of water in any specific situation constitutes a nuisance is determined by a jury on a case-by-case basis, but in the overwhelming majority of the cases reaching the courts, allegations of creation of a nuisance have been rejected (*South Carolina State Water Assessment*, 1983: 30-31).

There is even greater uncertainty with regard to groundwater. No court decisions pertaining to groundwater can be found in the judicial records of South Carolina (Dukes and Stepp, 1968: 20). Since there is no statutory law on the subject (with the exception mentioned below), it is inferred that the common law holds. The common law treats groundwater in the same way as minerals are treated, and the owner of the land surface is presumed to have the right to extract whatever useful natural resources lie beneath the surface unless the mineral rights have specifically been severed and transferred to another party. This means that the landowner can tap groundwater beneath his or her land in any way that is feasible and can extract that water to the maximum extent possible, including (presumably) extracting water at such a rate as to reduce the water available from his or her neighbors' wells.

While, at first glance, these laws regarding water use may appear primitive, they have served South Carolina well for many years. In a state like South Carolina, where water is relatively abundant, few conflicts over the use of water arise, and there is no need for a detailed delineation of the rights to make use of water. Indeed, a more complex system of water law such as that prevailing in the arid western regions of the United States would have required the expenditure of tax monies to maintain an administrative structure that would be very seldom used. Just as it makes no economic sense for South Carolina to maintain equipment for snow removal to clear roads when the rare heavy snows fall, it has made little sense to maintain a sophisticated system for adjudicating conflicts over our superabundant water resources.

Developments of Statutory Law. In the late 1800s, the General Assembly began passing laws aimed at expediting drainage, and a series of statutes pertaining to drainage, sanitation, and construction of levees were enacted in the first quarter of the twentieth century (*State Water Assessment*, 1983: 36). Viewed from the ecology-informed perspective of the late twentieth century, many of these laws appear to be ill-advised. The Drainage or Levee Districts Act of 1911, for example, states:

> It is hereby declared that the drainage of swamps, drainage of surface water from agricultural lands and the reclamation of tidal marshes shall be considered a public benefit . . . (*State Water Assessment*, 1983: 36).

But, in general, until about 1950, the state gave little official attention to management of the state's water resources.

The early 1950s were a period of intense drought in the Southeast, and the shortage of water caused by that drought served to focus new attention of South Carolina's water resources. In 1954, a Water Policy Committee (created by the General Assembly in 1953) recommended that South Carolina abandon the riparian doctrine and substitute by statute the prior appropriations system of water law that is widely used in the western United States (*State Water Assessment*, 1983: 41). The prior appropriations system might best be described as a system of water rights based on "first come, first served." Water rights are registered in much the same way as deeds are registered. The party holding the highest priority (i.e., oldest) right is entitled to use his or her quota of water regardless of the effects on others. Holders of water rights under the appropriations system need not be riparian landowners, and, at least in theory, the water rights can be severed from landowner rights and sold separately from land.

Although the recommendations of the Water Policy Committee were supported by such conservative organizations as the South Carolina Farm Bureau, they excited enormous controversy. The General Assembly, after consideration of the recommendations in four separate sessions, finally rejected the recommendations in 1957 (Steirer and Hite, 1983: 9-10). By that time, the drought was over and rainfall had returned to normal in the state, eliminating the immediate problem that had given rise to possible reform in the state's water law. Perhaps the primary significance of the controversy was that it caused South Carolinians to take a long look at state water policy for the first time in more than 100 years, and out of that renewed interest grew most of the statutes related to water that were passed in the 1960s and 1970s.

Water Quality Policies

Legal Framework. The South Carolina State Board of Health began to assume responsibility for protecting drinking water as early as 1900, but the state took no actions regarding water quality until late in the 1940s. As state industrialization proceeded, however, there was growing awareness that stream quality was deteriorating. In 1949, Governor Strom Thurmond declared a moratorium on further use of the state's waterways until provisions could be made for cleaning them up. The moratorium was followed in 1950 by the first legislation to control water pollution in South Carolina.

Act 873 of 1950 set up the South Carolina Water Pollution Control Authority and gave that agency responsibility to "abate, control and prevent the pollution of the waters of the state" (Tinubu, 1986: 2-3). The South Carolina law was, at least in part, a response to the *Federal Water Pollution Control Act of 1948*, the first federal legislation on the subject. Although an inventory of the state's streams undertaken in 1952-53 by the State Water Pollution Control Authority demonstrated that pollution was a major problem in South Carolina, there was considerable reluctance to enact pollution control laws that were tougher than those being enforced in other states. South Carolina needed industrial jobs for the thousands of workers being displaced from agriculture, and feared that tough pollution control laws would unduly handicap the state in attracting industries. Hence, the original South Carolina pollution control law contained only relatively weak penalties for polluters.

Both the federal and state water pollution control laws have been amended many times. The most important amendments focus upon increasing the penalties on polluters. In South Carolina, the State Water Pollution Control Authority was merged into the State Board of Health and the latter agency had its name changed to the Department of Health and Environmental Control (DHEC). In most cases, the changes that South Carolina has enacted in its state pollution control law have been in response to federal initiatives.

The water pollution control program that emerged is a joint federal-state effort. Congress has declared that the primary responsibilities for preserving and protecting stream quality rests upon the states. In practice, however, basic policy is established by the federal government and the role of the states is limited to the details of policy implementation. The basic scheme involves classifying streams based upon their use. The required level of water quality for each stream varies with its use classification, but the federal government has generally insisted upon secondary waste treatment as a minimum requirement on all material being discharged to streams or bodies of water.

DHEC remains the principal state agency responsible for water quality, including administration of the state *Safe Drinking Water Act*, regulation of sewage disposal and administration of the South Carolina Hazardous Waste Management Act. The various relevant statutes confer broad powers upon DHEC to do whatever may be necessary to protect the health of the public and to "insure proper operation and function of public water supplies and waterworks," (*South Carolina Code*, 1976: 44-55-30) and take such actions as seem necessary to ". . . protect the health of . . . persons or the environment" (*South Carolina Code*, 1976: 44-56-50). While the existing statutes may require minor modification or refinement to allow DHEC to operate more effectively in some situations and to improve its enforcement of the law, the basic statutory framework for protecting the quality of South Carolina water is in place.

Groundwater Contamination from Waste Disposal. While pollution in some surface waters of South Carolina still remains above levels that many South Carolinians are willing to accept, the fact remains that South Carolina has made considerable progress in abating pollution in the state's streams and lakes. In the last two decades of the twentieth century, attention has shifted to concern about contamination of the groundwater. In some respects, the success we have had in reducing pollution in streams and other surface waters has contributed to the increased problems of groundwater contamination.

The policy problem is not so much a lack of necessary law as it is lack of the information required to enforce existing law. Because so little is known about South Carolina's groundwater resources, groundwater contamination is not easy to detect. Most of the problems to date that have been identified in the state can be traced to landfills or other waste disposal sites, although some problems result from leaks in underground petroleum storage tanks. Generally, the problems are not detected until people begin to notice that something is wrong with water being taken from wells.

In some cases, the source of contamination can be identified as an existing business or activity and those responsible for the problem can be held accountable. In many cases, however, the source of the contamination is a long-forgotten waste disposal site. In some cases, chemical analysis can pinpoint the contaminants as being residuals from use of agricultural chemicals, but those individuals who are responsible cannot be identified. Often times, when the source is traced to an abandoned waste disposal site, it is not clear who placed the waste products at that site. Indeed, contamination from abandoned waste disposal sites is often part of the pattern with regard to some of the most serious problems of contamination. In such cases, the responsible party cannot be identified and remedial action must be taken by DHEC and paid for by tax monies.

Just how serious is the problem of groundwater contamination? Potentially, it is quite serious. The difficulty in assessing the problem is that it may take many years for contamination to be identified. Movement of contaminants through the soil can be extremely slow, and the lateral movement of groundwater beneath the surface is often measured in feet (or even inches) per year. Hence, it is possible that contaminants introduced to the subsurface environment may not be detected for 10, 20, or even 50 or more years.

As of January 1, 1987, 12 hazardous waste disposal sites in South Carolina had been declared eligible for cleanup using so-called "Superfund" monies, federal funds made available through the Environmental Protection Agency for eliminating problems associated with the most threatening problems. According to the Greenville News, South Carolina had more "Superfund" sites per capita than any state in the country (*Greenville News*, 1987: B-1). It is not clear, however, whether the high density of such sites in South Carolina is an indication of an extraordinarily large number of potentially threatening situations in the state or an indication of the political skill and influence of South Carolinians in getting site approval for cleanups using Superfund monies. DHEC officials would like at least eight other known sites in the state to be included on the Superfund list (*Greenville News*, 1987: B-1).

Among the many technical problems in combating groundwater contamination are: (1) devising ways to prevent any further contamination of the subsurface environment, (2) devising effective monitoring of groundwater quality within budget constraints that recognize the many competing uses of the taxpayer's dollar, and (3) devising cost-effective remedial measures when contamination is detected.

The difficulties are such that some have proposed that a ban should be placed on all burying of waste products. That proposal may have merit, but, at least by implication, it poses a more fundamental question: if we are not to bury certain types of waste because of possible groundwater contamination, what are we to do with it? Some of the materials now being disposed of by burial were, before the advent of strong anti-pollution programs, simply discharged into streams. One alternative to burial or discharge into streams is incineration. Yet incineration creates a risk that toxic fumes or other gaseous material will pollute the air.

Matter can neither be created nor destroyed. All that is possible is to change its form. But so long as we remove materials from the environment, we shall also need to place the residuals from those materials back into the environment in either a solid, liquid, or gaseous form. The only choices are: (1) which form, (2) the location of the disposal site, and (3) the timing of disposal. Reduced to their essentials, most pollution problems center on these three choices.

Seen in this light, pollution of some sort is an inevitable result of technology. Rational policy, therefore, might best be concerned not with eliminating pollution, but with minimizing the amount of damage that pollution causes. That is, the policy problem is to reduce waste products to a form that can be disposed of at a site and a time where the least amount of damage will be done. No one has yet found a practical solution to that policy problem. Until such a solution is found, DHEC must be encouraged to find better ways to enforce existing laws regulating burial of waste and must be provided with adequate budgetary resources to carry out its mission.

Saltwater Intrusion. A special type of groundwater contamination of particular interest in coastal South Carolina is saltwater intrusion. So long as there is no pumping of water from wells, the freshwater in the underground aquifers moves slowly toward the sea, often finding an outlet in undersea springs on the continental shelf. But if wells are sunk and considerable freshwater extracted from an aquifer, a low pressure center is created and the groundwater flows toward the low pressure. Saltwater from the ocean enters the aquifer through fissures and also flows toward the center of low pressure at the wells. Sustained high rates of pumping from wells, therefore, can draw saltwater into the aquifers and, eventually, brackish water will begin to appear in the water drawn from those wells.

To date, saltwater intrusion has been a relatively minor problem along the South Carolina coast. But scientific evidence is accumulating that the problem is likely to become increasingly serious in some coastal areas. Special attention has been focused upon Hilton Head Island and the Savannah area. Both Hilton Head and Savannah depend upon wells for their water supply. The sustained pumping at Savannah has reversed the underground flow of water and saltwater is entering the aquifer under Port Royal Sound off the northern end of Hilton Head Island. If the pumping rates on Hilton Head and at Savannah continue, that saltwater will be drawn under Hilton Head and begin to start appearing in the island's well water by late in the present century. What should be done? Efforts can be made to stop the high rate of pumping at wells supplying the Savannah area, but with continued growth on Hilton Head Island, such efforts could, at best, only delay the time when saltwater will appear in the Hilton Head water supply. Efforts might be made to limit further growth on Hilton Head. But unless the rate of pumping at Savannah is reduced, the result still would only be delay of the time of reckoning. Efforts at water conservation on both Hilton Head and at Savannah would also delay the appearance of saltwater in the water supply, but not eliminate the basic problem.

If Hilton Head and Savannah continue to grow, the only real option is to find an alternative supply of water, possibly from the Savannah River. The difficulty with this last option is that surface water, such as that which would be taken from the Savannah River, requires more treatment than does groundwater to bring it to drinking water standards. The greater the amount of treatment, the higher the cost. So the price of continued growth in many coastal areas like Hilton Head will be an increased cost of water.

Water Supply Issues

The problems of groundwater contamination are both those of water quality and water supply. But they are only part of the water supply problems South Carolina faces as the twentieth century draws to a close. While the state has more than enough water to meet all the water supply needs for the foreseeable future, it must find a way to make that water available at the places where it is needed at a reasonable cost.

Water Use. While the state's population is growing and, thus, increasing the demand for water, some decline is expected in the quantity of water required by manufacturing. The demand for water for irrigation of agricultural crops and golf courses will grow over the next fifteen years, but the total growth of water use in the state between 1985 and 2000 is expected to grow at a rate of only about 0.8 percent per year (compounded). Indeed, in 14 of the state's 46 counties, the total amount of water used is expected to decline during the period 1985-2000 (*Outlook for Water Resource Use in South Carolina*).

This picture of abundant water does not mean that sufficient water supplies might not be a problem in some localities within the state. In particular rapidly growing communities on the coast and in the suburbs around Charleston, Columbia and Greenville/Spartanburg may need to go further and further away to tap water sources. Act 90 of the 1985 General Assembly provided a mechanism for communities to undertake interbasin transfers of water. This mechanism will prove useful in allowing these relatively few communities with water supply problems to meet their needs.

Yet, in the main, most South Carolina communities should be able to meet their future water needs from local sources without having to resort to interbasin transfers. As noted earlier, information on groundwater resources is scanty, but conservative estimates of sustainable groundwater yields suggest that 80 percent of the communities in the state can meet foreseeable water needs from locally-available groundwater sources alone.[1] Continued contamination of groundwater represents a threat that might jeopardize future water supply needs. Hence, vigorous programs to prevent any further contamination of groundwater are important to guarding the state's future water supply.

Periodic drought is the other major threat to the state's water supply. Localized droughts with economic impacts on agriculture occur in South Carolina with a frequency of about every one to three years. More serious droughts of statewide and regional significance occur about every 25-30 years. The most recent experience with a severe drought was in 1986.

The most serious economic effect of the 1986 drought was on agriculture and forestry. Clemson Professor Mark Henry estimated that the impact of the 1986 drought on agriculture and forestry resulted in a net reduction in personal income in South Carolina of $166 million (Henry, 1986). Other economic losses were suffered from reduced ability to generate hydroelectric power and from reduced waste assimilative capacities of streams. Losses were also incurred in certain water-related recreational activities (such as raft rides on the Chattooga River) and in certain stresses created on pumping machinery of water supply systems. All of these losses were serious, but little could have been done to have prevented the most serious losses — those impacting agriculture and forestry. Considered against the totality of the South Carolina economy, the losses associated with the 1986 drought represented less than one percent of total personal income.

The lessons of the 1986 drought are that the state can afford to spend very little on any program to prevent or mitigate drought problems. A drought management policy is, in essence, an insurance policy. There are annual premiums associated with keeping the machinery in place and in working order to function when drought occurs. If the most serious drought on record produced economic costs of less than one percent of personal income, it makes little sense to spend substantial sums to prevent such losses. Moreover, not all of the losses incurred in 1986 could have been prevented by any conceivable strategy. The *Drought Response Act of 1985* is the basic law in South Carolina related to drought management, and, except for a few minor flaws, it showed in 1986 that it can work rather well. While some minor perfecting amendments to the law may be needed, the existing apparatus in

South Carolina for dealing with drought appears to be satisfactory and cost effective.

Organization of Water Supply. The most promising way to improve the abilities of South Carolina to deal with drought emergencies may be found in rethinking the organization of water supply in the state.

The organization of water supply in South Carolina is characterized by a high degree of decentralization with many relatively small, free-standing systems governed by local boards. Almost three-quarters of South Carolina's population depends upon publicly-owned water systems to provide daily water needs. There are more than 300 water supply systems in the state, of which 193 are owned by municipalities. The 22 largest municipalities serve 1.2 million people and account for 55 percent of the retail population served by public systems. The remaining municipal systems account for 25 percent of the population served by public systems (about 550,000 people). About 430,000 people in South Carolina obtain water from a variety of other public systems — water districts, water authorities, or nonprofit water companies (Tinubu, 1986: 3-7).

This decentralized organization developed for historical reasons that have to do with the limited powers of South Carolina counties prior to the 1973 changes in the state constitution, and with a variety of federal programs for subsidizing building of local water supply systems. One major factor has been the availability of low-interest loans from the Farmers Home Administration to systems serving populations of 10,000 or less. The Appalachian Regional Commission has also been an important source of funds for systems located in six counties in the Piedmont, providing grants of between 50-80 percent of the cost of capital projects. The state has supplemented these federal funds through the Rural Improvement Program and the South Carolina Water and Sewer Grants Program. In effect, these low-interest loans and grants have allowed many of the state's water supply systems to escape from the need to recover most capital costs through charges placed on the water they provide (Tinubu, 1986: 3-7).

Reductions in federal assistance, however, pose serious threats to many South Carolina water supply systems. So long as the federal government was willing and able to subsidize capital outlays through grants and low-interest loans, South Carolina water systems had little need to worry much about using up their capital. Most systems generate only enough revenues to cover immediate cash expenditures, and do not make prudent allowances for depreciation. So they are not generating sufficient revenues to cover long-term costs. As lines and other capital facilities need to be replaced or expanded, many systems face serious financial difficulties that threaten their continued ability to provide service.

The plain fact is that more than half the water supply systems in the state are eating up their capital faster than they accumulate new capital. A recent study indicates that price increases on the order of 150 percent are needed if the average water supply system in the state is to generate sufficient revenues to recover all costs (Wiggins, Woodside and Womer, 1986). This means that if the minimum monthly (per meter) charge for basic water service is $7, it would need to be raised to $17.50. It also means that if the average South Carolina family pays about $20 per month for water, the bill would need to be increased to about $50 per month.

If federal assistance to water systems is eliminated, or drastically curtailed, substantial rate increases of the order described above will become inevitable. While few South Carolina families are likely to welcome higher water bills, many will be able to adjust their budgets sufficiently to pay those bills. Low-income families, however, may experience considerable hardship in meeting even the minimum charges. Thus, if local systems are to be financially self-supporting, the state will either need to: (1) accept the fact that a substantial number of families are being deprived of water because of an inability to pay, or (2) devise some new scheme for subsidizing water supply through public assistance programs.

There are strong reasons why water systems should be self-supporting. The most important of these is that full-cost pricing of water is required to assure that water is used efficiently. Nevertheless, the social problems associated with depriving some families of water because of an inability to pay are substantial. Aside from humanitarian concerns, families with inadequate water supplies are more likely to contract diseases that might be spread throughout the entire community. Hence, some new scheme to subsidize the costs of providing water to low-income households will be needed.

In fact, low-interest federal loans and grants have been subsidizing the costs of providing water. The current system is not efficient, however, because it not only subsidizes water for low-income households but for all customers, regardless of those customers' abilities to pay. The existing subsidy programs are providing $7.5 million or so annually in grants alone for water systems. An undetermined amount is also provided through the lower interest rates charged on Farmers Home Administration Loans. Yet, if the basic monthly water bill (assuming full-cost pricing) were $17.50, only $2.3 million annually would be required to provide all low-income households in South Carolina with a voucher sufficient to meet their bills for the basic service. Such vouchers, provided as an addendum to public assistance payments, could be remitted to the water supplier in payment for service. The water supplier would, in turn, remit the vouchers to the state treasurer and receive reimbursement. The result would be a net savings on public water outlays and incentives for greater efficiency in water use.

Reorganization of the water supply system in the state might also have some promise in holding down the costs of providing water where and when it is needed. There are substantial economies-of-scale in water harvesting and treatment. All but a few of the large number of independent systems in South Carolina appear to be too small to realize these economies-of-scale. A number of the smaller systems purchase water on a wholesale basis from larger systems nearby and such an arrangement allows both the buying and selling systems to realize more economies-of-scale. In some cases, regional systems to supply water on a wholesale basis have also been established, the most notable case being the Beaufort-Jasper Water Authority. Regional systems that leave retail distribution of water in the hands of local community systems but centralize the harvesting and treatment of water have many advantages, both for holding down costs and for improving the flexibility of authorities' ability to deal with local water shortages such as those that occur in a drought. Elimination of subsidies for construction of small local systems will force many areas in South Carolina to consider seriously the advantages of a reorganization that separates the retail distribution of water from other functions.

Comprehensive State Water Policy

Policy as a Concept: Among those who play active roles in natural resource management in South Carolina, it has long been common to hear talk of a need for a "comprehensive state water resources policy." In 1966, the General Assembly created what is now known as the South Carolina Water Resources Commission and gave it the task of developing such a policy for consideration by the General Assembly. Piece by piece, the Commission has been developing a water policy for South Carolina, but no clearly understood, comprehensive policy has emerged.

One of the reasons there is no comprehensive policy is that the very concept itself is vaguely understood. Although many give lip-service to the need for policy, there is no consensus on what the particulars of the policy should be. Shaping a policy requires making strategic choices which will not please all those who want a comprehensive policy but prefer (for reasons altruistic or selfish) a policy shaped around a particular strategy. In a large sense, policy is strategy.

The central need for a water policy in South Carolina arises from the many programmatic responsibilities of various agencies dealing with water, two of the most active of which are DHEC and the South Carolina Coastal Council. As originally envisioned, the Water Resources Commission was to serve a coordinating role over the programs of agencies until a comprehensive policy could be agreed upon. Those who drew up the legislation that established the

Commission did not intend that it should become an agency with its own programs (Hite, 1986). But the Water Resources Commission, itself, has increasingly been drawn into programmatic activities, including administration of the *State Scenic Rivers* program, the *Groundwater Capacity Use Act*, the *Interbasin Transfer Act* and the *Drought Management Response Act*. As an active player in water resource management in the state, the Water Resources Commission can no longer serve as a referee in dealing with problems of interagency coordination. So programmatic decisions by various agencies are shaping policy, willy-nilly, without any rational effort to see that programs complement, rather than conflict with, one another.

Policy Choices. At the risk of some oversimplification, there are two basic models, or strategies, that South Carolina might adopt for a comprehensive state water policy: (1) one in which water is treated as the common property of all the people of the state, and in which the access and use of that water requires explicit permission and oversight by a government agency; or, (2) one in which water is treated as a commodity like any other, capable of being private property and bought and sold in the marketplace, subject to basic ground rules laid down by statute.

Both of the models, as described above, are capable of considerable modification and nuance, and in fact, various fusions of the two are possible. The historical trend on the treatment of natural resources in Western Civilization has been toward treating them as a commodity of private property, particularly as a resource becomes scarce relative to demand. Such an approach generally has been found to provide the most efficient use of the scarce resource in satisfying human wants. But it does not necessarily provide for a fair distribution of the benefits flowing from use of that resource.

The first model can, at least in principle (if seldom in practice), provide for a distribution of benefits that will be perceived by most people as fair. Yet our experience with bureaucratic allocation of resources teaches us it is often terribly wasteful. Therefore, using the two models to build a water resources policy is an attempt to balance efficiency and fairness, taking some pieces from one model and some from another.

South Carolina has long had so much water relative to the uses to be made of it, there was little need to worry much about efficiency. So perhaps it is to be expected that the policy toward which we have drifted has been one that treated water as a common-property resource. For the foreseeable future, it is likely that most of South Carolina will continue to have a superabundance of water relative to need. Yet the spare margin will diminish if the state continues to grow and there will be a need to move toward greater efficiency in water use. If the state has failed to incorporate some market mechanisms in its water policy, it may be very difficult for water programs to adjust as conditions of supply and demand change. At a minimum, policies requiring water supply systems to be financially self-sufficient, recovering all costs from fees, would assure that some of the costs of growth in particular communities are made explicit and that possible localized problems of water scarcity are made evident in the incipient stages.

In any event, the current drift toward water policy is much less to be desired than explicit and rationally-argued choices about what that policy should be. Statutory responsibility for proposing such a policy continues to remain with the Water Resources Commission. It is a heavy and politically difficult responsibility, particularly given the apathy (except during periods of drought) that South Carolinians seem to have toward water policy. The burden on the Commission is increased by the vested bureaucratic interests it now has in protecting its own programs. Nevertheless, it is very important that the Water Resources Commission press on with the task of devising a basic water policy for consideration by the General Assembly.

Summary and Conclusions

The superabundance of water in South Carolina has allowed the state the luxury of not developing an elaborate set of water laws to resolve conflicts over use or a large bureaucracy to manage water resources. Until serious pollution problems began to emerge in the middle of the twentieth century, South Carolina has been able to operate on the basis of ancient common law in dealing with water problems.

Beginning in 1950, the state found a need for new statutory law to control stream pollution. The drought of the early 1950s caused South Carolinians to consider seriously abandoning the riparian doctrine of water law governing use of surface streams. While, at the critical juncture, the General Assembly backed away from such a drastic break with tradition, a significant body of statutory law focused on water has developed in South Carolina in the last half of the twentieth century. In most cases, these new laws have been aimed at dealing with specific water problems. No comprehensive state water policy has yet emerged.

There is wide agreement that such a policy is needed. The need is particularly acute because of the structure of South Carolina government, with its strong legislature, weak governor, and many agencies. The Department of Health and Environmental Control, the Coastal Council, and the Water Resources Commission, together with a dozen or more other agencies, have all developed active programs focused on management and use of the state's water resources. There is no consensus, however, regarding what should constitute the principal components of a state water policy.

While South Carolina faces no immediate problems in having an adequate water supply, localized problems have occurred and will increase as the state's population expands. Groundwater contamination, and saltwater intrusion into the aquifers particularly along the coast, represents a growing problem. Perhaps the most serious immediate problem is the delicate financial condition of many of the state's more than 300 public water supply systems. Some of these systems are using up their capital without appropriate measures being taken to replace that capital. The pending withdrawal of federal subsidies for water supply systems will probably either force the state to pick up the financial burden of subsidizing water infrastructure or, alternatively, force many systems to make large increases in rates being charged water users.

The choice between state subsidies or financial self-sufficiency by local water supply systems will, inevitably mean a major policy decision regarding water management in South Carolina. Financial self-sufficiency by local systems would introduce market mechanisms into water allocation and provide for adjustments that increase, over time, the efficiency of water use in South Carolina. Yet, if such a policy is adopted, it will also create some economic hardship among low-income families faced with higher water bills unless appropriate income transfer arrangements can be made. Even with such transfers to aid low-income families, the political liabilities associated with higher and higher water rates may mean that a policy of financial self-sufficiency is not politically feasible. The alternative of state subsidies for water systems will place severe strains on an already strained state budget.

It is dealing with these growing financial problems of South Carolina's water supply systems that force South Carolina to develop some sort of water policy. The choices made in attacking this problem will be with the state for generations. If we are wise in making those choices, we should be able to assure that many generations of future South Carolinians will be able to pay as little attention to water resource management as South Carolinians have been able to give that management in the past.

Notes

[1]The estimate is based on work in progress by Janardan Khatri-Ghhetri, doctoral student in applied economics at Clemson. Khatri-Chhetri obtains his estimates by assuming the average yield in existing wells in given aquifers and assuming one well per every ten square kilometers. While the estimate is crude and does not account for whether current average withdrawal from wells is lowering the water table, it is based on a rather low density of wells per unit of area. In the absence of better data on groundwater, the Khatri-Chhetri estimates seem conservative and useful for planning purposes.

References

Code of Laws of South Carolina, (1976). 44-55-30.

Dukes, Gene and James M. Stepp (1968). *South Carolina Laws, Policies, and Programs Pertaining to Water and Related Land Resources.* Clemson University, Water Resources Research Institute.

Henry, Mark S. (1986). "The Personal Income Impact of the South Carolina Drought." Clemson University, Department of Agricultural Economics and Rural Sociology, Draft Report.

Hite, James (1986). "State Water Policy in South Carolina." Presentation at South Carolina Water Week, Hilton Head Island, S.C., September 2-3.

Petition to General Assembly. Spartanburg and Union Districts, 1812. South Carolina Archives, 1812-03-0087.

Report of House Committee on Internal Improvements (1835). Public Improvement Files, 1831-1859, Petitions Enoree River. South Carolina Archives (December 21).

South Carolina State Water Assessment (1983). South Carolina Water Resources Commission, Report No. 140 (September).

Steirer, William and James C. Hite (1983). "The Evolution of Southern Water Law: An Historical Perspective," in *Future Waves: Water Policy in the South.* Mississippi State, Miss.: Southern Rural Development Center.

The Situation and Outlook for Water Resource Use in South Carolina, 1985-2000: A Second Year Interim Report (1986). Draft Report prepared for the South Carolina Water Resources Commission. Clemson University: Strom Thurmond Institute of Government. (Cited as *Outlook for Water Resource Use in South Carolina.*)

Tinubu, Gloria B. (1986). "The Financial Stability of Publicly Owned Water Systems in South Carolina." Unpublished Ph.D. dissertation. Clemson, S.C.: Clemson University (August).

Greenville News (1987). "Waste Mop-Up Plodding Along Despite Danger." (January 5): B-1.

Willins, C. Don, B. Perry Woodside and N. Keith Womer (1986). "A Financial Description and Evaluation of Public Water Systems in South Carolina." Working Paper 082586. Clemson University: Thurmond Institute of Government (August).

5

South Carolina's Coastal Zone: Finding a Balance Between Man and Nature

Robert S. Pomeroy

Introduction

From its northern boundary at Little River Inlet to its southern boundary at the Savannah River, the 190 mile long South Carolina coast offers its residents and visitors a diverse, dynamic and unique opportunity to take advantage of all the amenities people seek from the shore. This diversity is evident in each of the eight counties which make up the coastal zone — Horry, Georgetown, Berkeley, Charleston, Dorchester, Colleton, Beaufort and Jasper. In addition to its political subdivisions, the South Carolina coast can be divided into four distinct regions using both an economic and a physiographic classification.

Economically, the coast north of Georgetown, with Myrtle Beach as its core, is a major recreation and tourism area. The region is a mix of high density hotels, motels, condominiums, campgrounds and amusement establishments, as well as older resorts such as Pawleys Island and Atlantic Beach. This first region is referred to as the Grand Strand. From just south of Georgetown south toward the Isle of Palms is about 50 miles of coast devoted to game management and environmental preservation. This second region includes the Yawkey Estate, the Cape Romain Wildlife Refuge, and the Santee Coastal Reserve. The Charleston area, which is the major population and commercial trade and industrial center of the coast, is the third coastal economic region. The urban growth from Charleston spills over into Sullivan's, James and Johns Islands and inland toward Summerville. To the south

---

Robert S. Pomeroy is a faculty member in the Department of Rural Sociology and Agricultural Economics at Clemson University.

of Charleston is the fourth region which is composed of a series of barrier islands, some of which, such as Kiawah, Seabrook and Hilton Head, have been developed as resort complexes.

Physiographically, the shoreline from the North Carolina line to the Winyah Bay is characterized by a wide beach cut by only a few small inlets. This first region is classified as mainland coast and corresponds with the area described above as the Grand Strand. From Winyah Bay southward the coast is composed of barrier islands and salt marshes. The Santee River Delta (Cape Romain), the second region, is the largest delta system on the East Coast of the United States. The lower delta is covered with an extensive salt marsh. The third region is drumstick-shaped barrier islands with sand dune ridges such as Capers Island, Bulls Island, Isle of Palms, Sullivans Island, Kiawah Island and Hilton Head Island. These barrier islands typically have stable interiors composed of well developed, vegetated beach ridges. The fourth region is nondrumstick-shaped barrier islands which are primarily thin strips of straight, sandy shoreline that are rapidly migrating landward. These areas include Morris Island, Edingsville Beach and Bay Point.

Each of these regions, whether defined politically, economically or physiographically, offers its own potentials and problems. For this reason it is important to view the coast of South Carolina as individual economic or physical regions, as political subdivisions, and as a single entity.

The coast of South Carolina is also unique in that unlike its neighbors, North Carolina and Georgia, much of the coastal zone is not restricted from development either by regulation or as a preservation area. While it is true that approximately 25% of the South Carolina coast is protected as game management and environmental preserve, the majority of the remaining land is not encumbered by severe development restrictions. In North Carolina a strong coastal management program has restricted development, while in Georgia much of the coastal region is protected as natural preserves. With increasing demand for access to coastal areas for development throughout the nation, this situation puts added pressure on the remaining undeveloped areas along South Carolina's coast.

The coast is an area of dynamic change and this is true not only for the biological and physical components of this region, but also for its economic, institutional and demographic components. The coast of South Carolina is currently in a period of change which will impact upon its character far into the future. Problems and opportunities exist which will require careful thought, discussion and management. This chapter will review several important factors vital to understanding present and future trends in the coastal zone of South Carolina and will show how these factors are relevant to a program of coastal zone management.

South Carolina's Coastal Heritage

To understand the coast's present and future, it is important to first understand its past. The present day character of coastal South Carolina is a product of its past and so we will begin with a brief history of the coast.

The Spanish first landed somewhere on the coast of South Carolina in 1514 and established the first European settlement in 1526 in the Winyah Bay area. The Indian population that they encountered generally lived in villages and had developed a fairly diversified agriculture, although hunting was still an important activity. The Spanish report that they found the Indians to be expert seamen, using canoes and fishing in Port Royal Sound. The concept of private property did not exist and the land and water were essentially a common property resource, open to all to use.

This first Spanish settlement failed, as did a later French Huguenot settlement near Parris Island. The Spanish did, however, maintain forts on Parris Island throughout the rest of the sixteenth century.

By the seventeenth century, the English had laid claim to all of the lands along the coast and Charles II established land grants to the territory. In 1670, Charles Town was established, becoming the first successful settlement in the region. As the English settlers moved along the coast they established temporary, then permanent, trading camps with the Indians. This eventually led to the establishment of Beaufort in 1710 and George Town in 1729. As the Englishmen settled they began to displace the Indians and change the land use and economy of the coast. A private property rights system was established.

Cattle were introduced by the English settlers and they flourished in the coastal areas. The cattle were allowed to roam freely in the woods and utilized natural forage. The Indians, who were used to hunting freely in the woods, began to shoot the cattle as free game. This relatively insignificant action led finally to war with the Indians along the coast and a major defeat for them. The Indians were driven further and further inland, leading to an opening up of the coastal region for permanent agriculture and the beginning of the plantation era.

Rice was introduced in the early eighteenth century and remained the most important agricultural crop along the coast until the Civil War. Rice was grown in impounded areas of fresh water and brackish water marsh. The rice plantations stretched from the rivers around Winyah Bay, south along the coast to the Edisto, Combahee, and Savannah rivers. The rice plantations changed the landscape along the rivers and wetlands of coastal South Carolina and were primarily responsible for the introduction of a large number of black slaves.

During the early eighteenth century, Charleston began its rise to prominence as a major port and trading center. A wealthy merchant class developed, exporting rice and, eventually, cotton.

While rice altered the land use and economy of much of the coast it had little impact on the sea islands. While some livestock was grown on the islands, it wasn't until the 1740's that they had a cash crop, indigo. Indigo, however, did not last long as a major crop and soon after the Revolutionary War it was replaced by sea island cotton.

The growing of sea island cotton brought about another major land use change along the coast in that the sea islands were cut over to create more fields. The sea island cotton also matured the plantation economy of the region and institutionalized slavery.

During the early nineteenth century, Charleston began to lose some of its prominence as a commercial center. New railroad connections did, however, eventually increase trade through the port. While there was some industrial activity along the coast before the Civil War, it never flourished due to the continuing profitability of the plantation economy.

The Civil War had disasterous impacts on the state and the coastal region. Following the Civil War, the sea island cotton and rice plantations which once predominated in the coastal region began a steady decline. The large plantations were purchased by private individuals and timber companies. Land values began a long and steady decline.

It should be noted that throughout the period of coastal development in South Carolina the timber industry played an important economic role in the region, as it does today. Following the Civil War, the Beaufort/Port Royal area began to prosper as a port. Fertilizer and lumber became the major industries of the coastal region during this time and remained so until the mid-twentieth century. The Charleston Navy Yard began its rise as a major economic sector along the coast and served as the base for future industrial growth. The mid-twentieth century saw the development of improved transportation along the coast and the attraction of new and diversified industries.

South Carolina commercial fishing concentrated primarily on oysters and finfish through the nineteenth and early twentieth century. By the 1920's these fisheries had begun to decline and shrimping became the primary fishery for South Carolina fishermen by the 1950's.

In order to escape the mosquitoes and the related maladies that they transmitted, plantation families would escape to the coast from May to November. Pawleys Island was used for recreation by 1768 and summer homes were built by 1790. Summer communities also began to appear on islands in the Santee River delta, Murrell's Inlet and Debordieu Island and in Moultrieville, near Charleston. By the middle of the nineteenth century seaside resorts were fashionable throughout the Waccamaw Neck and Grand Strand area and Folly Beach. As cotton and rice cultivation began to decline, the old fields were used for hunting. Through the early twentieth century hunting clubs flourished and hunting these areas remains popular today. An improved transportation system and air conditioning increased tourism and recreation activity along the coast. Resort and retirement development rapidly followed and with it a rise in land values. Recreation and tourism development began its long and steady rise as a major industry along the coast.

Storms have regularly struck the South Carolina coast, often with devastating effect. One of the first recorded hurricanes struck Charleston in 1686 and resulted in saving English colonists from a Spanish invasion, although it devastated crops, boats and buildings. During the nineteenth century, about 19 storms of hurricane intensity reached the South Carolina coast. Over 20 hurricanes have affected the state, directly or indirectly, in the last 80 years, although only 5 or 6 had great impact on lives and property. The most recent hurricane to cause severe damage along the coast was Hazel, which struck in October 1954. One person was killed and there was an estimated $27 million in property losses. Smaller, so-called northeasters, storms have regularly caused erosion and property damage along the coast.

Demographic Profile of the Coastal Zone

The dynamism of South Carolina's coast is not only evident in the biological and physical processes which are continually reshaping its character but in the population dynamics which are having a similar effect. During the past fifteen years (1970 to 1985) there has been phenomenal growth in the coastal zone. Berkeley County has had a 114% population increase during this period; Dorchester County has had a 123% increase in population; and Horry County has had a 74% increase. During this period the population of the eight coastal counties increased by approximately 50%, an increase of over 250,000 people. The population of the eight coastal counties is projected to increase by 36% in the next fifteen years (1985 to 2000) compared to a projected total state population growth of 26%. Anyone who has visited the coast recently has observed first hand this growth and its impacts. An examination of the characteristics of this growth brings to light some interesting trends about how the coastal zone of South Carolina is changing and what has been and what will be the effects of this change.

Census figures are available for the coastal counties of South Carolina beginning in 1850. These figures are shown in Table 1. Population growth in many of the coastal counties remained relatively stable during the latter half of the nineteenth century and the first half of the twentieth century. Beginning in the 1940's the population growth which currently exemplifies the coast began, with the Charleston metropolitan area, Horry County, and the Hilton Head area of Beaufort County being the growth leaders.

69

FIGURE 1.   POPULATION CHANGE – COASTAL COUNTIES: 1980 TO 2000

LEGEND: CHANGE   ⛏ < 1000   ▩ 1000 TO 5000
                      ▩ 5001 TO 10000   ■ > 10000

SOURCE: Clemson Univ. and Census Bureau

All of the eight coastal counties are projected to have double digit population growth between 1985 and 2000, with the counties of Dorchester, Berkeley and Horry experiencing the greatest growth. Dorchester and Berkeley counties, included in the Charleston Standard Metropolitan Statistical Area (SMSA), are projected to grow by 77% and 56%, respectively; and Horry County is expected to grow by 47%.

Five Census County Division's (CCD), cities or communities within a county, in the coastal zone have projected population increases of over 10,000 inhabitants for the period 1985-2000. These include the Beaufort-Port Royal CCD (Beaufort County), Cross Creek and Goose Creek-Hanahan CCD's (Berkeley County), Mount Pleasant CCD (Charleston County), Summerville CCD (Dorchester County), and Conway, Conway East, and Myrtle Beach CCD's (Horry County). These projections indicate that the historic growth areas of the Charleston SMSA, the Myrtle Beach area, and the Beaufort-Hilton Head area will continue to lead the growth in the coastal region.

In 1920, approximately 16% of the state's population lived in the coastal region. This remained stable until 1950 when 18% of the state's population

70

Table 1. Population of Coastal Counties, South Carolina 1850-1980

County	1850	1860	1870	1880	1890	1900	1910	1920	1930	1940	1950	1960	1970	1980
Beaufort	38,805	40,053	34,359	30,176	34,119	35,495	30,355	22,269	21,815	22,037	26,993	44,187	51,136	65,364
Berkeley	—	—	—	—	55,428	30,454	23,487	22,558	22,236	27,128	30,251	38,196	56,197	94,727
Charleston	72,805	70,100	88,863	102,800	55,903	88,006	88,594	108,450	101,050	121,105	164,856	216,382	247,645	276,974
Colleton	39,505	41,916	25,410	36,386	40,293	33,452	35,390	29,897	25,821	26,268	28,242	27,816	27,622	31,776
Dorchester	—	—	—	—	—	16,294	17,891	19,459	18,956	19,928	22,601	24,383	32,276	58,761
Georgetown	20,647	21,305	16,161	19,613	20,857	22,846	22,270	21,716	21,738	26,352	31,762	34,798	33,500	42,461
Horry	7,646	7,962	10,721	15,574	19,256	23,364	26,995	32,077	39,376	51,951	59,820	68,247	69,992	101,419
Jasper	—	—	—	—	—	—	—	9,868	9,988	11,011	10,995	12,237	11,885	14,504
State Total	668,507	70,308	705,606	995,577	1,151,149	1,340,316	1,515,400	1,683,724	1,738,765	1,899,804	2,117,027	23,822,594	2,590,509	3,121,820

71

resided in the eight coastal counties. Each subsequent decade has seen a steady increase in this ratio, with the coastal region having 20% of the state's population in 1960, 21% in 1970, 22% in 1980, and 23% (784,800) of the total state population of 3,436,300 in 1985. By the year 2000 it is projected that over 25% of the state's population will live in the eight coastal counties.

It should be noted that on peak weekends duing the summer months the population in the eight coastal counties climbs to over 1,000,000 people. The population of Horry County, for example, almost doubles during these peak summer weekends.

Within the framework of these general population trends and projections, there have been other less observable but equally important demographic changes occurring along the coast. One of the most striking is the shift in the racial makeup in these counties. For example, in Beaufort County in 1930 the population was composed of 29% whites and 71% blacks. This ratio has shifted through the subsequent years, reaching a balanced ratio sometime in the 1950's and being almost reversed in 1985 (67% white and 31% black). While this shift is most dramatic in Beaufort County, the same patterns are observable in each of the remaining seven counties. The black population has remained relatively stable, due primarily to outmigration, while the white population has risen sharply, due partly to inmigration. This shift corresponds with the decline in cotton sharecropping during the 1950's and the subsequent move north by blacks.

The counties of Beaufort, Berkeley and Dorchester have all experienced large net inmigration rates during the last 20 years. This has been one of the major factors involved in the tremendous growth rates in these counties. During the last ten years all of the coastal counties except Charleston have had positive net inmigration. It is expected that inmigration will continue to be a factor in the growth along the coast. Resort and retirement communities will attract people to Horry, Georgetown and Beaufort counties and the continued growth of the Charleston SMSA will bring people to Berkeley and Dorchester counties.

This inmigration to the coastal counties by retirees has brought about an aging of the coastal population. During the decade 1970 to 1980, for example, the age class 15-64 in Beaufort County increased by 26%, while the age class 65+ increased by 57%. On a subcounty level, as would be expected, the majority of this increase in the 65+ age class occurred in the Hilton Head area. Similar trends are observable in Horry county. On a whole inmigration for retirement purposes tends to increase the median age of the population, while inmigration for economic reasons tends to lower the median age. In general, the former is occurring in the Hilton Head area and parts of the Grand Strand region, while the latter is occurring in the Charleston area. These age shifts will have impacts on the demand for a variety of public and private services, such as medical care.

Beaufort County has one of the highest per capita personal income levels in the state, yet it is above the state average for number of persons below poverty level. While two of the eight coastal counties are ranked in the top ten in the state in per capita personal income, six of the eight counties are above the state average in the number of people below poverty level. This type of income inequality is observable throughout the coastal region, due primarily to small pockets of both wealthy resort and retirement communities and poor indigenous groups. As the economic and demographic makeup of the coast changes, this type of income shift will become more prominent, that is, a large upper income group, a smaller middle class, and a large lower income class.

The eight coastal counties of South Carolina will continue to experience substantial population gains during the next 15 years. This population growth will bring about a shifting demographic profile in the region with changes in the age and income makeup of the population. These population shifts also raise several important public and private policy issues.

As mentioned above, the growth of the coastal population will bring about a greater demand for a variety of public and private services. For example, much of the older population group in the coast are individuals from out-of-state who have chosen to retire in places such as Hilton Head and Myrtle Beach. Many of these people are wealthy and come from areas which provide a high level and variety of government services. More pressure will be put on local and state government to provide improved and expanded levels of public services. Many small local governments in the coastal region often are not able to meet these demands and will need technical assistance to improve their managerial and financial skills. Increased demand for public services will also be felt from other new residents to the state and from the population increase in general.

As the demographic and economic structure along the coast shifts there will be impacts upon the indigenous population of the coast, many of them poor black and white families. For many of these individuals and families, change, such as increased taxes and finding new jobs, could be difficult.

Change also brings about a threat to lifestyle. Many people in the coastal region are sensing that increasing population is threatening their quality of life along the coast and many who have been apathetic to these changes are now taking action to preserve the coastal amenities which first attracted them to the coast. Two recent examples of this are the incorporation of Pawley's Island as a city so that residents have more control over growth and the development of a growth management strategy for Hilton Head Island.

The Coastal Economy

The economy of coastal South Carolina has been characterized by major shifts in its economic sector composition through the years and these shifts continue today. The coastal economy today is more diversified than in the past, being centered around several key industries including tourism and recreation, agriculture, the federal government and manufacturing.

Throughout the coast of South Carolina, tourism, recreation, and resort and retirement development have become the region's largest and fastest growing industry. This is reflected in broad economic terms, in 1985 spending by visitors to South Carolina's coast amounted to more than $2 billion or about two-third's of total travel and tourism spending in the state, and in demographic terms, Horry County and the Hilton Head area of Beaufort County are not only the top generators of transient lodging rentals in the state but are among the fastest growing areas of the coast and the state.

The jobs created by tourism, recreation, and resort and retirement development are primarily those in the retail trade and service sectors, that is, a mix of retail stores, hotels and motels, eating and drinking establishments, amusement facilities, real estate, and health services. While large numbers of new jobs are being created, many of these retail trade and service jobs are relatively low wage and as jobs in this sector increase it tends to widens the income gap discussed above. Many of these jobs are seasonal in nature, although this is changing as the industry matures and becomes more year-round. As new jobs are created people are commuting long distances to work and the impacts are felt in the larger geographic areas.

Associated with this increase in tourism and resort and retirement development is the construction industry. New construction for residences, hotels and motels, and shopping centers is on the increase and there is a large amount of capital formation along the coast.

The growth from tourism, recreation, and resort and retirement development has been good for the coast, creating new jobs, strengthening the economic base of the region, and providing more amenities for residents and visitors. Yet, there are costs associated with this development as well. As discussed above, many feel that the quality of life along the coast is deteriorating. The public sector is being required to provide more and improved levels of services from new roads to better police protection. The exact costs and benefits from this economic activity has of yet not been calculated but it is an issue which needs to be addressed. This industry is in a boom period now but the momentum of new development cannot be maintained forever and eventually will flatten out. We need to be aware of this situation and its consequences.

The federal government is a major employer within the coastal region, especially in Beaufort and the greater Charleston area. This is primarily due to a number of military installations in the region. The coastal zone contains approximately 60 percent of the total civilian employment in South Carolina and 70 percent of all the military personnel in the state. Throughout this century, the Charleston Navy Yard has benefited the coastal economy. During World War II, the Yard employed about 26,000 people. Although after the war the shipyard went out of the construction business, it remained the area's largest industry. Through the influence of the legendary Congressman Mendel Rivers, the Charleston Naval Base complex was to become a major operating base as the focus of the nation's submarine ballistic missile program. With the Air Force Base at Myrtle Beach and Charleston, and a Marine Corps base and air station at Beaufort, the Federal government is a major employer in the coastal region and helped lay the base for the industrial development in this region.

The 1950's saw the beginning of a major statewide initiative to attract new industries. Up until this time, except for the fertilizer and lumber and paper industries, manufacturing was not a major sector of the coastal economy. Improved transportation facilities, including upgrading of port facilities at Charleston, North Charleston, Georgetown and Port Royal, assisted in attracting a mix of new industries to the coast. Steel, chemical, textiles, machinery, and transportation equipment manufacturing firms have located along the coast due to access to an international port, good highways and ample supplies of fresh water. Manufacturing industries are concentrated in the three county Greater Charleston area, Colleton County and Georgetown County.

Agriculture, forestry and fisheries continue to be important sectors of the coastal economy. The plantation economy has given way to modern agriculture along the coast. Fresh market tomatoes and other vegetables, particularly in Beaufort and Charleston, are a major coastal crop. Tobacco is the coastal region's most valuable crop, especially in Horry and Georgetown counties. Soybeans and corn are less important along the coast than in other parts of the state. It is interesting to note that besides having a thriving tourism industry, in 1985, Horry County was ranked as the number one agricultural county in the state in terms of cash receipts from farm marketing. Coastal agriculture is in a period of transition due to the financial crisis facing agriculture. The future of agriculture along the coast will also be impacted by urban encroachment, competition for water for irrigation, and new wetlands or "swampbuster" legislation.

Over 60% of the coastal region is forested and vast tracts of land along the coast are either federally owned or are owned by timber companies, particularly in Berkeley, Dorchester and Charleston counties. Forestry and the lumber industry has traditionally been a major sector of the coastal economy and it continues to play an important role in the regional economy today.

As with agriculture, the commercial fishing industry along the coast is also in a period of transition. More fishermen than ever are vying for what many feel is a declining or stabilizing fishery resource and many are having financial problems. Resource management is becoming increasingly more essential, especially with competition from recreational fishing. Finfish, shrimp, blue crab, oysters and clams remain the predominant species. Most South Carolina caught seafood is shipped out of the state. A positive trend for meeting the growing nationwide demand for fish is the development of aquaculture. The coastal region of South Carolina has the potential for the development of an aquaculture industry using a variety of cultural methods. Aquaculture could be conducted in upland ponds, brackish water and salt water ponds, and in open water enclosures.

The trend in the coastal economy is toward a larger percentage of the labor force employed in service and retail trade activities. These businesses are primarily servicing the expanding tourism, recreation and resort and retirement development along the coast. This is a major shift in the economic structure of the coastal region of the state and will have profound impacts into the future. While the shifts are good we must be aware that these growing sectors will eventually stabilize. It is also important to note that as these relatively low wage jobs increase it tends to strengthen inequitable income distributions in the region. While these sectors need to continue to be promoted we must be aware of the consequences and plan for a continued diversification of the coastal economy. Reliance on one particular sector can lead to problems.

The Coastal Environment

The coastal region of South Carolina is rich in natural resources, including moderate climate, dramatic scenic qualities, productive wetlands, fertile soils, wide beaches, fish, wildlife, water, and minerals. These resources are valuable for a variety of uses, including residential development, recreation, transportation, agriculture, industrial development, preservation, and others. Often these uses become competitive and conflict arises.

Unlike any other ecosystem, the broad interface between land and water known as the coastal zone is an area where production, consumption, and exchange processes occur at high rates of intensity. Ecologically, it is an area of diverse and dynamic biogeochemical activity but with limited capacity for supporting various forms of human use.

As human activity along the coast of South Carolina has increased, so have environmental disturbances in the region. Many of these disturbances are isolated and limited in scope, while others are of much broader concern and must be understood in terms of long range, cumulative impact. In an interdependent coastal ecosystem, however, it is imperative to understand the impact of a single disturbance on other factors in the system or management will very likely fail.

A number of important coastal resource and environmental issues, having both immediate and long-term impact, are of concern in the state. Two of particular interest both from a resource and economic standpoint have to deal with beaches, that of beach erosion and beach access.

Beaches move and coastlines change. The beach-dune complex is one of the earth's most dynamic environments. The beach is always changing and migrating in accordance to factors such as waves, sea level change, the shape of the beach, and sand supply. As discussed briefly above, the South Carolina coast has three types of beach: mainland (such as Myrtle Beach), barrier with sand dune ridges (such as Hilton Head and Isle of Palms), and thin, retreating barriers (such as Morris Island). In many parts of the coast natural beachfront movement and inappropriate location of development have brought about a conflict resulting from beach erosion. There is currently a great deal of debate at both the local and state government levels as to the most appropriate means to deal with this problem. Both structural (such as revetments, groins and rip-rap) and nonstructural (such as retreat, nourishment and setback lines) methods for addressing the problem are being discussed. Neither the federal nor the state government has adopted a consistent policy on beach erosion, although there is work currently ongoing in that direction. The economic and aesthetic value of the state's beaches make it imperative that a strategy be developed. Nonstructural methods, such as a coastal setback line and limited nourishment of high value beaches, and citizen education about the potential dangers of erosion would make a sound policy base.

As urbanization has increased along the South Carolina coast, public access to beaches and other natural areas has decreased. There is concern that in many cases access to valuable public resources is being limited to the well-to-do. As growth continues in the coastal region there will be greater demands for public recreation access, especially to beaches and boat ramps. State and local governments have endeavored to ensure public access to coastal resources, but have often been restricted by lack of funds and authority to increase access. A dilemma between preservation and access to natural areas also exists. As private development of the coast increases, developers should be encouraged, either voluntarily or by regulation, to ensure areas of public access to beaches and other natural areas. In areas where public money is used to enhance a natural resource, such as beach renourishment, access should be established. Funds at both the state and local government levels should be made more readily available to identify and acquire significant

77

coastal natural and recreational lands and to ensure access to these areas. Incentives should be established for private landowners to provide access or to transfer valuable areas to government.

The Santee River Delta (Cape Romain) is the largest delta complex on the East Coast of the United States. An extensive salt marsh covers the lower delta plain. This salt marsh makes up but one part of an extensive vegetated tidelands and wetland system along the South Carolina coast. Vegetated tidelands include the intertidal areas between the normal high water and low water marks. Wetlands are those areas above the mean high tide mark. Marshes are one of the most productive ecosystems on earth and serve many uses including wildlife and aquatic species habitat, flood protection, cleansing of water, and shoreline stabilization. Wetlands, whether fresh- or brackish-water, serve many of the same values as the vegetated tidelands in cleansing runoff waters and regulating their flow. Unique to South Carolina and several other South Atlantic coastal states are rice field impoundments. Land along the coastal rivers, beyond the salt water reach of high tide, were enclosed or impounded in the 1800's for rice production. Rice is no longer grown on a commercial scale in these impoundments, but the water in many impoundments is still manipulated to attract waterfowl, for mariculture, and for pasturage. State laws and regulations specifically address the protection of vegetated tidelands, although a clarification of state policy toward protection and preservation of these valuable resources is needed. Similar levels of protection do not exist for freshwater wetlands. An inventory of wetlands is needed and an articulation of protection and management policy is necessary. With an emerging aquaculture and mariculture industry the issue of reimpounding impoundments has arisen. A variety of federal and state agencies are involved in this issue. With the number of former impoundments along the coast no currently undisturbed areas need be impounded. Former impoundments can be repaired and maintained for a variety of uses. A state policy on the value of this resource and its management is needed.

Water supply and quality is the key to maintaining a sound socio-economic and environmental base in the coastal area. Increasing population and economic growth in the coastal region has put more pressure on coastal water resources. The demand for water in the coastal zone is expected to increase, especially for irrigation of agricultural crops and golf courses. There is no imminent water shortage in an absolute or hydrologic sense in the coastal zone, although the problem is in ensuring that there is enough potable water in locations where consumers need it. As growth continues in the coastal region the transfer of water from other water basins may be necessary. The organization of water delivery in the coastal region is characterized by a high degree of decentralization with many small, freestanding systems. This myriad of water systems may make the interbasin transfer of water difficult.

Groundwater is a major source of water for domestic uses along the coast. Groundwater problems are beginning to be encountered in the coastal region, especially in Hilton Head. Sustained pumping has caused a tremendous drawdown of groundwater in this area resulting in potential supply and saltwater intrusion problems. Alternatives such as water conservation and taking water from the Savannah River are being explored.

Maintaining water quality, with increasing growth and development along the coast, is also a critical water resource issue. This is especially true with increased interest in aquaculture and mariculture. Runoff from urban and agricultural areas and occasional violations of wastewater discharge permits contribute to water quality problems in sensitive coastal water environments. In coastal areas where land prices are at a premium, environmentally acceptable sites to locate landfills will be increasingly hard to find. Unsuitable lands, such as wetlands, have often been used. Solid waste disposal problems will continue to be an important issue in coastal areas in the future. Competition for waterfront space has also caused water quality problems, especially over conflicts between marinas and shellfish beds. In some coastal areas, water quality exceeds the designated water quality standards. Action is necessary to upgrade the classification of these waters where eligible. More information is also needed on the assimilative capacity of waters in the coastal area so that better siting and development decisions can be made.

While not fully realized as of yet, the coast of South Carolina has potential for offshore mining of phosphate and for oil and natural gas extraction. Any mining operation is required to obtain a permit under the S.C. Mining Act. Potential for conflict and environmental problems from these operations does exist and need to be understood and prepared for.

The declaration by the Federal government in 1983 of a 200 mile exclusive economic zone off the nation's coast could have important implications for coastal states. The ocean three miles from shore is controlled by the states and twelve miles by the Federal government. With the passage of the Law of the Sea Treaty, the United States, which did not sign the treaty, declared ownership of oil, gas, and other hard minerals on the ocean floor, and control of fisheries out to 200 miles. As the jurisdictional questions are handled and defined, there could be important impacts on and benefits to coastal states.

One issue which has not received enough attention, but will need to be addressed more fully as the coast continues to grow is coastal hazards. This includes a variety of potential problems resulting from the winds and waves of storms and sea level rise. Further public knowledge of potential hazards from coastal storms and close local-state corporation is necessary to reduce loss of life and property.

A great deal of research has been conducted through the years to gain a better understanding of the complexities of coastal ecosystems. To support management and regulatory activity in the state, continued baseline information on a number of vital coastal resource and environmental areas should be collected and analyzed. These include beach erosion trends, acreage and location of tidelands, wetlands and impoundments, and water assimilative capacity, as well as the economic value of coastal resources. We have learned much about the coastal ecosystem, but there is still much more to learn.

Coastal Zone Management in South Carolina

South Carolina is rich in coastal natural resources. The plantation era and slow industrial growth in the coastal zone protected these resources from the impacts of development felt in other East Coast states. Increasing population growth along the coast and growing concern over degradation of coastal resources led many coastal states, during the 1960's and early 1970's, to enact legislation that established authority over use of coastal wetlands. By 1972, every state on the east coast, except South Carolina, had enacted such legislation. During this same year Congress enacted the Coastal Zone Management Act (CZMA) to encourage the states, through the availability of federal grants, to extend this authority throughout the entire range of their coastal zones. While South Carolina was slow to act on its own to enact a wetlands protection law, Federal incentives prompted state officials to develop a more broad based program for coastal resource protection.

In 1973, the state created the South Carolina Coastal Zone Management and Planning Council and assigned it the task of developing a comprehensive coastal zone management program that would meet the requirements of the CZMA and enable the state to receive funding. At this time, the State did not have sufficient authority to control land and water uses within its coastal zone. Through the Budget and Control Board, the State exercised control in the coastal zone only over the tidelands and submerged lands and this was not enough authority to meet the requirements of the CZMA. In 1973, the General Assembly began work on a law to give the State more control over the resources and activities in the coastal zone. After four years of debate, the South Carolina Coastal Zone Management Act of 1977 emerged.

The Act establishes the South Carolina Coastal Council, an administrative body composed of eighteen legislators and citizens, and charges it with two basic duties: (1) to develop, administer, and enforce a State coastal zone management program; and (2) to exercise regulatory control over various activities within certain areas of the coastal zone. The basic policy of the Act is "to protect the quality of the coastal environment and to promote the economic and social improvement of the coastal zone and of all the people of the state."

South Carolina's coastal zone encompasses "all coastal waters and submerged lands seaward to the State's jurisdictional limits and all lands and waters in (eight) coastal counties...." In general, anyone desiring to "fill, remove, dredge, drain or erect any structure on or in any way alter any critical area" within the coastal zone must obtain a permit from the Coastal Council. The Coastal Council, however, has direct permit-issuing authority only within four types of statutorily defined "critical areas." The critical areas are defined as coastal waters, tidelands, beaches, and primary oceanfront sand dunes. The definitions of these terms by the Coastal Council determine the extent of the Council's regulatory jurisdiction under the Act. These definitions will not be addressed here, although it should be stated that the meanings of many of the terms are not clear and the Coastal Council has restrictively interpreted the geographic scope of its authority. Permitting rules and regulations have been established by the Coastal Council for activities in the critical area. Many specific activities are statutorily exempted from the council's permit process.

While direct permitting authority of the Coastal Council is limited to the critical areas, indirect management authority of coastal resources is granted to the Council in the eight coastal counties. Within this area the Coastal Council staff shall review any project requiring a state permit, Federal activities, licensing, or funding in order to determine its consistency with the S.C. Coastal Management Program. Additional regulatory functions are performed by various other state and local agencies under a "networking" approach. This approach involves a memoranda of understanding between agencies that they agree to administer their programs in accordance with the coastal management program.

The coastal council has established a set of resource policies and management authority guidelines for each activity of coastal concern both within and outside the critical area. These include a wide range of activities from residential development to dredging to energy facilities. The Coastal Council utilizes a "performance standards" approach to managing activities in the coastal zone which deals with the impact of an activity rather than the activity itself. Upon request the Coastal Council will also prepare Special Area Management Plan's for specific areas in the coastal zone. These plans are part of the Coastal Council's technical assistance program to local governments along the coast. Besides being a regulatory body the Coastal Council staff provides planning, management and scientific assistance to assist local governments in managing the coastal resources within their jurisdiction.

In addition to the Coastal Council, a state government agency, there are several other levels of government which have authority on the coastal zone. At the federal government level the most pervasive presence is the Army Corp of Engineers which administers the federal permit program for activities in navigable waters. The Environmental Protection Agency also has regulatory authority in the coastal zone through a variety of laws including the *Clean Water Act* and the *Clean Air Act*.

At the state level, in addition to the Coastal Council, the principal state agencies with jurisdiction in the coastal zone are the State Budget and Control Board (nontidal, navigable waters), the Department of Health and Environmental Control (air and water pollution control), the Land Resources Conservation Commission (mining operations), the Water Resources Commission (surface and groundwater), and the Department of Wildlife and Marine Resources (fish, game, and rare and endangered species).

Although not a governmental body, there are three regional councils of government functioning in the coastal zone. These regional councils are not regulatory agencies but provide assistance to local governments in planning for growth and development. The regional councils are multi-county.

Perhaps the most important government level are county and municipal governments along the coast. While most local governments along the coast have not taken an active role in coastal zone management or in land use planning in general this trend appears to be changing. As discussed earlier, many communities, such as Pawley's Island, are incorporating themselves so that their residents will have more say and responsibility in managing their growth. This is a very positive sign. The future of the coast will rest not on a single state government agency but with a coordinated and complementary coastal zone management program involving both state and local government. A great deal of assistance is now available to local governments in the coastal zone to develop planning and management programs to protect natural resources and community amenities.

As the coastal zone management program in South Carolina matures we are beginning to see changes and positive results. We are now seeing the Coastal Council beginning to give more coastal management responsibility to local government. Since much of the growth related activity along the coast is out of the critical area and thus the Coastal Council has limited authority over the activity, local governments must begin to take more responsibility, This process needs to be encouraged and supported through continued technical assistance from the state and a coordinated permitting program.

Interagency permitting also needs to be coordinated and streamlined to reduce some of the time and problems of getting a permit.

The Coastal Council is beginning to look at new and innovative ways to reduce conflicts between developers and regulatory agencies. One method, called mitigation, provides a framework to deal with potential conflicts before they end up in court.

As local governments begin to take more responsibility for planning and management it will hopefully reduce some of the load on the Coastal Council staff to begin to address other issues. One of the most important will be the preparation on a long range outlook and plans to guide coastal development. As has hopefully been pointed out in this chapter, the coast is going through many changes and the implications of these changes need to be fully considered and addressed. The various parts — economic, demographic and natural resource, must all be viewed as a whole to guide growth and change along the coast.

Looking Toward the Future

Change is an integral part of the coastal environment. The dynamic nature of coastal ecosystems is a fact of nature. Economically and demographically the coast of South Carolina is changing. It is projected that the population of the coast will continue to increase through the end of the century. Many of these new residents will be non-natives. They will require new and improved levels of services from both the public and private sectors. As growth continues it will put more pressure on fragile natural resources. Conflicts will arise from these changes, as will opportunities.

The public's perception of the coast is changing in South Carolina. People are beginning to become aware of the consequences of unmanaged growth. There is concern about a deterioration of the quality of life along the coast. People are not relying solely on the government to deal with change but are getting more personally involved with shaping their future. Change can be directed and controlled, but it will require education and planning not reaction.

The coast of South Carolina is a truly unique and wonderful place. The amenities it offers cannot be duplicated anywhere in the world. The complexities of coastal zone management issues — demographic, economic, natural resource, require an integration of many facets of each issue. Change can be positive if we are informed and involved.

References

Graber, P. H. F. (1984). "The Law of the Coast in a Clamshell. Part XV: The South Carolina Approach." *Shore and Beach* 52:2 (April): 18-25.

Wilson, H. S. (ed.) (1982). *Coastal Development: Past, Present, and Future.* Proceedings of a Conference, December 3, 1982. Charleston, S. C.: The South Carolina Sea Grant Consortium.

Wyche, B. W. (1978). "The South Carolina Coastal Zone Management Act of 1977." *South Carolina Law Review.* 29:5 (September): 666-703.

6

Public Education in South Carolina: The Struggle From Mediocrity to Excellence

Richard C. Kearney and Terry K. Peterson

Introduction

Until very recently, the story of public education in South Carolina was that of a resource-poor state doing badly. Historically, South Carolina has ranked at or near the bottom on almost all indicators rating the 50 states on resource commitment and quality in education. In 1984, the state took a bold step forward with enactment of the Education Improvement Act (EIA). The EIA has been recognized nationally as a "model" of education reform. Some observers feel that positive results are already being noted from this far-reaching and comprehensive attack on a traditionally backward state education system.

After a brief look at the history of public education in South Carolina and in the United States, this chapter will describe current education policy in the States. Special attention will be devoted to the Education Improvement Act, including the forces that led to its passage and its intended outcomes, as South Carolina attempts to move from mediocrity to excellence in this critical policy field.

Historical Background

Originally, the explicit purpose of schooling in the United States was to further Protestant religious beliefs and institutions among settlers in the colonies. (The first widely used textbook was entitled *Spiritual Milk for*

Richard C. Kearney is an associate professor in the Department of Government and International Studies at the University of South Carolina. Terry K. Peterson was Governor Richard Riley's Executive Assistant for Education Policy. He currently is on the staff of Winthrop College.

Babes Drawn from Both Breasts of the Old and New Testament). Early education efforts were privately funded and mostly reserved for the children of the wealthy and well born.

The principle of free and mandatory public education evolved over some 200 years, as state and local jurisdictions asserted increasing responsibility for schooling. In 1850, Connecticut became the first state to mandate free public education. Two years later, Massachusetts passed the first compulsory school attendance law. Other states soon followed these innovators with legislation of their own.

Regional differences in the quality, scope and nature of public education soon developed, with New England serving as the leader and the South as the laggard. Although Charleston, South Carolina was the site of the first public school in America, until the Civil War private education was predominant in the southern states. Publicly financed schooling was aimed mostly at orphans and children of the poor. The traditionally weak southern public education systems were further held back following the War by grinding poverty and the race problem.

Under the Tenth Amendment to the U.S. Constitution, public education is a field reserved to the states. However, education in many states has largely been an activity carried out and funded by local governments, primarily school districts. States have exercised oversight in education policy and set some minimum standards applying to all local education jurisdictions but, until recently, non-southern states delegated most responsibilities to localities. In the South after the War, local districts lacked sufficient resources to fund and administer public education. As a consequence, a system developed of strong state centralization in education. Southern states provided most of the funding for education systems and made important decisions on such matters as curriculum, textbooks, and teacher training and compensation. This pattern of state centralization continues to prevail today in a majority of the states of the old Confederacy.

Like her sister states, South Carolina had a limited public education system that was made worse by the ravages of the Civil War. In response, South Carolina developed one of the most highly centralized education structures in the nation. As we shall see later, recent policy changes have further strengthened the state role in educating South Carolinians.

How Public Education is Organized Today and Who is Involved in Making Policy

The basic local unit for providing public education in South Carolina today is the school district. There are one or more school districts in each county; a few cross county lines. Each district is governed by a school board. Most boards are elected by the voters of the district. However, in several districts the school boards are appointed, generally by the local representatives to the state legislature, a practice that is slowly being phased out. A superintendent is responsible for the day to day management of the schools, including personnel, finance, transportation, facilities and so on. Generally, the superintendent is employed by the school board; however, in a number of districts the superintendent is elected, a practice that is also being phased out.

State authority over education is exercised through the governor, the General Assembly, the courts, the State Superintendent of Education, the State Department of Education, and the State Board of Education. The *Superintendent of Education*, who is the chief state school officer, is elected every four years on a statewide ballot. He acts as head of the *State Department of Education*, which is the organization responsible for day-to-day operations of public elementary and secondary education at the state level. The State Department provides curriculum guidance, technical assistance, training aids, and testing assistance, and sets minimum standards for school districts. It also sets standards for all teacher training institutions. In essence, the State Department of Education is the administrative arm of the state in education and the principal policy making body. The *State Board of Education* is responsible for oversight and regulation of the school systems of the state. In practice, its policy making role is much more limited than that of the State Department. Except for one member appointed by the governor, the State Board members are elected by the General Assembly.

There are other important policy actors in the field of public education. *Taxpayers* are concerned with the cost of public schooling since they fund most of it through their property, sales, and income taxes and desire positive results for their tax investments. *Students* seek an educational environment which is interesting and challenging and where discipline policies are reasonable and fair. *Parents* want to be sure that their children are receiving an adequate education. *Educators* wish to be granted the authority to make operational decisions in the activities of their school and their classroom and, of course, to win higher pay and fringe benefits for their work. Finally, *voters* make their influence felt through electing school boards, the state superintendent, the legislature, and the governor. These elected officials, in turn, make budget, tax, and policy decisions affecting the schools. In some instances, South Carolina voters have the opportunity to participate directly in policy making through citizen referendums on school financing decisions. It is important to understand that while all the policy actors noted above make demands on the schools, they do not always speak with a common voice; they are sometimes found in intense competition with one another over resources and policy decisions.

The role of the national government in public education is limited and, under the Reagan Administration, diminishing. The United States is almost alone among nations in that it treats education as a subgovernment function. Nationally funded and operated systems are the norm. The federal role in U.S. education has always been limited, although federal activities did pick up during the 1960s and 1970s, with passage of the Elementary and Secondary Education Act of 1965 and the Education of All Handicapped Act of 1975. These and other national programs did not provide general aid to education, but rather were targeted at specifically identified problem areas in existing state-local programs, such as poverty-ridden schools and the special needs of handicapped students. Today most of these efforts have been merged into a block grant called The Education Consolidation and Improvement Act.

During the 1960s and 1970s the federal government took the lead in education reform and innovation. It offered grants for state and local program experimentation; disseminated statistics, research findings, and policy information; and provided technical and consulting aid to state departments of education and to school districts. In 1979 the Carter administration created a U.S. Department of Education to coordinate federal activities in public education. During this period the federal portion of total school expenditures grew from 4.5% in 1960 to 9.0% in 1980.

However, President Reagan substantially reduced the federal presence in public education. By 1984 only 6.4% of education funding came from Washington. Reagan attempted (unsuccessfully) to abolish the new U.S. Department of Education and eliminated or substantially cut back funding for several federal programs. It was obvious that education policy initiatives, reforms, and funding increases would have to come from the state and local governments for the duration of the eighties.

For the past decade there has been a clear trend toward increased state activity in the field of education. The local school district is still the major unit of government for delivering public education services, but education policy making and funding are being concentrated at the state level. The dramatic shift in sources of funding provides evidence of this trend. Although the states vary greatly in their contributions to the schools, the average state share has been growing for many years. In 1920 local sources funded 83.2% of education expenditures, and the states only 16.5%. By 1975 the state portion had risen to about one-half. This increasing state role may be attributed to the effects of taxation and expenditure limitations that have caused reductions in property tax revenues, the recent withdrawal of the federal government from education financing, and the apparent incapacity of local education districts to respond adequately to the complex challenges of the past 20 years.

The overriding issue in public education is money. The link between spending and educational quality is widely accepted. For the poor states, like South Carolina, a move to quality education requires a strong state role in funding. And since "he who pays the piper calls the tune," more state policy and program intervention is certain to accompany increased financing.

Education Reform in the 1980s

As the decade of the eighties dawned, a national realization of the generally unsatisfactory condition of American public schools began developing. Numerous problems had developed in the schools since the early 1970s. White flight from troubled central cities and continued opposition to integrated schools resulted in the emergence of private white "segregation academies." Education standards in the public schools declined with an increasing number of "social promotions" and "soft courses," while the special needs of the handicapped and the gifted were sometimes ignored. Declining scores on college admission tests provided ample evidence of decreasing basic skill levels among the nation's students. The teaching profession suffered from poor motivation due to low pay, low status, unruly students, and disinterested parents. The near crisis in public education led the National Commission on Excellence in Education to state in its 1983 report, *A Nation at Risk*, that:

> If an unfriendly foreign power had attempted to impose on America the mediocre performance that exists today, we might have viewed it as an act of war. . . . We have, in effect, been committing an act of unthinking, unilateral educational disarmament.

Awareness of these and related problems seemed to be reaching a peak just as the national government's financial and programmatic contributions to public education were being substantially reduced by President Reagan. De-emphasis of public education by the federal government, together with local government's growing inability to cope with the problems plaguing them in the schools, meant that the reins of education improvement fell into the hands of the states.

The states have responded admirably. Following publication of *A Nation at Risk* and several similar reports sounding the alarm bell on poor schooling, state officials across the U.S. established more than 275 task forces within a year's time. From 1982 to 1984, 40 states toughened graduation requirements, 36 increased student testing, 21 implemented performance based incentives for teachers. Teacher salaries were substantially increased in a majority of states; some raised taxes to finance higher salaries. All 50 states implemented some type of education reform. The depth of state commitment to education improvement was evident in Texas, where a new requirement that students must pass all courses in order to participate in extracurricular activities ("no pass, no play") was implemented and sustained even in the face of emasculation of high school football teams — unthinkable merely a year earlier.

The southern states, with the exception of Florida, have rarely been known as policy innovators. They tend to lag their sister states in addressing common problems through public policy. In the case of education reform, however, the southern states have surged ahead of the rest of the country. Of course, educational quality has always been lowest in the South, so these states have further to go just to catch up with other regions. Still, the education reform movement in the South during the 1982-1986 period, championed by progressive governors, has become almost a Holy Grail. The states are aggressively pursuing education improvement not only for its own sake, but also because of the tight link between educational quality and economic development in an increasingly technological world.

South Carolina's major contribution to educational reform became law in 1984, as the South Carolina Education Improvement Act (EIA). This Act, determined by a Rand Corporation consultant's study to be the most comprehensive single piece of education legislation passed by any state, has been held out as a model for the rest of the country. The EIA has dominated the education policy agenda in South Carolina since 1983, and will continue to be the single most important aspect of education policy well into the future. The remainder of this chapter discusses the campaign for passage of the EIA, its policy components, and preliminary results.

The Education Improvement Act of 1984

Although the EIA is a dramatic step forward for South Carolina, the move to raise the quality of public schools actually began in the mid-1970s. The performance of the State's schools was very poor, regardless of how measured. Many teachers were ill-prepared for the classroom, educational resources were scarce, and student standardized test scores were among the nation's lowest. Problems were most severe in poor, rural school districts, where a low tax base afforded precious little funding for the schools.

The first of three pieces of legislation intended to attack the problems of state schooling was the Education Finance Act of 1977, which created a 7-year program to provide additional resources for all elementary schools and to increase state financial aid to impoverished school districts. The second bill, the Basic Skills Assessment Act of 1978, required the State to develop tests to measure the effectiveness of the curricular and tests used to teach the basic skills. Finally, the Teacher Certification and Evaluation Act of 1979 imposed strict new standards for teacher certification, contract qualification, and entrance into teacher education programs.

State officials generally were pleased with the results of the three programs, but it was clear that much remained to be done if South Carolina was to catch up with the rest of the country in public education. A third of South Carolina's children still did not meet minimum performance standards. SAT scores remained the lowest in the U.S., and the State was last in per pupil funding.

Formulation and Enactment of the EIA

The Education Improvement Act had its origins in an ill-fated effort at a modest education reform introduced by Governor Riley early in 1983. In order to boost the cause of education, Riley and his staff proposed an alternative to a proposal being offered by some legislators to balance the state budget and give property tax relief through a one cent increase in the sales tax. Because property taxes were being increased statewide in response to reassessments mandated by "Act 208," Riley proposed dividing three ways the estimated $180 million in new revenues. Education would receive one-third, property owners would receive one-third in tax relief, and local governments would be allocated the remaining portion. The other, legislative proposal had basically ignored education.

Despite quite a bit of energy spent on the bill by the governor and his staff, it failed miserably. However, some very important lessons were learned from the failure, lessons that became crystal clear during a spring 1983 meeting between Riley, staff members, and several prominent business leaders. The businessmen told Riley that they could not support the bill, but noted in passing that if the entire 1 cent sales tax increase were to be devoted to education alone, they would be in favor of it, particularly if the business community could have a voice in formulating the education reform plan. There the idea of the EIA was born. The effort would be focused on allocating revenues from a sales tax increase to education alone, and the active involvement and support of the business community would be sought from the beginning. Obviously, greater attention would have to be given to gaining legislative support as well.

In order to organize the description of events characterizing development and enactment of the EIA, a three stage framework will be used: policy formulation, mobilization of support, and policy enactment.

Policy Formulation

The development of specific proposals to be included in the EIA was made the responsibility of two task forces whose members were appointed by the Governor. The Committee on Financing Excellence in Public Education was comprised of 25 educators, legislators, and private sector representatives. It became known as the Page Committee after the name of its chair, William

Page, Executive Vice-President of U.S. Shelter Corporation, former chairman of the Greenville School Board, and long time friend and political supporter of Riley. Two major tasks were assigned to the Committee: to develop a program for excellence in public education in South Carolina, and to evaluate a funding strategy to implement the program.

The second task force, composed of 39 top-level businessmen, industrialists, educators, legislative leaders and representatives from the Governor's office, was called the Business/Industry/Legislative/Education Partnership. Its duty was to act as a sounding board to recommendations from the Page Committee and, in general, perform a political function in gaining support for the education reforms proposed by the Page Committee. The Governor personally chaired this Committee, and the State Superintendent of Education Charlie Williams served as vice-chairman.

Building on several broad goals for education improvement submitted by Governor Riley, the Page Committee eventually came forward with eight "Action Recommendations," as follows:

1. *Raise student performance by increasing academic standards at all grade levels.* Included here were recommendations for increasing graduation requirements, strengthening student discipline and school attendance, providing special programs for talented students, offering more relevant vocational training programs, and developing special programs for handicapped students.

2. *Strengthen the teaching and testing of basic skills.* Such actions would include requiring an exit exam for graduation, enacting a promotion policy, and providing extra help to students needing to improve their basic skills.

3. *Elevate the teaching profession by strengthening teacher training, evaluation, and compensation.* Included here were such actions as improving teacher recruitment strategies, raising salaries, and developing teacher incentive programs.

4. *Improve leadership, management, and fiscal efficiency at all levels.* Included here were proposals to improve the recruitment, training, and evaluation of school administrators.

5. *Guarantee results by implementing strict quality controls and rewarding productivity.* Recommendations here included measuring school performance, improving planning, monitoring progress, correcting problems in seriously impaired districts through intervention by the State Board of Education.

6. *Create more effective partnerships* between the schools and parents, the community, and business organizations.

7. *Provide school buildings* conducive to improved student learning (repairs, renovation, and new construction).

8. *Provide the financial support necessary to achieve educational excellence in South Carolina's public schools.* Increase the sales tax by one cent to raise $210 million for public education.

During its deliberations over more than four months, the Page Committee analyzed an earlier South Carolina report prepared by the Superintendent of Education, national reports on educational reform, as well as studies made available by the Education Commission of the States. The total policy staffs of the State Department of Education and Governors Office were at the disposal of both task forces. All told, 64 specific recommendations were detailed by the Committee. The Chairman of the Subcommittee on Financing, State Senator James Waddell, insured all possible financing alternatives were considered including a state lottery, paramutual betting, an increase in the income tax and freezing all new appropriations for other areas of state government. It became obvious that only the sales tax was politically feasible and could generate sufficient revenues to fund the recommended improvements.

The two task forces were useful not only in drawing up a program for education improvement, they were also very important vehicles for building an early consensus on the specifics of reform among a wide variety of special interests that held conflicting views and objectives on controversial issues like teacher incentive pay and the evaluation of teachers and administrators. The early, constructive participation of significant interests within the education community, the private sector, and state government would be a key for reform supporters when the EIA was taken through the doors of the State House.

When on several occasions dissension threatened to deadlock committee work, the Governor intervened personally, holding meetings at the mansion with participants to let them blow off steam away from the prying eyes of media representatives. There was constant fear of a public explosion of differences. Toward the end of the committee's work one education association seriously considered filing a dissenting report. Such an open, public dissent likely would have provided an access point for opponents of the EIA to kill or substantially modify the plan in the legislature, but a working consensus was finally established in the Page Committee.

Mobilization of Support

The 1983 failure of education reform had indicated the need for the Governor and his staff to "do their homework" before embarking on a strategy for mobilizing support sufficient for passage of the EIA. Following the creation of the task forces, a three pronged approach was implemented to gather information.

First, it was decided to probe public opinion on education in South

Carolina. A Columbia public relations firm, Chernoff/Silver and Associates, volunteered its services in exchange for expenses only. During July and August, 1983, 496 people across the state were surveyed by telephone on their opinions regarding perceived problems in education and potential solutions, including a means of financing education improvement. Results demonstrated widespread public awareness of the education problems in the State and indicated a strong public acceptance of the need to commit a substantial amount of new money to resolving the problems. Eighty-three percent of the respondents said that the low quality of education in South Carolina was an embarrassment; about 75% agreed that they would be more likely to vote for a legislator who supported a tax increase for education.

The second prong of the approach to data gathering involved taking a delegation of legislators judged to be supportive of education reform to the annual meeting of the Education Commission of the States (ECS) in Denver and another delegation to the Southern Regional Education Board (SREB) meeting in Asheville. The ECS and SREB are organizations of governors, legislators, and educators. Their objective is to improve the quality of public education at all levels and to encourage the dissemination of policy innovations in the field. Both delegations of South Carolina legislators spent several days attending meetings with their peers from across the U. S. and holding discussions on education reform. All willingly joined the Governor's team and later would provide effective floor and committee leadership for passage and monitoring of the EIA.

The third effort to gather information was to send two of the Governor's top staff members (the legislative liaison and the chief education advisor) to Mississippi for consultation with Governor William Winter and his staff. Winter, like Riley, had failed in an early attempt to win education reform (in 1982), but had been successful the next year in gaining passage of a comprehensive education reform package. As it turned out, the Mississippi trip was fruitful, for it led to the discovery of an effective strategy for mobilizing public support for reform.

Thus, before the EIA had been officially drafted and introduced in the legislature, a tremendous amount of work had taken place. Opinions of all significant interests had been sought and expressed within a formal forum. A nation wide information search had been carried out, and the citizens' opinion had been tapped through a statewide survey. In addition, a consensus had been reached on the general parameters of a reform package later to be known as the Education Improvement Act. In the process, numerous important individual and group actors inside and outside of state government had joined the Governor's team.

The next step was to move forward with mobilization of public support for the reform package. It was here that the Mississippi experience proved valuable. In his own education campaign, Governor Winter had scheduled a number of forums across the state for speeches and presentations on public education. These forums were quite successful in garnering public support and participation. A much expanded version of the forums was utilized in South Carolina, with seven well-organized forums held at regional locations from September 15 to October 5, 1983. A carefully designed format was followed in each location, involving meetings during the day between the Governor, State Superintendent of Education and other high State officials and teachers, business people, and influential citizens. In the evening, following speeches by politicians and education notables, small group discussions were held with the public on how to implement the eight general goals of reform. It was estimated that 13,000 people attended the forums, and that another 15,000-20,000 individuals were contacted during related activities.

Throughout the mobilization of support for the EIA, the cooperation of two groups was deemed essential. The first, the education community, was divided by a variety of viewpoints on numerous issues. The strategy of the Governor's staff and the leadership of the two task forces was to encourage participation of the diverse education interests throughout the process while, at the same time, minimizing public conflict during the consensus building activities. As noted, when dissent escalated to a dangerous level, the Governor would step in as a peacemaker.

The second critical interest, also prone to fragmentation, was the business community. One segment of the business community offered its support for education reform from the beginning, making substantial financial contributions to fund the citizen survey, forums, and other mobilization expenditures. This segment recognized a clear relationship between the quality of the State's education system and the pace of economic development. The 1 cent sales tax increase dedicated solely to public education represented a long term commitment that would prove attractive to firms interested in locating in South Carolina.

The other, conservative segment of the business community, composed primarily of textile interests and retail merchants, was opposed to government spending generally and particularly to any tax increase. Moreover, many in this segment had not supported Riley during either of his gubernatorial campaigns because he was perceived to be too "liberal" and not strongly "pro-business." This element, which held a slight majority in the State Chamber of Commerce's Board of Directors, refused to grant the State Chamber's full endorsement to the EIA. Undeterred, the Governor's supporters instead successfully worked through the metropolitan chambers of commerce to build support in the business sector. Many local chamber leaders were to serve as business liaisons in the seven forums.

A final public mobilization effort was implemented one week after the

Page Committee issued its recommendations. Governor Riley kicked off the campaign by appearing on statewide television on November 22 to announce his "New Approach to Quality Education" in an unprecedented 30 minute address carried over all state networks. Also, staff laid the groundwork for legislative lobbying by initiating contact with citizens who had attended the forums. In addition, a speaker's bureau was created for presentations to organizations interested in education reform, and a toll-free "hotline" and telephone bank were established to answer questions and to maintain citizen contacts. Meanwhile, during the last month before the legislature was to convene, a public relations campaign was begun, funded with a $100,000 contribution from the business community and directed by Chernoff/Silver and Associates. Paid advertisements were developed in support of the education program and its proposed source of funding. The advertisements were attention-getting and quite effectively done. The theme was "a penny for their thoughts." In one commercial a pregnant woman was shown mailing a letter to her legislator and noting that her unborn child's future was too important not to support education improvement. Another presented a blue-collar worker who decided to skip a bowling match to attend the Governor's forum on education reform. Public pressure on legislators thus began to build for the final phase of policy enactment.

Policy Enactment

As the South Carolina General Assembly prepared to commence its work in January 1984, it was clear that passage of education reform would be an uphill struggle. Results of a poll by a local newspaper indicated that only about one-third of the legislators felt the bill would pass. A head count by the Governor's legislative liaison found only 37 votes in the House of Representatives firmly committed to the EIA. Even more discouraging was the fact that almost the entire leadership of the House was opposed including the Speaker and almost all key committee chairpersons. Only the Chair of the House Education Committee was a supporter. However, the Governor's staff and other chairpersons of education improvement had just begun their carefully designed, multifaceted assault to gain necessary legislative support.

It had been decided by the Governor and his top staff that the drive for education reform would be operated like an election campaign. It would involve total commitment of the Governor and staff members to the almost complete exclusion of all other pending legislation. Soon, the Governor's total concentration on education became painfully evident to legislators, lobbyists, and other participants in the legislative process who sought the Governor's favor or support. According to one such participant, "No matter what you tried to discuss with Riley, he always turned it into a forum on the education package."

A second strategy involved developing a core of legislative supporters to spearhead the education campaign in the legislature generally and especially in the House Ways and Means Committee. A group of legislators soon emerged to help the education improvement effort. They became know as the "Smurfs" because they were mostly young, relatively inexperienced legislators who were not in formal leadership positions. The Smurfs, together with two more experienced House members — one on the key Ways and Means Committee and the other known as a "master strategist" in managing bills through the legislative maze — directed the strategy on a day to day basis in the House. They also met daily with the Governor and his staff to plan broader strategy.

Meanwhile, the public "campaign" for education reform began in earnest. A telephone network was put in place to contact school administrators, teachers, PTAs, School Advisory Councils and those people who had attended the seven forums held during September and October, asking everyone to call their legislators and express their support of the bill. Certain recalcitrant legislators on Ways and Means were "targeted" to receive 50 to 100 calls each. Operating the telephone network were volunteer operators directed by a professional hired with private funds. During this time period, lobbying teams from key committees sat in committee rooms and in the gallery, with Ann "Tunky" Riley, the Governor's wife, sitting right up front.

The EIA emerged from the Ways and Means Committee essentially intact, although funding for programs was reduced drastically. On the House floor, after several diluting amendments were defeated, the EIA supporters slowly gained support for the bill. Each component of the eight Action Recommendations was considered item by item, then voted on. The highly organized Smurfs bombarded other legislators with information in support of the bill. Finally, after nine weeks of debate and intense pressure from a massive citizens lobby for education improvement, the EIA passed the House with funding of $195 million. Only three of the 64 original items set forth in the Governor's New Approach of Education had been deleted.

In the Senate, the leadership of that body, as well as the Lieutenant Governor, who presides over the Senate, were supporters of the EIA. Opposition led by two interest groups, the South Carolina Textile Manufacturers Association and the Retail Merchants Association, was overcome by EIA supporters, as were final efforts to change the method of financing the bill. Following slight substantive amendments, the EIA passed the Senate and was sent to the House-Senate conference committee for resolution of differences between the two houses. Finally, on June 22, 1984, the General Assembly gave final passage to the EIA. Governor Riley signed it into law six days later.

Early Results From The Education Improvement Act

At the time of writing this section it was too early to know the long term impact of the Education Improvement Act; however, initial results were very encouraging.

SAT scores in South Carolina, while still too low, led the nation in points gained over the past several years, even though 50% of high school graduates were tested (a very high proportion). In the wake of a controversy in Washington, D.C. regarding whether private or public schools contributed to the gain, the South Carolina Governor's Office conducted a study which found the SAT gains were almost entirely attributable to improvements in the public schools' student scores. South Carolina saw a 25 point gain for all students (compared to the national gain of 15 points), but public school scores increased 32 points. For a comparison, in Washington, D.C., there was a 20 point overall gain with an increase of only 4 points in the public school scores. While the impressive improvement in South Carolina can not be attributable only to the EIA, clearly it has been an important factor, along with the series of earlier reforms.

In addition to SAT scores, basic skills and academic skills test scores showed remarkable gains in South Carolina during the three years since the Education Improvement Act effort was launched. The gains were found in all grades, in all subjects and on all tests. The annual gains have been 2-5 times greater than gains prior to initiating the reform movement in South Carolina. All categories of students, including low achievers and minorities, have made substantial progress since the education reforms have been in process. Critics of the reform movement in the early 1980's contended that some of the components of reform, such as higher standards and testing programs, would create new barriers blocking progress of "at-risk" students. The package of reforms in South Carolina has avoided this problem and in fact is helping at-risk children make meaningful improvement.

In the first years of the Education Improvement Act, the non-attendance and truancy rates in South Carolina schools were cut by one third. As a result, South Carolina students attended school almost a week longer than the national average even though the school year was roughly the same length. Good attendance pays off now in fewer classroom interruptions and later in dependable work habits.

Finally, what do teachers think of the reforms? In a number of states teachers were bitterly opposed to the changes resulting from reform legislation. In such circumstances, even if the reforms are good, they probably won't work. In an August, 1985, random sample poll of teachers in South Carolina, almost 80% said they (1) felt better about being a teacher "as a result of the South Carolina Improvement Act," and (2) felt that South Carolina Improvement Act money is well-spent and has improved the quality of public education. Ninety percent of the teachers believed that education is improving in South Carolina and that the annual salary adjustments will help the profession remain attractive to teachers in the field and will attract more college students with greater ability to enter the teaching field.

Conclusion

Polls taken in the 1980's indicate that the people of South Carolina and the nation believe that teaching and learning are serious business. They believe that the education of our children is a necessary base for economic vitality, social mobility, personal development, and an improved quality of life in our state.

It appears that South Carolina is on the right track for making this happen through the Education Improvement Act. South Carolina did what many believed to be impossible. Long term, successful implementation will require time and hard work from educators, policymakers, students, parents and citizens. From 1924 to 1933, South Carolina attempted to implement a major education reform package, but due to implementation problems that act was repealed. Sixty years later it appears that South Carolina has the commitment to implement fully one of the most far-reaching educational reform efforts in the United States. The well-being of the economy and the people of the state depends upon it.

References

Kearney, Richard C. (1987). "How A Weak Governor Can Be Strong: Education Reform in South Carolina." *Journal of State Government.* Fall.

Siegel, Peggy (1985). "School Reform Momentum Continues" *State Legislatures* (March): 11-14.

National Commission on Excellence in Education (1983). *A Nation at Risk.* Washington, D. C.: U. S. Government Printing Office.

7

Crime and Corrections in South Carolina: The Problem of Prison Overcrowding

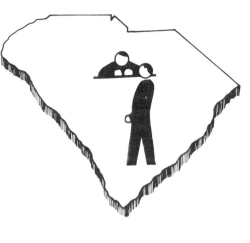

Philip Jos and Mark E. Tompkins

Introduction

South Carolina state government has faced a series of criminal justice system controversies in the 1980's, framed by litigation over conditions in the prison system and budgetary constraints limiting the state's options for responding to this litigation. We hope in this paper to provide a historical perspective that will help explain how these controversies, and South Carolina's current criminal justice policies, have evolved and how they are likely to shape future criminal justice policy in the state.

Crime and Punishment in South Carolina, 1970-1980

The 1970's saw a dramatic increase in reported crime in South Carolina, as illustrated in Figure 1. Between 1970 and 1980, the state's crime rate rose from 2,067 index crimes (essentially those for which the F.B.I. has kept statistics over the years) per 100,000 population to 5,439 per 100,000, a 163 percent increase. In the 1972 to 1975 period alone, the state's reported crime rate doubled. These increases were due, in part, to improved reporting techniques and to demographic trends in the state, including the fact that the so-called "baby-boom" population (those born between 1947 and 1968) had

---

Philip Jos is a faculty member in the Department of Political Science, College of Charleston. Mark E. Tompkins is a faculty member in the Department of Government and International Studies at the University of South Carolina in Columbia. This chapter is a revised version of an earlier Public Affairs Bulletin.

reached the age of peak criminal activity (many crimes are committed by young adult men). Migration into the state and a more active tourism industry may also have contributed to this change.

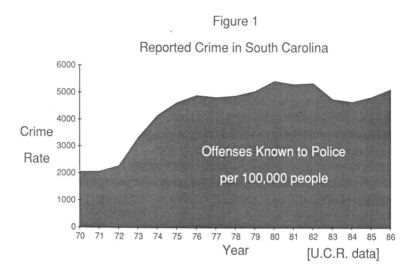

Figure 1

Reported Crime in South Carolina

Crime Rate

Offenses Known to Police per 100,000 people

Year

[U.C.R. data]

During this same period, the state's prison population has also grown dramatically. Since the early 1970's, South Carolina has sentenced an increasing percentage of its citizens to state-run prisons. For example, the state's incarceration rate (the number of sentenced prisoners in state penal institutions per 100,000 population) increased from 118 in 1971 to 238 in 1980. Over this period, the average inmate population in the state's Department of Corrections surged from 2,705 to 8,865. These increases were especially noticeable in the mid-1970's when the state assumed the responsibility for housing many prisoners who had formerly been held in county facilities. For example, the average inmate population grew 78% from 1974 to 1976. (By mid-1985, only nine counties were operating separate prison facilities.) Figure 2 displays the changing incarceration rate for the state over the same period as Figure 1. As it shows, the rate continued to grow in the 1980's, even though crime rates had leveled off.

Crime and Punishment in South Carolina, 1980 To The Present

Although the state's crime rate leveled off in 1981 and 1982, then actually dropped during 1983 and 1984, the public's concern with crime apparently grew. Both in South Carolina and across the nation, there was a growing feeling that violent criminals were not being punished appropriately and that

Figure 2

Incarceration Rate in South Carolina

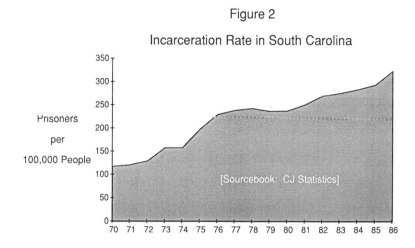

the victims of crime were being overlooked. In 1981, 80% of a sample of Americans responded that "most crimes go unpunished." The rehabilitation of criminals was seen increasingly as less important than swift and certain punishment. The percentage of Americans' favoring the use of the death penalty, for example, rose from 40% in 1966 to greater than 60% in 1981. In 1985, Joseph Carl Shaw became the first person to be executed in South Carolina since 1962. The formation of Citizens Against Violent Crime (CAVE) and its efforts to influence policy in the General Assembly provided further evidence that many South Carolinians felt that crime was not being dealt with adequately. The concerns expressed by CAVE, and the related national interest in cutting back on the reduction of sentences, led to increased interest in longer sentences which could not be shortened by parole.

State decision makers have responded to the change in public mood. In recent years, criminals have been more likely to receive prison sentences, the sentences they receive have been getting longer, and probation and parole have been employed more sparingly. As Figure 2 suggests, the rate of incarceration, which began its climb during the 1970's, has continued to grow.

South Carolina has been particularly aggressive in employing incarceration as a response to crime. Figure 3 shows the rate of incarceration in South Carolina and a number of neighboring states. As it suggests, the rate in this state is noticeably higher than it is in neighboring states, such as North Carolina and Georgia, and it is much higher than the national average. Throughout the last decade, South Carolina has incarcerated people at a higher rate than all but a handful of other states in the nation. These changes in incarceration rates are exacerbated by the fact that longer sentences are being given. Once imprisoned, inmates were less and less likely to have their sentences shortened by parole. For example, the percentage of parole applications which were approved dropped from 58.4% in the middle 1970's to 27.5% in 1985-1986.

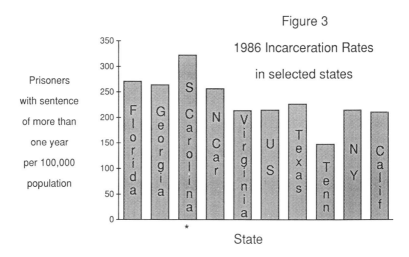

Figure 3

1986 Incarceration Rates

in selected states

Prisoners with sentence of more than one year per 100,000 population

State

When we compare crime rates for these same states, however, it becomes apparent that these differences are not produced by higher levels of crime. Figure 4 shows the rates in neighboring states for comparison. In fact, the state's crime rates are rather typical of the nation and no worse than those in neighboring states, where long-term incarceration is less commonly employed as a response to crime.

As a result of these forces, the prison population in South Carolina has continued to grow through the 1980's, as shown in Figure 5. At the end of June, 1988, the Department of Corrections had 13,976 people under its jurisdiction. This represented dramatic growth, not only from the 1970's, but also from 1980.

Figure 4

Reported Crime Rate

in selected states

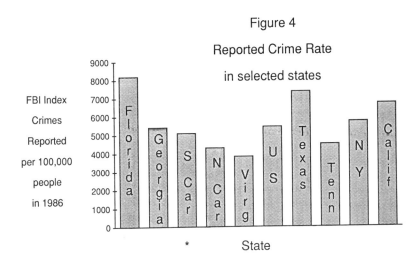

FBI Index Crimes Reported per 100,000 people in 1986

* State

Figure 5

Number of People Supervised

by S.C. Dept. of Corrections

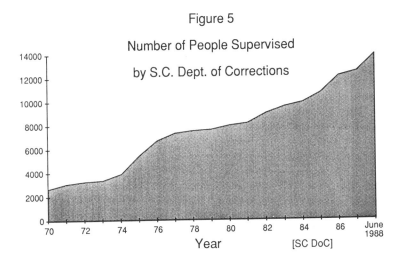

Year   [SC DoC]

Consequences For Corrections In South Carolina

An Expanding Correctional System. As might be expected, the proportion of state funds going to corrections has increased as state officials attempt to keep up with the inmate population. In his March 1985 message to the General Assembly, then-Governor Riley pointed out that the additional costs of building new prisons had become the single largest new expenditure by the state, after education.

The personnel and budgets of the primary components of the South Carolina corrections system have grown tremendously in recent years. The Department of Corrections is the largest component of the state correctional system. Not only has the number of inmates grown dramatically but the costs of proper supervision for inmates have more than doubled in the last decade, as they have across the country. In the current fiscal year, the Department of Corrections has a budget of more than 159 million dollars, more than twice the budgetary allocation it received ten years earlier, and by June 30, 1988, it employed 5,138 people. The Department of Parole and Community Corrections had responsibility for over 26,000 clients in the 1987-1988 fiscal year, 22,633 of whom were serving probated sentences, 3,009 of whom were on parole, and 941 of whom were in early release programs. Over the past ten years the number of agents employed by the Department has grown from 146 to more than 370. This Department now administers a budget in excess of 22 million dollars (with more than $12,590,000 coming from the state and most of the remainder coming from cost of court fees and fees generated by the Department's programs). In this fiscal year, the Department of Youth Services budget is more than $30,839,000. Even with this growth, the corrections system is severely taxed as the associated agencies attempt to keep pace with the growing number of criminal offenders assigned to them.

Prison Overcrowding. By the late 1970's and early 1980's, overcrowding in South Carolina had reached a point where many feared a federal court takeover of the prison system. In 1980 the state's prisons, on average, housed 52% more inmates than existing institutions were designed to accommodate. The overcrowding was so severe in some prisons that cells designed for one person were occupied by three inmates. At the Midlands Correction and Evaluation Center, for example, as many as three inmates were confined in cells with 35 square feet of floor space. Other institutions in the system were also overcrowded and there were simply too many inmates to supervise. As has been found to be typical in such a situation (see, for example, Cox et al., 1984), violent incidents became more common and more difficult to control. As it became more difficult to control the prison population, the work of the correctional officer became more difficult as well. Since the pay for correctional officers is low, (as the result of a bill passed in the 1988 Session of the General Assembly, a trainee will receive $14,082 beginning in January of 1989, compared with a reported beginning salary for a police officer in Columbia of $17,927 and $18,616 for a beginning public safety officer in Spartanburg), this makes a difficult job even more unattractive. These problems make it more difficult to attract qualified applicants and more difficult to retain the trained officers already working.

Early Legislative Responses to Overcrowding

By 1980 the Governor's Committee on Criminal Justice, Crime and Delinquency was warning of the increasingly costly problem of prison overcrowding. Their recommendations for reducing overcrowding focused on providing judges with alternatives to prison sentences for nonviolent offenders. A step in this direction was taken with the passage of the *Parole and Community Corrections Act of 1981*. This act mandated a statewide classification system for all offenders and expanded the sentencing alternatives available to judges. *The Community Corrections Act* established an intensive supervision program for probations and parolees and also expanded the ways in which inmates can reduce their sentences by earning "good time" credits and earned work credits (which allowed certain classes of offenders to reduce their sentences by one day for every two to seven days worked, depending on their situation). The bill also sought to alleviate prison overcrowding by allowing inmates to qualify for parole earlier in their terms (except for inmates convicted of murder, armed robbery, criminal sexual assault, assault and battery with intent to kill, and kidnapping).

Without passage of the *Community Corrections Act* it is likely that prison overcrowding would have become even more severe, but the fact remains that conditions worsened during 1981 and 1982. While the General Assembly did not formulate any comprehensive plan to reduce overcrowding, it did empower the governor to take decisive action to temporarily alleviate overcrowding by the early release of nonviolent offenders.

The Prison Overcrowding Powers Act of 1983 established a procedure providing the Governor with the ability to respond to severe overcrowding problems by declaring a State of Emergency which advanced the release dates of qualified inmates up to ninety days. This procedure had also been adopted in a number of other states faced with similar problems. Under South Carolina's procedure, the Board of Corrections could request such a release when they determined that the prison population had exceeded capacity for over 30 days. This request was considered by the Governor along with a report from the Board of Parole and Community Corrections which indicated whether or not all alternative programs which might relieve overcrowding were being utilized . The governor had three options: he could order a State of Emergency, decline to order a State of Emergency, or take no action at all, in which case a State of Emergency automatically took effect in 14 days.

Under a State of Emergency prison sentences were "rolled back" by the release of inmates certified as nonviolent offenders by the Department of Corrections. Once the population stays within its capacity for seven consecutive days, the State of Emergency would be terminated. However, if the Governor determines that the State of Emergency posed a threat to the public safety, he or she could terminate the emergency decree at any time. The act was first invoked on September 2, 1983, then again on three subsequent occasions. Once an emergency had been declared, the Department of Corrections identified those inmates who might qualify for early release; the inmate's proposed residence was checked by the Department of Parole and Community Corrections (since renamed) before they were released. Between September 16, 1983 and June 30, 1986, 1,453 inmates were released from Department of Corrections institutions directly into the EPA Program, while 2,117 were placed on the supervised furlow program earlier because of the Program. In the spring of 1986, the Department asked Governor Riley for an additional rollback, which he denied.

In 1986, the Act was significantly revised, so that a specific number of prisoners was proposed for release rather than sentences being rolled back. In addition the Department of Parole and Community Corrections used a risk assessment model, based on the inmate's past history and prison record, to predict the likelihood that they would commit another crime if released. Shortly after he took office in April of 1987, the newly elected Governor, Carroll Campbell, confronted a request for an additional early release affecting 1,152 prisoners. Ultimately, he agreed to the release of only 300 inmates, based on the number who could be released under legal restrictions and the number eligible for release who were not classified as being at "high risk" of committing additional crimes once released. It is apparent that while the EPA can be a valuable tool for resolving an immediate crisis in the capacity of the prison system, it will not be the long term solution for the prison overcrowding problem. What is needed is a long-range solution that either reduces the prison population or establishes new facilities to adequately house them.

Sentencing reform has received a great deal of attention from professionals in the corrections community as one element of a long-range solution. As early as 1980 a study of sentencing in South Carolina concluded that sentences given criminals in the state were inconsistent, with substantial disparities from one case to another and that the lack of guidelines given judges invited inequities and abuse. Pursuant to the study group's recommendations, a Sentencing Guidelines Commission was established with Frank B. Sanders, who would subsequently become the Executive Director of the Department of Parole and Community Corrections, as its director. The Commission and the Governor came to the conclusion that a serious effort to deal with sentencing disparities and prison overcrowding required sentencing reform. Efforts were made to pass legislation that would lengthen sentences for violent offenders while at the same time requiring judges to employ alternatives to prison for certain classes of nonviolent offenders.

Although a Sentencing Guidelines bill was introduced in both houses, the

General Assembly adjourned in 1986 without action on the legislation. The General Assembly has responded, however, to demands for aiding and supporting the victims of crime. In 1983, the South Carolina Crime Victims Compensation Fund was established by law to provide compensation for expenses for personal injuries suffered by victims of violent crime, although the program has not been fully funded to date. This legislation was amended in 1984 to establish a victim/witness assistance program and to reduce the threshold for compensable claims.

In 1984 the General Assembly also passed the *Victims and Witnesses Bill of Rights* which requires that victims be informed of court proceedings and available compensation and other services. The act further provides for the protection of victims and witnesses and requires judges to consider a "victim impact statement" at a sentencing or disposition hearing and at parole hearings. While the focus on victims may be long overdue, the presence of victims at trials and parole hearings may result in longer sentences and fewer parole approvals, thus exacerbating prison overcrowding.

In 1986, the General Assembly revised the provisions of the legislation governing emergency powers and passed the *Omnibus Criminal Justice Improvements Act*, which, among other things, established new mechanisms for diverting some offenders from the traditional system of long term incarceration. In 1988, responding to the initiative of Governor Campbell, the General Assembly substantially increased the funding devoted to the programs of the Department of Youth Services. It also passed legislation improving the pay and benefits for correction officers (including those in the Department of Youth Services). These efforts arose from the perception that more energy needed to be focused on the effort to avoid incarceration rather than increase it. To understand these efforts, we must first examine the pressures arising from the increasing demands made on the incarceration system.

The Prison Overcrowding Issue Emerges

By late 1983 and early 1984 officials were warning that unless the state took decisive action, South Carolina faced the prospect of losing control of its correctional system altogether. States that had failed to upgrade their prison facilities and address problems of overcrowding and adequate care for inmates, such as Alabama, Arkansas, Florida, Mississippi, Oklahoma, Rhode Island, Tennessee, and Texas, had already become the subject of federal court orders by 1981. As a result of the suits, generally brought on the basis of the Eighth Amendment's ban on cruel and unusual punishment, state legislatures sometimes lost control of even basic funding decisions regarding corrections, when the courts mandated specific prison systems appropriations in their orders. Moreover, federal monitors have been appointed in a number of states. These monitors have maintained a presence in the state's correctional systems and, for all intents and purposes, are empowered to run the state's prison system on a day to day basis. In Texas, where state corrections officials chose to oppose any court settlement that might have prevented the appointment of a federal monitor, attorney's fees had exceeded 1.8 million by 1987, and the state's prison system will continue to operate under the supervision of the federal courts for many years to come.

The Nelson Suit

Although South Carolina's corrections system had a far superior reputation making for good faith efforts to improve prison conditions compared to states like Texas, the prospect of a court takeover of the prison system was very real. In 1982 Gary Wayne Nelson, an inmate at the Central Correctional Institution in Columbia, sued, charging that the totality of conditions in all facilities operated by the Department of Corrections violated the 8th amendment. (This suit, it should be noted, followed earlier litigation and potentially affected all inmates, not just Nelson.)

Since the overcrowding problem was severe at CCI and in other state prisons, the Board of the Department of Corrections, and after consultation with the Governor, Attorney General and General Assembly, concluded that winning the Nelson suit was all but impossible. Aware of the costs of intransigence, the Department entered into negotiations, after authorization by the General Assembly, intended to settle the suit in a way which would prevent the appointment of a federal monitor and allow the state adequate time to comply with the settlement's provisions.

The Actual Nelson Settlement. In early 1984 lawyers for both sides had reached an agreement in the case of *Nelson v. Leeke*. In an effort to involve a broad spectrum of state officials in the decision, the settlement was negotiated with the knowledge of the Governor's office, members of the legislature and other responsible state officials. In May, the Budget and Control Board and the General Assembly were informed of the terms of the settlement and gave their approval. On January 8, 1985, the order was signed by all parties and after some minor objections from Judge Houck were addressed, the order was approved by the court, with full compliance contemplated by 1990.

The most fundamental issues addressed by the court order are: (1) the inadequate staff in the prisons, (2) the lack of inmate access to work programs, vocational training and the like, and (3) overcrowding. (Other issues included the operation of the state's institution for women, visitation policies, the use of physical restraints, food service, fire and personal safety, and sanitation).

With respect to the deployment of prison staff, the state agreed that prisoner/staff ratios would not fall below January 25, 1983 levels. Furthermore, the order requires that correctional officers be stationed so that they have visual or voice contact with the inmates at all times (except at pre-release and work release centers or during emergencies). As the result of the need to staff new prisons being constructed and to have more supervision of inmates in all facilities, the number of correctional officers employed by the Department of Corrections has more than doubled.

With respect to educational, vocational, and medical services and programs, the consent order requires that all inmates have the opportunity to engage in "full-time, meaningful work or program assignment for not less than 5 hours a day, 5 days per week," and that access to educational programs be maintained and offered at least two evenings per week. Prison libraries are to be made available at least 37½ hours, including two evenings. Emergency medical training for prison staff must be expanded and a team of medical consultants will review the Department's procedures, resources, training, and staffing for medical and psychological service.

The Nelson settlement requires an end to all triple-celling of inmates and allows double-celling only in certain facilities or in cells of a certain size. (The question of double-celling would be the focus of subsequent controversy.) The order provides that: (1) any inmate confined to a cell for more than 12 hours per day will be single-celled in a cell with at least 40 square feet of sleeping space in present institutions and 50 square feet in any future institutions, (2) inmates confined for less than 12 hours per day (those in the general prison population) can be double-celled but only if they are provided with 50 square feet of sleeping space each, (3) inmates confined to wards or cubicles (where individual living areas are not separated by prison bars) must be provided with at least 45 square feet of space per person (50 square feet at Manning and CCI), and (4) the housing units in existence at the time of the Consent Order will house no more than 7,385 prisoners within 5 years (in FY 1984, the Department of Correction's facilities held 8,539 prisoners on average). Since then, renovations and new construction have added additional capacity to the overall system.

While the state successfully avoided a court takeover of the prison system, the state must now honor its agreement which will largely govern South Carolina's corrections policy for at least five years and will subject the state to close scrutiny for even longer. The Nelson Consent Order amounts to a blueprint for the operation of the Department for the next decade. The order requires the provision of additional space for inmates (by implication, requiring the construction of additional prisons), hiring and training additional staff, and upgrading program services. While South Carolina has not yet come under court administration like a number of other states, the court retains its jurisdiction as it does in any case where on going compliance with a consent order is required. If the parties involved cannot agree about whether the consent decree is being properly implemented, a court-sponsored mediator may be called in to make recommendations to the court.

With respect to overcrowding, the settlement specified a plan for phasing in the order's requirements. Thus, for the state to comply with the decree, it had to halt virtually all triple-celling, provide the specified sleeping space for inmates at maximum or medium security prisons within 6 months of the completion of the Lieber and McCormick institutions (now in service), and provide all other inmates required sleeping space by 1990. The settlement provides that the state may not exceed the maximum prescribed population at an institution by more than 10%, and by no more than 5% for institutions housing more than 200 prisoners. Finally, the total prison system must operate within maximum capacities and no individual inmate can be improperly housed for more than 60 days in one calendar year.

For the first year after the settlement the state was able to comply with the requirements of the Consent Order, but by March of 1986 the number of people sentenced to serve time in South Carolina's prisons had risen so dramatically that the state was unable to meet the requirements of the decree for the total prison population. The state had anticipated an average net increase of 30 to 50 prisoners per month between December 1985 and December 1989, but by the middle of 1986 the Department of Corrections was receiving a net increase of 110 prisoners per month. This increase precipitated a court order requiring the state to reduce its prison population by 530 within two months. The Department of Corrections responded by releasing 132 inmates early and building several temporary wooden barracks to house the remainder of the excess inmate population.

The pressure on the prison system's capacity led the state to seek relief from one requirement of the Nelson settlement by allowing it to adopt double-celling in its new medium and maximum security facilities. While the cells in these new facilities did not meet the minimum space requirement for double-celling agreed to in the Nelson settlement, and some evidence exists that double-celling increased the tensions present in any prison (Cox et al., 1984), they were modeled after federal jurisdiction's facilities in which inmates were double-celled in comparable cells. Further, the Supreme Court had ruled in *Rhodes v. Chapman* (1980) that double-celling was permissible in some circumstances, when services and programs were provided to compensate for the reduced space (as they were in the South Carolina system). Accordingly, the state sought to use these cells in the same way. The implications of the resolution of this controversy were substantial, since double-celling in these facilities would reduce the need for additional prisons. This effort was supported both by the Attorney General, Travis Medlock, and the Governor, Carroll Campbell.

Estimates of the number of prisons which will have to be constructed in order to comply with the growing prison population and the Nelson settlement vary. The state has already added facilities at Lieber, McCormick, and Broad River, and it is currently constructing new facilities at sites in Allendale and Marlboro counties. A new men's prison and a new facility for women offenders, along with some renovations of existing facilities which will add capacity to the system, are authorized in the bond bill passed in the 1988 Session of the General Assembly. If the prison population continues to grow, even more facilities will be required. Each prison has been estimated to cost between 28 and 34 million dollars to build and 7 to 8 million dollars a year to operate. Even with this investment, it is virtually certain that the state will not be able to keep the prison population at legally acceptable levels in the long run without either another major commitment of funds for prison construction and operation to provide beds beyond 1990, or a change in the number of people sentenced to the Department of Correction's facilities or in the length of sentences they receive.

Control over each of these areas, the allocation of funds, the discretion given judges on sentencing alternatives and available prison terms, and probation and parole policy ultimately reside with the General Assembly. For this reason, the year long debate over the *Omnibus Criminal Justice Improvements Act* originally focused on developing long-range solutions to the problem of prison overcrowding. By the time of ratification, however, the bill's implications for the overcrowding problem were anything but clear.

The Omnibus Criminal Justice Improvements Act of 1986

In March of 1985, just two months after the settlement of the Nelson suit, Governor Riley presented a package of criminal justice proposals to the General Assembly. Once again, he noted that South Carolina's criminal justice system was "in critical need of repair" and that the burdens on the corrections system would continue to grow. Recognizing the changing political climate, Riley said,

"There can be no doubt anywhere that this state will continue to lock up dangerous offenders and will lock them up for longer than ever before. To do this we must use our prisons wisely and use punishments other than prison for minor offenses where possible. Therefore it must be the state's correctional strategy to insure there is always a prison bed available for the violent offender and to require as many nonviolent offenders as possible to repay their victims and their communities through restitution and work."

113

The Riley package was directed towards three goals: alleviating prison overcrowding, increasing support and assistance for crime prevention efforts, and sentencing reform. Convinced that a reliance on building new prisons as a way of dealing with overcrowding would "create a new class of victims in the state — the taxpayer," the Riley proposal stressed longer sentences for violent offenders coupled with providing alternatives to prison for nonviolent offenders. (In FY 1985-86, 55.7% of the inmates in the custody of the Department of Corrections had, as their most serious offense, crimes against people, including homicide, sexual assault and other sex offenses, kidnapping, robbery, assault, or arson, or charges involving dangerous drugs. On the other hand, 39.9% had, as their most serious current offense, various property crimes, such as burglary or larceny, or fraud, or a traffic offense. The remaining cases are less easily classified.) As it stood, judges usually faced a choice between a probated sentence which would return the offender to the community, or sending a first-time nonviolent offender to prison. Riley proposed, and the General Assembly ratified as part of the Omnibus Crime Bill, the establishment of programs aimed at these offenders. The bill established "restitution centers," community based residential facilities where nonviolent offenders are required to live and work as a condition of probation. Judges were also given the option of suspending a nonviolent offender's sentence and sentencing him to 90 days in a "shock probation program," after which he would be subject to intensive supervision by the DPCC. The shock probation centers require strenuous labor and are designed to give those in the 17-24 year old age group a taste of prison life which might discourage future criminal behavior. Finally, probation programs were expanded so that judges could impose new conditions on probations such as curfew restrictions, house arrest, submission to urinalysis and/or blood testing, and performing public service work.

While these programs provide alternatives to prison, their effect on prison overcrowding remains uncertain primarily because the legislature, as it had in the past, rejected sentencing reform. The sentencing reform proposals would have placed offenses into nine different categories based on their seriousness and specified maximum terms for each. The proposals would also have limited the discretion of judges in imposing sentences, requiring judges to impose longer sentences for violent offenders and less prison time for others (but requiring greater use of restitution centers, public works, and new forms of probation for nonviolent offenders). Without these provisions the use of alternatives to prison is up to individual judges and it is difficult to predict what the impact of program availability will be on prison overcrowding.

Moreover, the elimination of sentencing reform from the bill was only part of a gradual shift from an emphasis on prison overcrowding to a concern with toughening criminal sanctions. The intervention of the CAVE group during

Senate consideration of the bill in April of 1985 not only helped undermine support for sentencing reform but also helped convince legislators to strengthen further those sections of the bill designed to get tough on those convicted of violent crimes. In its final form, the bill required that persons convicted of murder in which one or more aggravating circumstances are present must receive either the death penalty or a sentence of life in prison without possibility for parole until the service of 30 years (20 years where no aggravating circumstances are found). Offenders convicted of a violent crime while in possession of a gun or a knife may receive a non-parolable consecutive or concurrent 5 year sentence. In addition, a variety of restrictions are placed on inmates convicted of violent crimes; these include: (a) no possibility of parole after the second conviction for a violent crime; (b) life imprisonment without parole after their third conviction for a violent crime; (c) less frequent parole hearings (every other year rather than every year) and a two thirds vote of the parole board (instead of a simple majority) to obtain parole; (d) no release on supervised furlough; (e) no release under emergency powers provisions applied to prison overcrowding; (f) no participation in the community penalties plan; and no reduction in sentence for taking education courses.

Consideration of the bill in the House reflected an increasing emphasis on toughening penalties as well and the House also deleted a provision which would have shifted offenders convicted of nonviolent crimes and sentenced to less than a year from state prisons to county jails. In many other states, these offenders are handled at the local level. The governor's office estimated that this provision alone would have saved the state the cost of building two prisons.

By the time the bill passed the General Assembly in May of 1986 it no longer had the support of the Prison Overcrowding Project (a panel of legislators, prison and parole officials, and others). "The bill just does not address prison overcrowding, as we see it," remarked Project Executive Director Ken Long. State Senator Tom Smith likewise lamented that "we have not done a thing to solve the real problem of (overcrowding in) the maximum security prisons." The Department of Corrections was also skeptical as to whether the bill would help to reduce the number of inmates being sent to the state's prisons.

In subsequent months, the prison population did, indeed, continue to grow. This led to another request for "emergency powers" based releases of inmates to relieve overcrowding, this time to the new Governor, Carroll Campbell. He declined to authorize the requested release of all 1,152 inmates, arguing that many of those affected were classified as "high risk" by the Department of Parole and Community Corrections. He also pointed to legislation which limited the number of inmates who could be released per month as restricting the extent of any further releases that could be authorized. He did, however, agree to release 300 inmates, classified as lower risk.

The inmate population continued to increase. As a result, when the state failed to meet the timetable for reducing overcrowding in January of 1988, Judge Houck ordered the state to begin early releases of approximately 700 inmates. These inmates were still being double-celled, although the Consent Decree specified that this practice would be ended by this time. This ruling was appealed to the 4th U.S. Circuit Court of Appeals, where Judge Houck's order was first stayed pending a hearing, then, on April 27, 1988, a three judge panel agreed to permit the state to double-cell inmates in five new institutions (McCormick, Broad River, and Lieber, and the new facilities under construction in Allendale and Marlboro). In June, the full appeals court refused to reconsider this ruling. If this decision stands, it would add 2,104 beds to the system's capacity according to the Department, saving the state the costs of constructing nearly three new facilities. These additional inmates would still require the state to hire new staff and to provide support services for them, adding to the overall costs of running the system.

The Search for Alternatives . . .

This continuing controversy has increased policy-makers' interest in finding alternatives to costly incarceration. The *Omnibus Criminal Justice Improvements Act of 1986* required what has become the Department of Probation, Parole, and Pardon Services to develop a number of alternatives to incarceration. This led to several new and modified programs, aimed at providing alternatives to long term incarceration for first offenders and non-violent offenders.

The resulting system created a continuum of sanctions to be applied to convicted criminals. Ranging from most to least severe, these are shown in Table 1.

Judges are afforded a range of sanctions, to provide them with sentencing options. Perhaps the most noteworthy of these options are the programs for Shock Probation and Restitution Centers, which were created as the result of the 1986 legislation. These options afforded judges sanctions which did not expose offenders to hardened criminals in the state's prisons but provided punishments which, it is hoped, will provide both a rehabilitative and deterrent effect.

These programs are also substantially less expensive than long term incarceration. The State Reorganization Commission has estimated the comparative costs of three sentencing options: (a) one year of incarceration (estimated at $11,472), (b) ninety days of shock probation followed by one year of intensive probation (estimated at $3,933.55), or (c) one year of

Table 1
Continuum of Criminal Sanctions

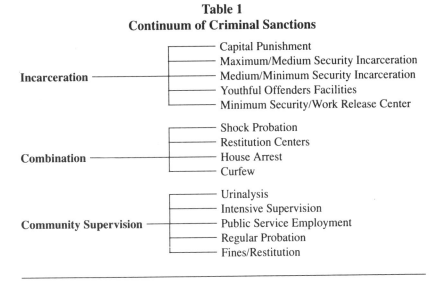

Incarceration
- Capital Punishment
- Maximum/Medium Security Incarceration
- Medium/Minimum Security Incarceration
- Youthful Offenders Facilities
- Minimum Security/Work Release Center

Combination
- Shock Probation
- Restitution Centers
- House Arrest
- Curfew

Community Supervision
- Urinalysis
- Intensive Supervision
- Public Service Employment
- Regular Probation
- Fines/Restitution

intensive probation followed by two years of regular probation (estimated at $1,602.35). Thus, if these programs have the same impact as incarceration, they would be desirable simply for being cheaper alternatives. It is also hoped, of course, that they will prove more effective in discouraging recidivism.

Advocates of shock probation programs also argue that the brief period of intensively supervised incarceration (which involves a heavily regimented environment, and strenuous manual labor and physical exercise) will "shock" a young offender whose future is not yet established out of future criminal behavior. The program was implemented in South Carolina in 1987, so firm evidence on its impact is not yet available, although studies are now underway under the auspices of the State Reorganization Commission. It is not yet clear, for example, whether judges are willing to divert offenders who would otherwise be incarcerated into the program nor has enough time passed to determine whether or not it does deter program participants from committing further crimes. Nationally, comparable programs were first undertaken in Georgia and Oklahoma in 1983. While they have become increasingly popular with state policy makers anxious to find alternatives to long term incarceration, John J. DiIulio, a nationally known expert on correctional administration, has argued that definitive studies of the value of these programs have not been done yet.

The first restitution center opened in November of 1987. The restitution center program affords judges an opportunity to respond to the needs of victims as well as to the need for punishment and deterrence. It, too, offers an alternative to incarceration — one that again reduces the burden an offender places on society, while assessing a penalty for the crime committed. Finally, it also avoids exposing some offenders to a prison environment, where more impressionable people may learn patterns of behavior that lead to further crimes. Nonetheless, this program got underway slowly; in the first five months of the center's operation, only 27 offenders were placed in it, but in the next four months, more offenders were sentenced to it and a waiting list has developed.

The apparent limitations of corrections programs have focused interest on the factors that may lead to crime in later years. This interest has enhanced support for reforms in the educational system. It also sparked interest in Governor Campbell's proposals for enhancing the role played by the state's Department of Youth Services.

The Department of Youth Services Initiative

As Governor Carroll Campbell and his staff contemplated the problems created by the overburdened correctional system, another element came to the fore. The Department of Youth Services' facilities had long been overcrowded and inadequate for the complex responsibilities that the Department faced. By 1987, a serious threat of litigation over this issue had emerged, which raised the possibility of court intervention into this agency's administration. Moreover, it became increasingly apparent that more could be done with juvenile offenders served by this Department than the current budget and programs allowed.

The Department serves a complex mix of status offenders and those committing crimes against people and property, involving some 16,006 referrals from the courts in FY 1986-87. The programs it administers for youths range from traditional incarceration to community-based services. A noteworthy number of children passing through these programs subsequently commit crimes as adults. For example, Governor Campbell pointed out in his September 1987 address to the Joint Legislative Commission on Children that one third of those currently sentenced to death had been involved in the juvenile justice system. At the same time, data gathered by the Department suggested that children going through the innovative Marine Institutes program operated by the Department were three times less likely to be incarcerated for a new offense than those handled in the traditional programs.

Accordingly, Governor Campbell proposed a significant increase in support for the Department and its programs. In particular, he urged the General Assembly to support the creation of three new Marine Institutes as an alternative to expanding the facilities available for traditional incarceration.

These institutes provide intensive remedial, vocational and life skills training for troubled youths, with the ultimate goal for them being the attainment of a G.E.D. and placement in a job.

In his address to the Joint Legislative Commission on Children, the Governor said:

"Guiding us in our efforts to address these concerns must be the goal to house at D.Y.S. only those children who clearly must be there. Alternatives to institutionalization must be developed and used for all children who do not need to be placed in a corrections setting. And for those who are placed at D.Y.S., adequate facilities and services must be provided so that children are treated humanely and given an opportunity to turn their lives around."

The General Assembly accepted the Governor's recommendation, funding all three new Marine Institutes. It also authorized new capital spending for the Department and added a number of new correctional officers the Governor and Department had requested, although not as many as had been sought initially. In addition, higher pay and an improved benefit package for correctional officers was approved.

Future Prospects

Although state policy makers continue to work on the problems posed by the corrections system, it seems clear that the state will have to continue to devote substantial energy to the corrections system. While seven new prisons are now being added to the system, the price tag assigned to them of about thirty million dollars reflects only a part of the problem involved. The expenses of bonded indebtedness probably double the costs of building a new prison. Adding operating costs, each of these prisons may cost over 300 million dollars over a 30 year period.

Once the Nelson suit deadline is met in 1990, the state will face another set of critical choices. Without building additional prisons or taking action to control the prison population, South Carolina will rapidly return to the crisis conditions of the early 1980's and face perhaps even more radical court intervention.

While it seems likely that additional prisons must be constructed over the next five years, a long-range strategy that relies heavily on prison construction to reduce overcrowding has some serious drawbacks. As noted earlier, prisons are quite expensive to build and operate. In fact, it currently costs more to house and care for a prisoner for a year, $11,472, than it does to attend a public college or university for a year. (For example, U.S.C.'s *Bulletin* estimates the costs of attendance for the 1987-1988 academic year, at $6,066, including tuition, fees, room and board, books, transportation, and personal expenses, for a resident student.) Moreover, the costs of housing inmates are likely to rise. While South Carolina's current costs compare quite favorably with other states (see Figure 6), in the future we can expect these costs to move closer to the national average, which now stands at about $16,000 a year.

Figure 6

Average Cost per Inmate in

Selected Southern States

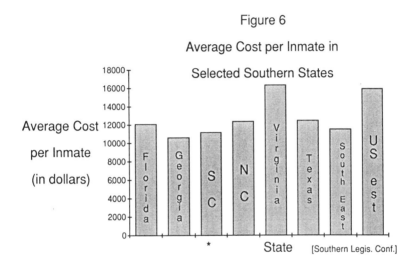

Present demographic and political trends suggest that the state's prison population will continue to grow for some time. As Dean William J. Mathias of USC's College of Criminal Justice observes,

"Criminals now impose two types of costs on society. Initially, their crimes impose economic and psychological costs on their victims and on society. Once convicted, their punishment imposes additional costs as funds which might otherwise be used to support improved education, health care and other critical public needs, must now be used to pay for expensive imprisonment."

As a complement to a reasonable plan for constructing additional prisons, the state must consider ways of controlling and reducing South Carolina's prison population. As we have seen, there are essentially two approaches to reducing populations: "back-door" strategies which accelerate the release of inmates, and "front-door" strategies which reduce the intake of prisoners.

Back-door strategies include early release programs, supervised furloughs, expanding opportunities for inmates to reduce their sentences by earning "good time" credits, and more frequent use of parole. The increasing reluctance of governors to order early releases of inmates, especially as the inmate population becomes increasingly limited to violent and dangerous offenders, suggests that this mechanism will play less of a role in controlling the prison population in the future. At the same time, the judicial system has demonstrated that this remains an option, if safe and reasonable conditions are not maintained within the prison system.

The current political climate also makes a more liberal use of parole unlikely, although programs like the Department of Probation, Parole, and Pardon Services' intensive supervision of parolees may make parole a more acceptable option. The Department has also implemented parole guidelines coupled with the use of a risk assessment procedure which provides more information and a better and more consistent basis for the assessment of the risk presented by a candidate for parole. Apart from this process, prison officials are very supportive of programs which allow inmates to reduce their sentences by participating in educational and vocational programs. While the rehabilitative effects of such programs have been overestimated in the past, it is both legally and practically important to provide opportunities for meaning- ful activity to inmates who will eventually return to the community. Apart from the possibility of rehabilitation, corrections officials find such programs to be indispensable for managing a prison. The especially dangerous inmates are often those who have lost all hope and have no incentives to obey prison rules.

Finally, while the idea of shorter sentences is particularly unpopular at the moment, there is research which suggests that the severity of a sentence has less of a deterrent effect than the certainty of being sentenced to prison. If, however, the aim of longer sentences is not deterrence, but simply punishment or revenge, then some difficult choices must be made about the use of taxpayer's money. Adding only one month to the sentence of each of the 7,000 prisoners admitted every year, for example, has been estimated to create the need for an additional prison which would cost taxpayers over 300 million dollars over a 30 year period.

Front-door strategies seek to divert the most marginal offenders from prison to alternative programs. Using programs like those incorporated in the 1986 Omnibus Crime Bill (including restitution centers and shock probation) provide a means to deal with offenders whose crimes are not serious enough to warrant a prison term but who should receive more than a stern warning and a probated sentence. It remains to be seen if South Carolina's judges and solicitors will make use of these alternative programs. It is also unclear whether the public and the General Assembly are willing to reform sentencing practices in a way that would require their use for qualified offenders. Other reforms, such as those aimed at the Department of Youth Services, and the

121

educational system, also play a role where they provide alternative life styles and better personal values for youth who might otherwise commit crimes as adults.

Whatever mixture of alternative reforms, prison population control and prison construction the state pursues, it has become clear that to do nothing is the most costly strategy of all. A failure to address the problem of prison overcrowding will mean that the state will continue to lurch from one crisis to the next, risking federal court intervention and undermining the criminal justice system's ability to punish criminals appropriately while insuring that they are treated humanely.

References

Blumenstein, Alfred (1983). "Prisons: Population, Capacity, and Alternatives," Chapter 13 in James Q. Wilson (ed.) *Crime and Public Policy*. San Francisco: The Institute for Contemporary Studies.

Brakel, Samuel Jan (1987). "Prison Reform Litigation: Has the Revolution Gone Too Far?." *Corrections Today* (August): 160-168.

Coxs, Verne C., Paul B. Paulus, and Garvin McCain (1984). "Prison Crowding Research: The Relevance for Prison Housing Standards and a General Approach Regarding Crowding Phenomena." *American Psychologist* 39: 1148-1160.

DiIulio, John J., Jr. (1987). *Governing Prisons: A Comparative Study of Correctional Management*. New York: The Free Press.

Glasser, Daniel (1983). "Supervising Offenders Outside of Prison," Chapter 12 in James Q. Wilson (ed.) *Crime and Public Policy*. San Francisco: The Institute for Contemporary Studies.

Greenwood, Peter W. (1983). "Controlling the Crime Rate Through Imprisonment," Chapter 14 in James Q. Wilson (ed.) *Crime and Public Policy*. San Francisco: The Institute for Contemporary Studies.

Jacobs, James B. (1977). *Stateville: The Penitentiary in Mass Society*. Chicago: The University of Chicago Press.

Peirce, Neal R. (1987). "No Bars, No Guns: Punishing Without Prison." *National Journal* (November 21): 2987.

Peirce, Neal R. (1987). "On Letting the Punishment Fit the Criminal." *National Journal* (December 5): 3107.

Silberman, Charles (1980). *Criminal Violence, Criminal Justice*. New York: Vintage Books.

Ziesel, Hans (1982). *The Limits of Law Enforcement*. Chicago: The University of Chicago Press.

8

Medical Indigence in South Carolina

S. Jane Massey

Introduction

Among the many challenges facing South Carolina is the one posed by its historically high poverty levels. The 1980 Census found that 16.6 percent of South Carolinians, or 500,363 persons, had incomes below the poverty level. Only eight states had higher rates of poverty. More recently, in 1985 South Carolina was ranked 46th among the states in per capita income. That means only four states had per capita income levels lower than South Carolina's $10,586 (*South Carolina Statistical Abstract 1986*). These statistics show a poverty problem which impacts a whole range of other state issues, many of which are addressed in this volume. Education reform, prison overcrowding, prospects for the rural economy, and even coastal zone management have been shaped, at least partially, by this central fact of South Carolina life: that a very large number of the state's citizens are poor.

One problem area in which the state's high poverty rate particularly is reflected is its citizens' health and medical care. For example, in 1982 South Carolina had the highest infant mortality rate (16.1 deaths per 1,000 live births) of all fifty states (*South Carolina Statistical Abstract 1986*). In addition to a large number of poor people and their attendant health problems, the state has had historically minimal public assistance programs. In 1983, South Carolina ranked 51 among 54 states and territories in its Aid to Families with Dependent Children (AFDC) payment level and 50th in its Standard of Need for qualifying for public assistance. The result was a large number of people who had neither public nor private resources available to pay for health care; that is, people who could be termed medically indigent. A study produced by the Toomey Company, a private consulting firm under contract with the state, found that hospitals in South Carolina shifted some $69 million in costs in 1983 to cover care for the poor and medically indigent — a good indication of the extent of medical indigence in the state. The

S. Jane Massey is associate director for research in the Bureau of Governmental Research and Service at the University of South Carolina. This chapter is an update of a Public Affairs Bulletin coauthored with Ann Chadwell Humphries.

123

Hospital Association found in 1981 that hospitals had to increase a patient's bill by an average of 20 percent per day to meet its financial obligations for uncompensated care (State of South Carolina, Office of the Governor, 1984).

This chapter will examine the problem of the medically indigent in South Carolina. The first section will consider who makes up the population of medically indigent. South Carolina's response to the problem will be considered in section two. In the final portion of this chapter future issues concerning uncompensated health care will be discussed.

What is Medical Indigence

In simplest terms, the medically indigent are those individuals who are unable to pay for their health care. These are individuals who have neither public nor private payment resources. Not surprisingly, low income groups face a high risk of medical indigence. In addition, there are those who would not normally be considered low income but who, because of catastrophic medical expenses, become medically indigent.

While the simple definition above tells us what medical indigence is, it does not adequately address the question of who the medically indigent are. This seems especially true in light of the availability of Medicare and Medicaid, and the widespread availability of employer provided health insurance and individual health policies. On the face of it, one might wonder how someone, even with a low income, could find themselves in the position of being unable to pay for necessary health care. Who are the approximately 36 million Americans who lack any kind of health insurance? (Roemer, 1987:7) To understand medical indigence better, we need to understand who is and who is not covered by public and private health care programs.

Medicaid. Medicaid is a joint federal and state health insurance program aimed at four specific groups of low-income persons — the elderly, the blind, the handicapped, and single-parent families with dependent children. States have a great deal of discretion in operating the program. Basically, the states are only required to provide Medicaid benefits to those people who qualify for Supplemental Security Income (SSI) and Aid to Families with Dependent Children (AFDC).

SSI is a federally administered program providing income assistance. The federal government determines eligibility. In order to qualify for SSI (and therefore Medicaid) a person must be poor and 65 years of age or older, have a corrected vision of 20/200 or less, or be physically or mentally handicapped to an extent that prohibits employment. Benefit levels are based on income, marital status and living arrangements.

AFDC is also an income assistance program but it is a joint federal and

124

state program in which the state determines income eligibility and benefit levels. AFDC support primarily goes to single (generally female) headed households with dependent children. Some states do provide some benefits to two-parent households if the primary income earner is unemployed, but the two-parent household program is a very small part of AFDC. Since states set the income eligibility criteria for AFDC (and therefore Medicaid) there is a great deal of variability in income level requirements. The income level requirements represent the maximum income a family can have and still qualify for AFDC assistance. As of March 28, 1984 federal poverty guidelines set the poverty level at $10,200 per year (or less) for a family of four. AFDC income eligibility standards then ranged from Vermont's $10,932 per year for a family of four to South Carolina's former standard of $2,748 for the same family type. In 1985, South Carolina increased its eligibility income limit to 50 percent of the federal guideline ($5,100 annually for a family of four based on the March 1984 guidelines). In doing so, South Carolina joined 32 other states whose eligibility limits are 50 percent or more of the federal poverty guidelines.

Based on the eligibility requirements of these two programs, only low income elderly and handicapped people and very low income single parent households with dependent children *must* be included in the Medicaid program. Apart from these groups who must receive Medicaid, states have the option of providing benefits to the "medically needy." The medically needy are those who fall into one of the four qualifying categories (elderly, blind, disabled, or part of a household with dependent children) who have incomes which are too high for participation in SSI or AFDC but whose incomes are not sufficient to pay their medical bills. Thirty states provide benefits to the medically needy (South Carolina established a medically needy program in the 1984 appropriations bill). But with or without a medically needy program, Medicaid generally leaves the childless poor, the working poor, and low income two-parent households ineligible for benefits. Because of the wide variations across the states in medicaid eligibility, Medicaid actually covers only about 50 percent of people whose incomes are below the federal poverty standard nationally. Medicaid is not, therefore, a comprehensive health insurance program for the poor (Altman, 1983: 109).

Medicare. The Medicare program was established to provide hospitalization and medical insurance for the elderly regardless of income. Anyone who is 65 years of age or older and who is also eligible to receive social security or railroad retirement benefits qualifies for Medicare. In addition to the elderly, some younger persons who suffer from chronic kidney disease or who are disabled and have been receiving social security benefits for two years or more are also covered. Virtually everyone over age 65 in the United States is covered by Medicare. However, Medicare does not cover all health care expenses. Physical therapy exceeding a set limit per year, routine physical examinations, prescription drugs, hearing aids, eyeglasses, dentures or dental care, and private duty nurses are among the items not covered by Medicare. In addition, Medicare recipients must also pay a deductible for hospital and other medical expenses. Sixty-nine percent of the people who are covered by Medicare also have private health insurance to fill gaps. That means, of course, that 31 percent of those covered by Medicare must use their own resources to pay for costs not included under the program. Therefore, there is some uncompensated health care even among those enrolled in the Medicare program.

Hill-Burton Act. The Hospital Survey and Construction Act, better known as the Hill-Burton Act, was enacted in 1946 to provide for the construction of hospitals and health facilities. Since 1946, almost $6 billion in grants, loans, and loan guarantees have been distributed to approximately 7,000 facilities. In return for Hill-Burton assistance, hospitals were obligated to provide a certain amount of free care to people whose incomes fell below federal poverty guidelines. Hill-Burton hospitals were also obligated to make their services available to everyone living in their geographic area. Thus the Hill-Burton Act has facilitated a significant amount of health care provision for the medically indigent.

The Hill-Burton Act is not, however, a solution to the problem of medical indigence. First, the federal government is no longer making funds available through this program. Secondly, hospitals had a 20-year free care and community service obligation under Hill-Burton. Many hospitals have now fulfilled that obligation and are at liberty to either discontinue or substantially reduce their free care programs. People who once received Hill-Burton free care may now have no medical resources. And finally, even while operating under Hill-Burton obligations, hospitals were never required to provide unlimited free health care. The amount of free care required was based on a formula which used the hospital's operating budget and the amount of federal assistance received. Fifty-nine South Carolina hospitals received Hill-Burton funds, eleven of those have already completed their free care obligations.

Veterans' Benefits. The Veterans Administration (VA) provides a wide-range of services which include medical care. Although VA health care benefits are primarily directed toward treating veterans with service-connected medical conditions, the VA does treat some veterans who might otherwise be medically indigent. Care in a VA hospital is provided on a bed-available basis for non-service-connected conditions if the veteran signs a statement that he/she is unable to defray the cost of comparable care. Veterans

126

with non-service-connected conditions are automatically eligible for hospital treatment if they are 65 years of age or older, receiving a VA pension, eligible for Medicaid, or a former Prisoner-Of-War.

The VA medical care program is not an insignificant provider of health care to those who are medically indigent. But, of course, VA care is not an option available to most people, since only veterans are eligible. In addition, since care for non-service-connected conditions is on a bed availability basis, there can be a long wait for nonemergency or elective procedures. VA hospitals and facilities are also generally located in metropolitan areas and access to them can be a serious problem for veterans in rural areas.

Employment Based Health Insurance. Private insurance is by far the most common way for Americans to cover their health care needs. Seventy-five percent of the population has private health insurance (*New York Times*, 18 February 1985). Over 80 percent of that private health insurance is employment based (e.g., company group health plans). Our current tax laws have done much to encourage this reliance on employment based health insurance. As it now stands, health insurance premiums are tax deductible for employers while benefits are not considered taxable income to employees. There has been some discussion, however, about making health insurance benefits taxable income. If this change occurs, some lower income employees might find it necessary to opt out of group health plans.

The pervasiveness of employment based health insurance has several implications for medical indigence. Prior to 1986, when a worker lost his/her job, typically his/her health insurance was also lost. This loss of health insurance came at a time when the individual or family was least able to afford the more expensive non-group health insurance policies. During the 1982-83 recession, the Congressional Budget Office estimated that of the 12 million people out of work in December 1982, 7.4 million had been laid off. While some of those 7.4 million laid off workers were able to at least temporarily retain their health insurance, 10.7 million people (dependents and workers) lost employer based health insurance (Hester, 1983: 42).

As part of the Consolidated Omnibus Budget Reconciliation Act (COBRA), signed into law by President Reagan on April 7, 1986, employers with 20 or more employees must now make extended health care benefits available to former employees and their beneficiaries for 18 to 36 months after death, termination of employment, and divorce. Dependent children of employees who become ineligible for coverage under the group plan because of age must also be offered extended health care benefits. However, employers *do not* have to pay for these benefits. The former employee or beneficiary may be charged up to 102 percent of the cost of the group plan. COBRA offers unemployed workers an important benefit since group health coverage will

127

normally be less expensive than individual insurance plans. Nonetheless, unemployed workers may find even group health coverage for themselves and their families too expensive. At the same time, the unemployed worker is also likely to have too many assets to qualify for a government health program like Medicaid. This could mean that even with COBRA protection, during periods of recession, when unemployment is high, medical indigence will increase. Such an increase in medical indigence might occur when the public coffers are also suffering from decreases in income tax and sales tax collections, thus making a governmental response more difficult (*Personnel Manager's Legal Reporter*, May 1986).

Another implication of employment based health insurance is its cost to business. Each year businesses spend about $77 billion for group health insurance. As group insurance costs have climbed, business has begun to look carefully at those expenditures. Some businesses have responded by requiring their employees to pay a greater share of medical costs in the form of higher premiums for dependent coverage or larger deductibles. This response to the high cost of group coverage has caused some employees to drop their family coverage, thus creating another potential for medical indigence. In addition, the high cost of group policies (especially for small groups) has discouraged some small businesses from even offering health insurance as a fringe benefit. In 1982, approximately 9 percent of employed workers were without health insurance.

And finally, as with Medicare, having private health insurance does not mean that all the recipient's health care costs are covered. Most traditional health insurance does not pay for preventive care. The individual is also responsible for the deductible and any items not covered by the insurance. Commercial insurance carriers pay, on the average, 92 percent of billed charges. The gap between insurance coverage and costs opens up the potential for uncompensated care (Greenman, 1984: 3).

Self Pay. For those people who are not covered by any of the programs listed above, two options exist. First, one may obtain private non-group health insurance. Typically these policies are more expensive than group policies and offer less adequate coverage. In some cases, it is also possible to obtain group insurance policies that are not employment based through professional or fraternal organizations. These policies may be less expensive than individual health policies, but more expensive than employment based group policies, since work based policies are often employer subsidized. About 20 percent of all people who have commercial health insurance have one of these two types of policies. Of course, in order to obtain this type of coverage, one must be able to afford the premiums — which in some cases can be substantial.

128

Apart from the types of coverage discussed above (Medicaid, Medicare, access to Hill-Burton care, Veterans Administration, or private coverage), the only other option is self-pay. Those people who use their own resources to pay the entire cost of their health care face a very high risk of medical indigence. In South Carolina, 7 percent of all inpatients are self-pay. It has been estimated that 85 percent of these self-pay patients will be "bad debt" cases (Jacobs and Alexander, 1983: 15). Many doctors and hospitals are, therefore, reluctant to take self-pay patients.

And finally, there is one other group who risks medical indigence. These are people who do have resources to cover normal medical care (insurance, savings, etc.) but who could not handle the cost of a catastrophic illness.

Based on the above descriptions of public and private health care programs, the composition of the medically indigent population becomes clearer. The medically indigent generally have low incomes; they may be unemployed or underemployed (part-time or casual labor); they are uninsured (or underinsured); and they do not qualify for government programs for the elderly, the handicapped, and dependent children. The ranks of the medically indigent include people like the 55 year old widow with grown children, no social security, and no job; the single mother of two, working privately for several households as a maid; and the construction worker and his family whenever he is in between building projects. It may be fair to say that most of the medically indigent really have "fallen through the cracks" in our health care system. They are people who do not have employment based insurance, cannot afford individual commercial policies, but are not poor enough or do not fall into the right categories to qualify for Medicaid.

The Impact of Medical Indigence

Traditionally, the cost of medical indigence (the dollar amount of uncompensated care) was handled "under the table" through cost shifting. That is, hospitals charged patients an amount equal to the cost of care received plus enough extra to cover bad debt patients. In this way, the cost of uncompensated care was spread across commercial insurance companies and self-pay patients. Medicare, and usually Medicaid, excluded the cost of bad debt, charity, and courtesy care from its reimbursement formulas.

Cost shifting as a strategy for handling medical indigence was not a serious problem as long as (1) the margin between costs and charges was small and (2) the health care system was not price competitive. Before 1969, the margin between costs and charges stayed between 5 and 7 percent. Between 1969 and 1979, that margin or cost shift increased to 15.3 percent. Thus, the margin between costs and charges has become uncomfortably large. Additionally, cost shifting has become less acceptable as both public health programs

129

and private insurers have sought to introduce (or reintroduce) price competitiveness into the health care market.

Complex reasons account for the increase in the cost of uncompensated care and the change in price competitiveness for health care. They are tied to a number of important changes which have occurred in our health care system over the past forty years. To understand how medical indigence is impacting the health care industry, it is important to review those changes and how they have led to the current problem.

Perhaps the biggest change in the American health care system has been the huge increase in the number of people gaining access to the system since World War II. That increase in access has occurred for both the poor and the nonpoor. The increase in health care access for the nonpoor began in the late 1940's when commercial insurers started to make medical insurance policies widely available. Over the next forty years, medical insurance became a customary part of employer fringe benefit packages. In 1940, only 12 million Americans (or nine percent of the population) had some type of hospital insurance. By 1950, 77 million people were insured and in 1976 that number had grown to 177 million. Now, 75 percent of the population has private health insurance.

While the pervasiveness of private health insurance has no doubt increased the amount of health care available to working and middle class Americans, it has also distorted the behavior of both consumers and providers of health care. Because health care is no longer paid out of pocket by the consumer, providers and consumers have become insensitive to the true cost of treatment. In 1950, patients paid for 50 percent of all hospital bills directly. Today, that figure is under 10 percent. The result of this price insensitivity has been to increase the incentive for providers to render treatment (regardless of its necessity) and decrease the incentive to limit hospital stays and tests to the minimum necessary. Third party (i.e., insurer) financed health care has been one factor in the large increase in the cost of health care and its share of GNP.

Increased access to health care for the poor and the elderly occurred with the passage of the Medicare and Medicaid programs in 1965. With the passage of Medicare and Medicaid, the federal government essentially entered into an open-ended commitment to provide health care benefits for the elderly, as well as increasing health care for the poor. That commitment was entered into at a point in American history when, in retrospect, a new demographic trend was beginning — the graying of America. The population aged 65 and over is now the fastest growing segment of our population, presently comprising 11 percent of the population. According to the South Carolina Hospital Association, people over the age of 65 use hospitals five times more frequently than those under 65. On the average, it costs 3.5 times as much to treat someone over 65 than it does to treat someone younger. For individuals 75 years and older, the cost is seven times greater. Therefore, the Medicare program in particular was vulnerable to rapidly increasing costs. And, in fact, the number of people served by Medicare and Medicaid, and the cost of that service, has increased dramatically. In 1967, Medicare and Medicaid cost $5.7 billion in state and federal expenditures. In 1981, the two programs cost about $73.4 billion.

The goal of Medicaid and Medicare was better health care for the elderly and the poor. However, in the process of providing better health care for the elderly and the poor, Medicare and Medicaid also introduced some distortions into the health care system. First, like private health insurance, Medicaid and Medicare tend to make the consumer of the health care less sensitive to cost. In addition, the payment schedule used until October 1983 was an open-ended cost-based reimbursement — payments were made based only on what was spent for patient care with few limitations. Hospitals therefore had no incentive to control costs. And finally, as hoped, Medicare and Medicaid brought many people into the health care system who otherwise would not have had access. But, in doing so, the demand for a limited resource — health care — increased, further increasing the cost.

Taken together, private health insurance, Medicare, and Medicaid succeeded in greatly expanding the demand for health care while, in effect, rewarding high cost treatment. In 1965, health care expenditures represented 6 percent of the Gross National Product (GNP). That figure had increased to 10.8 percent by 1984 and is expected to reach 13 percent by 1990. Hospitals account for 42 percent of total health care spending. In the twelve years between 1968 and 1979, annual hospital inflation averaged 15 percent, more than double the inflation rate for the rest of the economy during that period. It is not surprising, then, that health care spending in general, and hospital costs in particular, have been the target of government and business action to increase price competitiveness.

In addition to the large increase in health care demand and the concurrent weakening of price competitiveness, some other changes have impacted the health care industry. One change which has already been mentioned is demographic. The United States is made up of an increasingly older population, an older population which requires more health care. The health care industry has also experienced great technological changes. The introduction of items like CAT scanners, transplant technology, and microsurgery have increased the cost of medical care. While hospitals have had no incentive to be price competitive, they did not quit competing with each other. Rather than price, the prestige of the medical staff and the availability of the most modern equipment and facilities have been the competitive factors. This type of competition increases the operating expenses for hospitals and therefore increases hospital costs. And finally, an increasingly litigious American society, coupled with large damage awards by juries, have increased the cost of malpractice suits and malpractice insurance. In South Carolina, malpractice costs rose 500 percent between 1975 and 1983. The high incidence of malpractice suits has also impacted the way in which doctors practice medicine — providing an additional incentive for extra tests and procedures. It has been estimated that 30 percent of the price increases in health care can be traced to increasing service intensity. That means that a given patient is now receiving more procedures and more advanced procedures — a direct result of technology change and the increased risk of malpractice suits.

Aiding The Medically Indigent In South Carolina

In response to the pressing problem of medical indigence, the State of South Carolina took two major steps to address those needs. The two steps were (1) the establishment of medically needy coverage within the Medicaid program and (2) the passage of the Medically Indigent Assistance Act which expanded AFDC/Medicaid eligibility and established a Medical Indigence fund. This section will analyze these two actions and their impact on medical indigence.

The State's Response. The State's response to the problem of medical indigence began in January, 1982 when, reacting to the growing problem of medical indigence (made worse by a recession and high unemployment during the same period), Governor Riley directed his staff to look into the problem of medical indigence and to focus attention on the need for a comprehensive plan to address the problem. As a result, the Department of Health and Environmental Control (DHEC) prepared a study which analyzed the resources available to the medically indigent in South Carolina. Following this study, the Health Care Planning and Oversight Committee of the General Assembly; the House Medical, Military, Public and Municipal Affairs Committee; the Senate Medical Affairs Committee; and the Governor's Office formed a coalition to further investigate the scope of the medical indigence problem. On behalf of the coalition, the Health Care Planning and Oversight Committee commissioned a study by the Toomey Company. When the Toomey report was complete in March 1984, the Medically Indigent Subcommittee of the Health Care Planning and Oversight Committee held two public hearings and created an Ad Hoc Committee comprised of a variety of professionals to make recommendations based on the Toomey report and other information available at that time.

During this period in which attention was being focused on medical indigence, the General Assembly took an important first step toward a comprehensive response to the problem. In June, 1984, a medically needy program was funded as part of the state's Medicaid program. The General Assembly appropriated $18.8 million to provide Medicaid coverage to poor pregnant women and poor children who are members of intact families. These groups had been deleted from coverage previously when federal monies for the program were cut.

The following year (1985), the General Assembly considered the recommendations of the Health Care Planning and Oversight Committee and passed the Medically Indigent Assistance Act. The Medically Indigent Assistance Act made several major changes in care for the medically indigent in South Carolina.

The Medically Indigent Assistance Act expanded the number of people eligible for Medicaid. By changing South Carolina's Standard of Need for qualifying for AFDC from $2,748 per year for a family of four to 50 percent of Federal Poverty Guidelines ($5,100 per year) and by adopting the AFDC-Unemployed Parent (AFDC-UP) program, approximately 42,600 additional individuals were made eligible for AFDC and Medicaid. This strategy for addressing medical indigence allowed the state to take advantage of a favorable federal matching ratio. For every $100 in expanded services, the Federal share is approximately $73 (State of South Carolina, Office of the Governor, November 1984).

The Act also created a fund to provide medical care for those who do not qualify for other government programs but who are, nonetheless, medically indigent. The Medically Indigent Assistance Fund is financed by assessments from each general hospital in the State and by an assessment against each county. The money is collected and distributed by the State to cover claims made by hospitals for the treatment and care of eligible persons. The establishment of the Medically Indigent Assistance Fund was effective January 1, 1986.

In addition, the Act mandated that "no person, regardless of his ability to pay or county of residence, may be denied emergency care…" This section's intent was to insure that no one would be turned away from receiving emergency care because of medical indigence.

The fourth step taken by the Act was to implement a prospective payment system for Medicaid and for the new Medically Indigent Assistance Fund. The goal of prospective payment systems is to provide an incentive for hospitals to deliver health care efficiently.

And finally, the Medically Indigent Assistance Act implemented a process to contain hospital costs and to control hospital rate schedules. The State Health and Human Services Finance Commission is to publish each August 1 an "annual target rate of increase for net inpatient charges for all general hospitals in the State." If the hospital industry exceeds the annual target rate of increase, the financial reports of each hospital exceeding the target will be reviewed. The Commission may penalize a hospital by limiting its future rates of increase. After three consecutive years of exceeding its target rate, a hospital may be barred from receiving Medically Indigent Assistance Fund payments. It would still be required to pay its annual assessment for the fund. The Act also includes some data collection and special study requirements which should lead to more and better information on the medically indigent and health care costs.

Implementation. The addition of the medically needy program and the passage of the *Medically Indigent Assistance Act* helped South Carolina make great strides in providing health care for the medically indigent. As with many new initiatives, however, the implementation and financing of these programs did not always proceed as expected. The State's commitment to the medically needy program only lasted about two years. The expansion of the Medicaid program by changing AFDC eligibility requirements did not produce the expected increase in people enrolling in the program. And the medical indigence assistance fund has run short of money each year since its inception. In addition, the *Medically Indigent Assistance Act* places a significant burden on county governments which needs to be considered. The Act also does not address the need for preventive or primary health care and does not address the problem of uncompensated health care provided to low income people who are covered by Medicare and employment based or private health insurance. Each of these issues will be discussed below.

The medically needy program focused on providing preventive care for children and prenatal care for pregnant women. The medically needy program was a relatively small program during the almost two years that it was in place. The February 1985 *Statistical Report* of the S.C. Department of Social Services showed 4,143 persons in the medically needy program. Pregnant women made up 725 of that group; the other 3,418 were children under 18. The February 1986 report listed 3,173 persons in the program. The program was eliminated March 1, 1987 in order to avoid a $24 million shortfall in the Medicaid program that fiscal year. In addition to eliminating the medically needy program, the state also reduced reimbursements to nursing homes, pharmacies, and hospitals. At the time of the medical needy program's elimination, the S.C. Hospital Association expressed concern about the ultimate cost of poor prenatal care. The issue of cost-shifting was also raised. Pete Reibold, board member of the South Carolina Hospital Association was quoted in the February 11, 1987 *State* newspaper as saying that "In essence, then, what the proposed Medicaid cutbacks will do is mandate a return to cost-shifting."

The expansion of Medicaid participation by relaxing AFDC eligibility requirements also did not fare as expected. When the *Medically Indigent*

Assistance Act was first passed, it was estimated that almost 43,000 additional individuals would be eligible for AFDC and Medicaid. However, looking at the number of persons enrolled in the AFDC program (and therefore participating in the Medicaid program) each February from 1979 through 1988, one will note that the number has been declining since 1981, no doubt largely due to a strong economy and improving unemployment rates. In February 1985, 120,585 persons were participating in the AFDC program. In February 1986, after the change in AFDC eligibility rules, 130,809 persons were in the AFDC program. In February 1987, one year after the rule change, the South Carolina AFDC program covered 130,078 persons. Only about 10,000 additional people actually came into the Medicaid program as a result of the eligibility changes. There has been a lot of speculation as to why such a relatively small number of people have enrolled in the AFDC/Medicaid program. The original estimate of 42,600 additional persons was, in retrospect, too high. James L. Solomon Jr., Commissioner of the Department of Social Services, speculated that the application process might discourage some eligible people from participating in the program, particularly if it is their first experience with the AFDC program (Salahuddin, 1986: 1-B). In any case, this portion of the *Medically Indigent Assistance Act* has been a disappointment.

The Medically Indigent Assistance Fund, on the other hand, has been very successful and has suffered from a lack of sufficient resources because of its popularity. Each year since the program's start, the fund has run out of money before the end of the fiscal year. That means that during the last one to three months of the fiscal year, no claims are processed or paid. Nonetheless, in fiscal year 1987, the first full fiscal year under the Act, 7,336 claims totaling $15,301,300 were paid (S. C. Health Plan and Oversight Committee, August 1987).

One interesting aspect of the *Medically Indigent Assistance Act* is its intergovernmental element. For some, the requirements placed on the county are perceived to be a problem. Through the Act, counties were mandated to provide $5.5 million dollars in matching funds for Medicaid services and to maintain and implement the Medically Indigent Assistance Fund (MIAF). The FY 87 and 88 county MIAF assessments each totaled $7.5 million. Counties are assessed their share of fund contributions based on property value, per capita income, net taxable sales, and claims against the fund by county residents. Each factor is given equal weight, making the formula at least mildly redistributive. The good thing about this approach is that it helps equalize what has been a very unequal effort by counties to address the needs of their medically indigent. Out of South Carolina's 46 counties, 14 budgeted no funds in 1982 for indigent health care. The remaining counties budgeted from $4 million (Charleston County) to $1500. The five counties with regional community hospitals provided 80 percent of all county indigent funding. The Medically Indigent Assistance Fund does address this inequity and does recognize through the formula the differing abilities to pay of the various counties. The problem is that counties are already facing growing demands on their scarce revenues. Anytime that the State imposes a financial mandate of this type without an accompanying decrease in some other obligation or an increase in revenue sources (through State aid or taxing ability), some counties will suffer a hardship in their own service delivery abilities.

In a study of State mandates prepared by the Bureau of Governmental Research and Service at the University of South Carolina for the S.C. Advisory Commission on Intergovernmental Relations, researchers looked at the financial impact of the MIAF program and Medicaid assessments on fourteen counties. When county expenditures for the medically indigent in FY 1985 (prior to passage of the Act) were compared to the MIAF administrative costs, plus the mandated Medicaid and MIAF assessments for FY 1987, the fourteen counties in the study fell into three distinct groups. For four of the fourteen counties, the FY 87 assessments, plus administrative costs, totaled less than the amount which they had spent on medical indigence in FY 85. Bamberg, Charleston, Colleton, and Richland counties spent $6.52, $20.35, $8.75, and $16.59 per capita, respectively, for assistance to the medically indigent in FY 85. In FY 87, the state mandated medicaid and MIAF assessments, plus MIAF administrative costs, ranged between $3.14 and $4.87 per capita for these counties. The two urban counties, Charleston and Richland, have also chosen to continue their higher levels of assistance to the medically indigent by continuing to appropriate additional funds for that purpose. Richland County appropriated $1.5 million in FY 87 for additional assistance. Charleston County appropriated over $7 million in FY 87 and FY 88 to support Charleston Memorial Hospital which primarily serves low income persons (Massey and Thomas, 1988: 39-47).

Two of the fourteen counties, Greenville and Sumter, experienced little change between their FY 85 expenditures for medical indigence and their mandated FY 87 expenditures. Of the eight counties in the study which were required to increase their efforts, five had to increase their expenditures by over 100% between FY 85 and FY 87. Florence county for example increased its spending by over $400,000. However, even the less dramatic increases, such as the $68,136 expenditure increase required of Dillon County, had an important budgetary impact in the smaller counties.

In order to evaluate the extent of the impact the program has had on county budgets, the study looked at the portion of general fund revenue that is being spent for the MIAF and Medicaid assessments and administration of the MIAF program in each county. That impact ranged from 3.67 percent of total general fund revenues in Richland County to .98 percent in Colleton. Based on the value of one mill of property tax (the amount of revenue that one mill will raise), counties estimated that the assessments represented from about 1.5 mills in Oconee County to about 4.5 mills in the poorer counties of Bamberg and Dillon. The timing of the mandate caused the financial impact to be particularly significant. The requirement by the State for counties to allocate a portion of their revenue for assistance to the medically indigent came at about the same time that S. C. cities and counties were faced with a loss of over $71 million in federal General Revenue Sharing funds.

Nevertheless, in discussing the mandate with county officials, most of the officials from the study site counties agreed that the assistance program was important for the low income citizens in South Carolina. There appeared to be fairly widespread support for the provision of the service. County officials disagree more with the requirement to pay into the Medicaid portion of the program than with the MIAF assessment. The Medicaid program was perceived to be a state function. Several of the county officials, while supportive of the program, believed that their county simply could not afford the program.

Another problem that has been pointed out about the Act is that it primarily focuses on acute care rather than on primary or preventive care. One problem inherent in poverty and in medical indigence is that people in these groups are generally not as healthy as others. Access to preventive care, diet, and education on health matters are all factors which contribute to this problem. The poor health status of the low income and medically indigent means that when people in these groups do seek medical care, they are often sicker than they would be otherwise. Their care is therefore more expensive and their hospital stays are longer. Given this situation, many health care professionals believe that primary care should be emphasized over acute care. While the Medically Indigent Assistance Act does mandate studies to consider programs which encourage and provide incentives for wellness and prevention, the thrust of the Act is actually acute care. Without programs which make preventive care available to the poor, the gap in the health status of the poor and the nonpoor can be expected to continue. Additionally, we will continue to spend public funds for acute care which might have been avoided through good primary care.

Conclusion

We cannot expect initiatives like South Carolina's recent legislation to solve the problem of medical indigence. Any final answer would require a resolution of the age-old problems of poverty, education, and public health. The problem of the medically indigent is, therefore, one which we can expect to continue to see in the future. In particular, more concern with preventive care can be expected. One proposal has been to establish Health Maintenance Organizations (HMOs) for the poor. Another proposal is for state and/or local governments to become more active as a direct provider of preventive care (e.g., well baby and well child clinics).

Another issue which can be expected to arise regarding the medically indigent is the extent to which a two-tiered health care system is evolving. With the increase in private not-for-profit and for profit hospitals we are already beginning to see patients with private insurance utilizing private facilities in greater numbers, leaving the public hospitals for the poor only. This kind of two-tiered system has some serious negative implications for the treatment of both the poor and the nonpoor. The ability of public hospitals to attract the best staff, philanthropic contributions, and funds for capital improvements could be endangered by this type of system.

In South Carolina, we can expect problems and controversies to emerge as the Medically Indigent Assistance Act is implemented. Counties, hospitals, health care advocates, and others may seek adjustments in portions of the Act. Additionally, the State will continually be forced to balance its commitment to aiding the medically indigent against the many other demands on the State's resources. The existence of competing needs such as education system improvement, prison construction, environmental protection, housing, and economic development virtually ensure that the problem of medical indigence will never be totally addressed. Therefore, the State's approach to assisting the medically indigent will of necessity be an evolutionary or incremental process.

References

Altman, Drew (1983). "Health Care for the Poor." *The Annals of the American Academy of Political and Social Science*, Vol. 465 (July): 103-121.

"15% of Americans Found To Lack Health Coverage" (1985). *New York Times* February 18: A13.

Bledsoe, Debra-Lynn (1986). "Panel Questions Equity of Indigent Care Funding." *The State* Columbia, SC. January 8: 2-C.

"The Changing System and the Medically Indigent" (1984). *Health Planning Times*, Vol. 3 (May): 2-6.

Demkovich, Linda E. (1984). "Hospitals That Provide For The Poor Are Reeling From Uncompensated Costs." *National Journal*, (November 24): 2245-2249.

"Doctor Criticizes Hospital Policies" (1985). *New York Times* February 7: A16.

Flandung, Thom (1986). "Indigent Care Fund To Run Out Midway Through Fiscal Year." *The Record* Columbia, S. C. July 16: 1-A.

Flanders, Danny C. (1987). "Medical Officials Warn Against Infant-Care Cuts." *The Record* Columbia, S. C. March 17: 1-A.

"Former Employees Entitled To Health Benefits Under New Law" (1986). *Personnel Manager's Legal Reporter*, (May): 1.

Greenman, Barbara W. (1984). "Cost Shifting: A Public Policy Debate." Unpublished Paper. Institute for Health Planning. Madison, Wisconsin. February.

"Helping The Medically Indigent: Some Coverage Better Than None" (1988). *The Urban Institute Policy and Research Report*, Vol. 18 (Winter): 10-11.

Hester, Ronald D. (1983). "Health Insurance and the Unemployed." *Urban Health*, Vol. 12 (November/December): 42-44.

Jacobs, Phillip and Greg R. Alexander (1983). "Hospital Reimbursement and Indigent Care: The Costs of a Nonpolicy." *Business and Economic Review*, Vol. 29 (March): 13-18.

Levin, Arthur (ed.) (1980). *Regulating Health Care*, Proceedings of the Academy of Political Science. Vol. 33, No. 4.

Malloy, James M. and David B. Skinner (1984). "Medicare on the Critical List." *Harvard Business Review*, Vol. 62 (November/December): 122-135.

Massey, Jane and Ann Chadwell Humphries (1986) "Providing Care For The Medically Indigent: The South Carolina Response." *Public Affairs Bulletin*, No. 32. Bureau of Governmental Research and Service, University of South Carolina. March.

Massey, Jane and Edwin Thomas (1988). *State Mandated Local Government Expenditures And Revenue Limitations in South Carolina, Part Four.* Prepared For South Carolina Advisory Commission on Intergovernmental Relations, Columbia, S.C.: S. C. Advisory Commission on Intergovernmental Relations, March.

Pope, Charles (1987). "Medical Cutbacks Ordered." *The State* Columbia, S.C. January 22: C-1.

Reed, David (1985). "Indigent Care Funding Off To Sluggish Start." *The News and Courier/ The Evening Post*, Charleston, S. C. October 27: 1-B.

Reem, Susanne (1985). "Abolishing the Barriers: Mainstreaming Indigent Patients Into Private Care Facilities." *Ambulatory Care* Vol. 5 (February): 8-13.

Roemer, Ruth (1987). "Access To Health Care By The Uninsured And Underinsured." *Review,* Indiana University School of Public and Environmental Affairs, (Fall): 7-11.

Salahuddin, Mobashir (1986). "Officials Amazed At Low Response To Health, Food 'Giveaway'." *The State* Columbia, S. C. April 14: 1-B.

South Carolina Department of Health and Human Services (1984). "Medically Indigent Funding Comparisons and Options." In-house Statistical Compliation. September 27.

South Carolina Department of Social Services (1979). *Statistical Report.* Columbia, S. C.: S. C. Department of Social Services, February.

South Carolina Department of Social Services (1980). *Statistical Report.* Columbia, S. C.: S. C. Department of Social Services, February.

South Carolina Department of Social Services (1981). *Statistical Report.* Columbia, S. C.: S. C. Department of Social Services, February.

South Carolina Department of Social Services (1982). *Statistical Report.* Columbia, S. C.: S. C. Department of Social Services, February.

South Carolina Department of Social Services (1983). *Statistical Report.* Columbia, S. C.: S. C. Department of Social Services, February.

South Carolina Department of Social Services (1984). *Statistical Report.* Columbia, S. C.: S. C. Department of Social Services, February.

South Carolina Department of Social Services (1985). *Statistical Report.* Columbia, S. C.: S. C. Department of Social Services, February.

South Carolina Department of Social Services (1986). *Statistical Report.* Columbia, S. C.: S. C. Department of Social Services, February.

South Carolina Department of Social Services (1987). *Statistical Report.* Columbia, S. C.: S. C. Department of Social Services, February.

South Carolina Department of Social Services (1988). *Statistical Report.* Columbia, S. C.: S. C. Department of Social Services, February.

South Carolina Division of Research and Statistical Services (1986). *South Carolina Statistical Abstract 1986.* Columbia, S. C.: State Budget and Control Board, Division of Research and Statistical Services.

South Carolina General Assembly (1984). "Final Report and Recommendations", Columbia, S.C.: Ad Hoc Committee of the Medically Indigent Subcommittee, Joint Legislative Committee on Health Care Planning and Oversight, September.

South Carolina Health Care Planning & Oversight Committee (1987). "Medically Indigent Assistance Fund County Experience FY 1986-87." Columbia, S. C.: S. C. General Assembly, August.

South Carolina. *South Carolina Medically Indigent Assistance Act. Code of Laws of South Carolina 1976, Annotated* (The Lawyers Co-operative Publishing Company, 1987), Title 44, Section 6.

South Carolina, Office of the Governor (1984). "Briefing on Indigent Care." Columbia, S.C.: Office of the Governor, November.

United States Congress (1984). House Committee on Energy and Commerce. *Report on Hill-Burton Hospitals and Their Obligations* Committee Print 98-JJ. 98th Cong., 2d Sess. Washington, D. C.: U. S. Government Printing Office.

United States Department of Health and Human Services (1982). *Your Medicare Handbook* Washington, D.C.: U.S. Government Printing Office.

"Unwanted by Hospitals, Stabbing Victim Dies" (1985). *New York Times* February 4: A8.

Wallace, Cynthia (1984). "State Legislatures Considering Ways To Finance Medical Care for Indigent." *Modern Healthcare* (December): 28, 32.

Wlodkowski, Bonita A. (1983). "Caveat Emptor in Health Care." *Political Science Quarterly*, Vol. 98 (Spring): 35-45.

9
South Carolinians' Political Attitudes

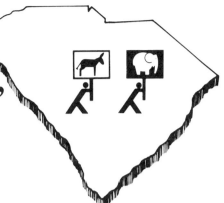

Michael A. Maggiotto

Introduction

Lincoln's poignant homily at Gettysburg offered a simple definition of democracy that has become a permanent part of the American political catechism. As children we learned it, and as adults we teach it: democracy is government of, by, and for the people. We enshrine the people above every competitor — be it state, class, party, or lineage. In this indivisible society, the people are sovereign and serve as the ultimate legitimators, actors, and evaluators. Government in all its forms and functions must be accountable to the people.

"The people" may be a sufficient formulation for theories of democracy, but the hard realities of politics require something more specific. Public opinion polls, using scientifically sound statistical methods, can provide us some of the best estimates of the popular interest — one specific measure of "the people." Public opinion polls are doubly useful measures. First, they are interesting in and of themselves as pictures of what people, in this case South Carolinians, think. Their accuracy provides us the evidence to sustain or challenge contemporary characterizations of the state. And second, they offer us a clear standard against which to judge the actions of governmental officials whom we have elected and who act in our name. Put simply, they are the data that allow us to assess public accountability easily.

Michael A. Maggiotto is associate professor of political science, Department of Government and International Studies, The University of South Carolina. Except as otherwise stated, the data for this chapter were gathered by Metromark, Inc., under contract with Columbia Newspapers, Inc., publishers of The State newspaper, and purchased by the Bureau of Governmental Research and Service for its archive. The author thanks Dr. Emerson Smith, President of Metromark, Inc., Mr. Clark Sarratt, Governmental Affairs Editor of The State, and Columbia Newspapers, Inc. for permission to purchase and to use these data. The author is similarly indebted to Dr. Charlie B. Tyer, former director of the Bureau of Governmental Research and Service, for authorizing the purchase of these data from scarce Bureau resources. Neither Metromark, Inc., Columbia Newspapers, Inc., The State newspaper, the Bureau of Governmental Research and Service nor their officers, editors, or employees are responsible for the views expressed below. The views and interpretations expressed are those of the author alone.

New South Partisanship In South Carolina

Political parties function as intermediaries between the people and the government, in western, representative democracies. Their platforms summarize the views of their members; their success in recruiting and electing candidates committed to those views is their primary goal and reason for being (Luttbeg, 1981: 115-178). Thus, attitudes regarding membership in political parties or party identification constitute one of the most important dimensions of public opinion (Campbell, et al., 1960: 120-167; Nie, et al., 1979). Examining partisanship, then, is a fitting place to begin our inquiry into "the people" of South Carolina.

The South has been regarded historically as a stronghold of the Democratic party. Table 1 presents the partisan distribution in South Carolina in 1985 and comparable near mid-decade figures for two other deep South states, Alabama and Mississippi, for two rim-South states, Texas and Florida, and for the nation as a whole.[1] These data reveal the portrait of the solid democratic south, in the 1980s, as faded and cracked. While identification with the Democratic party remains the most common response nationally and in each state in the table, except Florida, only in Mississippi does the democratic share approach 50 percent. In South Carolina, the proportion is nearer one-third than one-half. With these distributions before us and knowing that a person's party identification is very often a good prediction of the way he or she will vote, the electoral success of southern Republicans in congressional and senatorial contests and the persistent strength of GOP presidential candidates become much more understandable.

Table 1
Comparative Distributions of Party Identification

	S.C. (1985)	Ala. (1984)	Miss. (1984)	Tex. (1984)	Fla. (1985)	Nat'l. (1985)
Democrat	36%	39%	44%	38%	35%	38%
Republican	25	27	17	27	35	28
Independent	33	20	37	34	30	34
Other/Don't Know	6	13	2	1	—	—

We can refine this point further by keeping in mind two observations about politics in the South and one observation about how and when people become politically involved.

First, the South has figured importantly in the electoral calculations of every Republican presidential candidate since Barry Goldwater's successful foray south of the Mason-Dixon line in 1964. *Second,* the national Republican party organization has targeted the South, devoting much of its considerable financial resources and technical expertise over the last ten years to create and maintain viable state and local party organizations. Rather than emulate the Republican party's concentration on grassroots organization and political recruitment, the Democratic party occupied itself with the creation and amendment of party rules, during the same time period (Cotter, et al, 1984; Crotty, 1983; Polsby, 1983; Ranney, 1975).

Third, as a general rule, it is only after people have become eligible to vote that most begin to appreciate how useful partisanship can be in the evaluation of candidates, issues, and policies. It is at this time in a person's life when the political environment can have its most enduring impact. The nature of the times — its social coalitions and divisions, its economic strengths and weaknesses, its symbols and values — defines a combination of hopes, fears, and anxieties that may be "imprinted" on one's political consciousness, establishing, thereby, norms and expectations against which the future is evaluated. Thus periods of turmoil may create a political generation with non-partisan or antipartisan perspectives, just as periods of partisan dominance may encourage the adoption of and commitment to partisan values and identities among political initiates (Beck, 1976; Jennings and Niemi, 1974, 1981).

Putting these three observations together allows us to draw some conclusions about the relationship between age and partisanship among South Carolinians in the mid-1980s. This relationship appears in Table 2.

Table 2
Distribution of Party Identification by Age Cohort

	18-24	25-34	35-44	45-54	55-64	65+
Democrat	36%	36%	36%	40%	46%	37%
Republican	26	34	23	27	24	19
Independent	38	30	41	33	30	44
N = 508	106	120	88	70	67	57

It is clear from the table that the most solidly Democratic of the age groups into which the table is divided reached their twenties between 1942 and 1961. We might think of this period as the last retrenchment of the South. During the early 1930s, when elements of the oldest group came of age politically, the social and economic dislocations of the Great Depression had their greatest political impact. A political era dominated by Republicans at the national level. The South was a full and active partner in the New Deal Democratic coalition that emerged. But, after the 1938 congressional elections and Roosevelt's decision to run for a third term in 1940, the South began to pull away from the national Democratic party, to reassert its regional partisan identity. Only World War II kept the South from bolting (Ladd and Hadley, 1978; Sundquist, 1973).

After the war, the differences within the national democratic party between the dominant northern bloc and the minority southern bloc became increasingly manifest. Strain gave way to rupture with the Dixiecrat revolt of 1948. The revolt was symptomatic of the depth of southern racism and of the commitment of southern Democrats to a states' rights position that would preserve white dominance politically and economically.

The 1950s saw federal challenges to this position under a Republican presidency. Integration of the military, especially significant due to the number of bases located in the South, proceeded apace. That was followed by the Supreme Court's decree that *Plessey v. Ferguson's* formulation of separate but equal was inherently flawed. The Republican Chief Justice Earl Warren, speaking for the Court in *Brown v. Board of Education,* announced that the Constitution demanded that public schools be integrated with all deliberate speed. The NAACP's victory in *Brown* spurred action throughout the South; it breathed new life into the fledgling Civil Rights Movement. And when challenge came, as in the case of Orville Faubus' unwillingness to enforce integration in Little Rock, Republican President Eisenhower sent in federal troops. Moreover, under that same Republican administration, the first major Civil Rights legislation was passed in 1957.

Throughout the twenty-year period, then, the South appeared isolated from the rest of the nation. Its institutions were besieged; its traditions were reviled; its streets, parks, restaurants, hotels, and buses were becoming the battlefields of social protest. Unrepentent, unreconstructed, unflagging — the southern wing of the Democratic party symbolized the garrison South. This was the atmosphere in which the two age cohorts of South Carolinians with the strongest, most persistent ties to the Democratic party received their political imprinting.

The next younger age group reached political maturity during the most volatile decade in recent memory. The vista of John Kennedy's New Frontier dazzled us. But more, we thought that anything was possible, even placing a man on the moon, and that excited us. We believed. Dreams of equality catalyzed ethnic and racial minorities and polarized the majority. The federal government responded with the *Civil Rights Act of 1964* and the *Voting Rights Act of 1965*. We acted. In the abundance of our economic prosperity, we conceived a society where the quality of life was as important as the quantity of life's possessions, where we shared opportunity and outcome: Lyndon Johnson called it the "Great Society." We agreed.

But John Kennedy was assassinated, as were Martin Luther King and Robert Kennedy. Lyndon Johnson's crippled presidency did not survive for a second election. Hatred replaced hope for many, and cities burned. Those who could not cope with or stand fast against the hedonism of the Woodstock generation dropped out. And then there was Vietnam. As if in a Greek tragedy, our dreams revealed themselves as so much hubris, and we suffered accordingly.

The partisan tie was a close one. Kennedy and Johnson were Democrats who epitomized the liberal mentality of the national party. They were very different from state and local Democrats of the South who wore their conservative credentials proudly. Southern Democrats used their congressional seniority and wily grasp of parliamentary procedure to delay and deflect change. But the national tide overwhelmed them. Some, like the leader of the Dixiecrat revolt, Sen. Strom Thurmond, sought refuge in the Republican party. Others followed Gov. George Wallace in a third party challenge. The result was confusion. National Republicans, like Goldwater, echoed traditional southern virtues; national Democrats did not. National Republicans, like Nixon, paid assiduous attention to southern prerogatives; national Democrats did not. But state and local Democrats remained largely the same. In retrospect, the response to this confusion was predictable: next to the oldest cohort, the age cohort reaching political maturity between 1962 and 1971 contains the fewest partisans.

The cohort reaching political maturity during the 1970s contains the most Republicans identifiers. In percentage terms, the number of Republicans is insignificantly different from the number of Democrats. Recall that this cohort's first presidential choices involved the regional anathema, George McGovern, representing the liberal wing of the national Democratic party, and the sitting Republican President who was attempting to bring an "honorable peace" to Vietnam, to select Supreme Court nominees who were strict constructionists from the South, and to slow down the engine of social change that had roared through the nation, forcing aside traditional commitments to family, neighborhood, church, and school so revered in the South. Recall, at the same time, that it was this Republican president who was driven from office for offenses for which he has never recanted, loudly proclaiming his innocence and indicting his ideological enemies for magnifying grotesquely trivial acts of stupidity by subordinates, whom he loyally tried to protect, into a legal and political scandal. Recall too that this was the cohort whose first political experiences included the intensive Republican efforts at state and local mobilization which resulted in Republican footholds in Congress and in state legislatures and in a few governors' mansions. Recall as well that this cohort numbered among its earliest political memories the rebuke of a Southern democratic president by a northern liberal fellow Democrat who, while failing to win the nomination, fatally damaged Jimmy Carter's chances of defeating the Republican Ronald Reagan in 1980. Recall finally the bedrock principles of family self-reliance and local control; small, honest, waste-free government; economic expansionism; military prepared-ness; militant anti-communism; and God-fearing propriety in social mores on which Ronald Reagan stood and the Republican party platform rested in 1980. These were principles that seemed destined to unite the South and the West under the Republican banner and to banish liberal Democrats to the Northeast. Ronald Reagan's landslides did precisely that.

Why then is the youngest cohort, the one maturing now under the national aegis of the Republican party and witnessing the slow but certain growth of the state Republican party, so hesitant in proclaiming its Republican identity? The answer is related to the very age of the people in question. People under 25 are occupied with a number of activities which compete with politics for their attention: completing an education, serving a stint in the military, beginning a career, searching for a spouse, and starting a family. The uncertainties implied in each of these activities are made even more complex by the fact that these young people are often moving from place-to-place at the same time. Thus not only are their personal lives in a state of flux, but even their geographic location changes rapidly because of educational, military, or job requirements. The ties that bind one to a community physically and socially and that encourage one to take a serious interest in the outcomes of community politics take time to develop, time that is otherwise occupied among the young. Additionally, habits of political thought and behavior have not developed fully in the youngest cohort (Franklin, 1983; Franklin and Jackson, 1983). It would be fair to anticipate, however, that as members of the youngest age group settle down physically and socially and connect more securely with the communities in which they live — if only because their children are in school or their jobs place a premium on civic involvement — we should see an increase in political behavior and party identification that reflects the growing parity between the parties that we observe in the state's political environment. In short, the current political context bodes well for the future growth of the Republican party in South Carolina.

It should be clear by now that demographic characteristics play an important role in understanding the distribution of partisan attitudes. What is less clear, but of equal practical importance, is the composition effect of groups within parties. Thus it is important to know more than the age-partisan linkage. We must investigate the relationships of sex, race, education, and income-level to partisanship as well.

Table 3 shows that there are significant gender differences in the partisan distribution. Principally, men are much more likely to eschew partisan attachments and identify themselves as Independents than are women. Women, at the same time are more likely to call themselves both Democrats and Republicans than are men.

Table 3
Distribution of Party Identification
by Sex

	Male	Female
Democrat	35%	42%
Republican	24	29
Independent	42	29
N = 512	246%	266

Table 4 reveals an even starker contrast by race. Blacks are more than twice as likely as whites to call themselves Democrats, while whites are, in turn, nearly seven times more likely to identify with Republicans than are blacks. Democratic identification is the most frequent reponse for blacks. For whites, as for males, the most frequent is Independent identification.

Table 4
Distribution of Party Identification
by Race

	Black	White
Democrat	71%	29%
Republican	5	33
Independent	24	39
N = 510	120	390

Tables 5 and 6 illustrate South Carolina's participation in an old, national phenomenon: those occupying higher socio-economic status tend to affiliate with the Republican party. For both education and income, the higher the level the fewer the Democrats and the greater the number of Republicans; Independents show no consistent trend.

Table 5
Distribution of Party Identification by Education

	0 – 11 Grade	High School Grad.	Some College	College Grad.
Democrat	46%	42%	31%	30%
Republican	17	24	29	39
Independent	38	34	39	31
N = 511	120	176	99	116

Table 6
Distribution of Party Identification by Income

	0 – 13,000	13 – 19,000	19 – 25,000	25,000 +
Democrat	48%	53%	39%	27%
Republican	19	18	24	37
Independent	32	29	37	36
N = 486	108	93	95	100

These sociological distinctions contain important political lessons for each party. Thanks to the *Voting Rights Act of 1965* and its subsequent amendments, blacks register to vote at a rate comparable to whites in South Carolina. Combining black partisan loyalty, black registration rates, and the black proportion of the population produces a net contribution of blacks to registered South Carolina Democrats that approaches one-half. To be precise, in 1986, 48.6 percent of registered Democrats were black and 51.4 percent were white. By contrast, blacks constituted only 8.1 percent of Republicans, versus 91.9 percent for whites. It is clear that, for Democrats to be successful, they have to forge an enduring coalition of interests and respect between blacks and whites. Racial polarization spells defeat for Democrats.

The income and education data also contain ominous warnings for Democrats. The population of South Carolina is becoming better educated. With the passage of the Educational Improvement Act and the infusion of tax revenues into the public schools, the quality of education in the state will improve. We can anticipate more students appreciating the importance of post-secondary education in the future, as they seek to obtain the foundation for professional and business careers. The positive correlation between educational status and financial attainment on the one hand and Republican party identification on the other suggests that this trend will produce an increasing proportion of Republican identifiers and a decreasing proportion of Democratic identifiers in South Carolina. Moreover, since those with higher socio-economic and educational status tend to register and to vote in greater proportion than those with lower status, the electoral clout of the new wave of Republicans will have an especially potent effect.

These conclusions are simple extrapolations from the experiences of the rest of the nation over the last forty years. They are not immutable laws. Moreover, the results they predict must be qualified by attention to the impact of specific issues raised by party candidates during political campaigns. Important issues that touch the lives of citizens directly can have a profound effect on whether they participate and whom they support. These issues cannot be ignored, especially since elections — even those which set the political agenda for long periods of time — are often decided by small vote margins. A few percentage points either way can make a huge difference in policy now and, through the incumbency effect, policy in the future. It is important, therefore, to go beyond partisanship to examine the distribution of attitudes on issues.

Issues and Voters in South Carolina Politics

Several issues meet our criteria of political relevance by being important in some objective way and by touching the lives of many South Carolinians directly. Let us discuss each in turn.

Education. The largest single item in most state budgets is education. South Carolina is no exception. That alone is reason enough for close, annual inspection of public education's achievements and expenditures. However, beyond the normal disputes over the programmatic achievements and bureaucratic efficiency of big ticket agencies that engage legislators and editorial writers, South Carolinians have an especially good reason for paying attention to educational matters in the mid-80s: the *Educational Improvement Act* (EIA).

Passed in 1984, the EIA provided for a substantial increase in funding for public elementary and secondary education. More than $200 million was earmarked annually from a 25 percent increase in the state sales tax. The EIA generated widespread support for some obvious reasons. Parents saw that their children needed a better educational foundation in primary, middle, and high school, if they were to pursue post-secondary education leading to professional careers. Economic and political leaders saw that corporations contemplating a move to the sunbelt demanded a stable pool of technologically sophisticated workers from which to hire. Hi-tech service industries cannot function properly with a marginally educated workforce. Moreover, there is no reason for them to try in this highly competitive environment. They can locate elsewhere, in places that feature more far-sighted and committed governments.

To service these ends, the EIA provided funds to upgrade buildings, enhance teaching materials and equipment, and attract and retain qualified teachers and administrators. To insure the effective use of these funds, the EIA mandated state-wide pupil testing at regular grade intervals, culminating in an exit examination to achieve a high school diploma. Thus, opinions about education are of singular importance in the mid-1980s to evaluate the mood and the future course of South Carolina's progress.

Table 7 indicates that the citizens of South Carolina still target teacher inadequacies, in number and quality, as important problems. More than half identify a teacher shortage in the state, and less than half are willing to claim South Carolina teachers among the nation's best. Blacks are more likely than whites to cite the shortage of teachers as a problem. Yet blacks along with the less educated and the elderly are more sanguine, in general, about the quality of the state's teachers.

Optimism about the future is widely shared. Table 7 reveals confidence among South Carolinians that EIA expenditures have made a difference. And, more importantly, overwhelming numbers believe that the improvement will continue. These sentiments are most pronounced among women and minorities, but not confined to them. Clearly, in the minds of the state's parents and taxpayers, employers and employees, the crucial battle has been joined. Just as clearly, residents expect the outcome to pay rich dividends.

Table 7
Attitudes toward Public Education
in South Carolina

	Problem: Teacher Shortage	Teachers Among Best in Nation	More $ Has Improved Ed. Quality	More $ Will Improve Ed. Quality
Strongly Agree	35.4%	21.6%	26.0%	42.6%
Agree	21.2	20.7	30.1	32.3
Disagree	14.9	18.5	8.7	6.1
Strongly Disagree	14.8	25.3	16.6	9.8
Don't Know	13.7	14.0	18.6	9.2
N =	542	542	542	542

Crime and Punishment. Whether because of the much publicized war on drugs or because of actual increases in crime rates documented in earlier chapters, nearly half of all South Carolinians feel that the amount of crime is rising. This fear is most likely to be expressed by women. A slightly larger number of respondents feel that crime rates are about the same as the previous year. But, together, these categories account for more than 91 percent of respondents, as Table 8 indicates.

Crimes demand punishment, and punishment often means incarceration. With one of the highest per capita prison populations, South Carolina's jails are overcrowded. There are two logical solutions to this problem that would prevent suits claiming cruel and unusual punishment: build more prisons or release prisoners early. Of the two, the former is the public's overwhelming favorite, as we note in Table 8. We see too that a majority of this fiscally conservative state agrees with the proposition that more prisons should be built even if that means spending more money on the Corrections Department. The spending alternative receives greatest support at the extremes of the income and educational distributions. Those at the bottom are allied with those at the top of both the income and educational distributions in being more supportive of prison construction than those in the middle of each distribution, even in the face of a rising tax bill.

Table 8
Crime and Punishment in South Carolina

	Annual Crime Rate Is		Solve Prison Overcrowding By		Spend More, Build
Increasing	45.0%	Building Prisons	60.7%	Strongly Agree	43.2%
Steady	46.3	Release Prisoners	26.4	Agree	32.7
				Disagree	7.6
Decreasing	6.5	Neither	8.3	Strongly Disagree	11.8
Don't Know	2.2	Don't Know	4.6	Don't Know	4.8
N =	542		542		542

Table 9
Attitudes toward Capital Punishment

	Disposition Toward Death Penalty
Strongly Favor	52.7%
Favor	15.5
Opposed	5.5
Strongly Opposed	15.7
Don't Know	10.6
N =	509

	Type of Verdict Required		Governor's Power of Commutation
Unanimous	60.1%	Retain	53.2%
Two-thirds	31.6	Abolish	41.7
Don't Know	8.3	Don't Know	5.1
N =	509	N =	509

152

Capital punishment is a separate issue from prison construction. Nevertheless similarly large majorities of South Carolinians (more than two-thirds) favor imposition of the death penalty as favor prison construction. Males, whites, and those with higher levels of income and education are most favorably disposed toward capital punishment. More than half of the state's respondents (58.6 percent) are also unwilling to take the age of those convicted into consideration when determining whether the death penalty should be invoked. Blacks are the only major socio-economic or demographic group dissenting from this conclusion collectively. Nevertheless, these attitudes toward capital punishment do not appear to be indiscriminant choices born of unfocused anger over the rising prevalence of crime, because, for example, approximately 60 percent of respondents would require unanimous jury decisions, and more than half would retain the governor's commutation powers. Unanimity and commutation are especially important considerations among the state's women. These data are found in Table 9.

Economic, Social Welfare, and Moral Issues. More than 80 percent of South Carolina's registered voters believe the national debt is a problem. Only our younger citizens seem relatively unmindful of the economic juggernaut that the debt presents. Just under three-quarters of those registered voters who recognize a problem feel that the appropriate solution is a reduction in spending not an increase in taxes. Predictably, support for a tax increase declines with income. Support for tax increases can be found disproportionately among blacks and those with the lowest levels of education; nevertheless, the most frequent response for blacks and whites is a reduction in spending. But, the relationships between income and education on the one hand and spending reductions on the other are curvilinear: the lowest and the high highest levels of education and income are united against the middle levels in opposition to spending cuts as the solution. Thus the policy choice — spending or taxes — elicits support from very different clusters of people. They are not mirror images of the same problem in the minds of the voting constituency.

To speak of tax cuts or spending reductions is to manipulate symbols and values (Edelman, 1964; Elder and Cobb, 1983). That is an appropriate purpose of political debate. But the results of political debate often involve concrete decisions. Attitudes about abstractions may not be generalizable to specific cases.[2] As seen above, the priority of prison construction overrode the spending proscription.

Table 10
Attitudes Toward the National Debt

	Debt is National Problem		To Handle Debt
Yes	80.2%	Increase Taxes	10.9%
No	12.8	Cut Spending	73.9
		Both	10.9
Don't Know	6.7	Don't Know	4.3
N =	542	N =	422

Social service provision overrides spending proscriptions in the area of indigent medical care as well. The data in Table 11 provide a clear illustration of the service-spending trade-off. Nearly nine out of ten South Carolinians believe that medical care should be provided regardless of the patient's ability to pay. Women and minorities seem especially concerned that this outcome prevail, while only those with the highest incomes demure. In cases where the patient is unable to pay, the costs, respondents feel, should not be added to the bills of paying patients. Rather, government should pick up the tab. And, respondents feel this strongly enough to advocate higher taxes to pay for the additional services, a feeling held especially strongly in the black community, but less positively among the elderly. Thus there are definable limits to fiscal conservatism.

Another type of trade-off with both moral and financial implications involves Sunday blue-laws. Traditionally, severe restrictions were imposed on Sunday commerce in South Carolina to encourage observance of the Christian sabbath in worship and rest. As social mores changed, however, commitment to blue-law observance waned. No doubt that decline in blue-law popularity was related to the number of families where both spouses worked and for whom evenings and weekends represented the only convenient times for shopping. The rise in tourism, especially along the Grand Strand, provided another spur to change. Tourism, after all, is a seven-day per week service industry. Limiting Sunday sales could be costly in state sales, accommodations and nuisance tax revenues, as well as a depressing force on local economies in general. In May, 1985, the Sunday blue-laws were substantially

Table 11
Attitudes Toward Indigent Medical Care

Care Provided Regardless of Ability to Pay			
Strongly Agree	65.6%		
Agree	21.8		
Disagree	3.9		
Strongly Disagree	5.3		
Don't Know	3.3		
N =	524		

	Who Should Pay?		Taxes Increased To Pay
Government Subsidy	73.1%	Yes	74.9%
Raise Charges to Paying Patients	8.6	No	18.1
Don't Know	18.3	Don't Know	7.1
N =	524		524

changed to allow most forms of commerce after 1:00 PM. Tables 12 and 13 chart the opinions of South Carolinians before and after the change.

Before the legal change, three-quarters of respondents favored change, but most did not favor complete elimination of the blue-laws. As expected, approximately two-thirds felt they would take advantage of the extended shopping hours themselves. Only 28 percent felt that church attendance might be adversely affected by changes. Men, the young, and the better educated supported change — indeed outright elimination — most strongly. They were also among those who felt sure that they would take advantage of extended shopping hours. The better educated were joined by the better off in dismissing the impact of blue-law curtailment on church attendance.

Several months after the changes went into effect, South Carolinians were again asked their opinions. In the interval, slightly less than half had availed themselves of the new shopping opportunities, and only 21 percent felt that church attendance had been affected. Sunday shopping was positively correlated with income and education, as anticipated, and only the oldest refrained, significantly, from the new privileges. Men, despite adamant support for blue-law curtailment, shopped no more often than women. Thus the relaxation of shopping restrictions did not destroy the Sunday sabbath tradition, as many had feared.

Table 12
Attitudes Toward Sunday Blue-Laws
Before Legislative Change

	Position on Sunday Shopping
Eliminate Blue Laws	22.4%
Modify: Shop After 1:00 PM	53.2
Retain Blue Laws Unchanged	22.0
Don't Know	2.4
N =	509

Likelihood of Respondent Sunday Shopping		Blue Law Change Means Declining Church Attendance	
Very Likely	41.5%	Strongly Agree	17.1%
Somewhat Likely	25.9	Agree	10.8
Somewhat Unlikely	7.7	Disagree	28.3
Very Unlikely	22.4	Strongly Disagree	40.1
Don't Know	2.6	Don't Know	3.7
N =	509	N =	509

Religion plays an important role in the lives of South Carolinians. When asked, nearly 65 percent admit to attending church "often" and another 20 percent claim to attend "sometimes." Eighty-eight percent proclaim no doubts about God's existence. These are joined by another 4.5 percent who have some doubts yet believe in God and 3.5 percent more who express faith in the existence of a higher power but choose not to call that power "God."

Table 13
Attitudes Toward Sunday Blue-Laws
After Legislative Changes

	Respondent Shopped on Sunday		Church Attendance Declined
Yes	47.2%	Strongly Agree	11.4%
No	52.8	Agree	10.1
		Disagree	29.2
		Strongly Disagree	36.5
Don't Know	0.0	Don't Know	12.7
N =	542	N =	542

Against this background, we might anticipate certain reactions to important national issues, like abortion and school prayer, on the one hand and to important state issues, like legalized gambling, on the other. Specifically, we might hypothesize opposition to abortion and gambling and support for prayer in the public schools. Our opinion data allow for a test of these hypotheses.

More than half of South Carolinians favor banning abortions except in cases of rape or incest or in order to save the mother's life. This sentiment is negatively related to both income and education. Similarly, more than two-thirds of our respondents strongly favor prayer in the public schools, while another 16 percent are moderately in favor. The only dissent from this position is among some whites who are nearly three times more likely than members of minorities to object to school prayer. As Tables 14 and 15

Table 14
Attitudes Toward A Limited Ban On Abortions

Favor	56.6%
Oppose	36.0
Don't Know	7.4
N =	542

illustrate, substantial majorities among South Carolina's residents feel that the U.S. Supreme Court has erred in its interpretation of the Constitution or is out of step with the sovereign populace, at a minimum.

Table 15
Attitudes Toward School Prayer

Strongly Support	68.4%
Support	15.9
Oppose	4.9
Strongly	7.9
Don't Know	2.9
N =	509

The data in Table 16 strongly suggest that gambling falls into a different category than abortion and school prayer. Nearly two-thirds of South Carolina's registered voters approve of the idea of a lottery to pay for state programs. Men are more approving than women who are joined in their opposition by the old. Support for a lottery jumps to over 70 percent when the benefiting program is identified as public education. The young are the most supportive and the old are the least supportive of this initiative; Blacks are more likely to agree with the idea than whites; and the least and the most educated are less supportive than high school graduates and those with some college in their background.

Even when the state is not the revenue recipient, support can be generated for wagering. More than 60 percent of registered voters expressed approval of Bingo, although it must be acknowledged that this game is so often associated with churches and voluntary organizations that it may be considered a benign form of amusement in the minds of many respondents. Blacks are more likely to approve of Bingo than are whites, and the elderly are more likely to cling to older prohibitions against wagering than are the young.

Clearly, however, off-track betting, even in the context of a horseracing culture, as exists in South Carolina, is a different matter. And less than half of registered voters could support such a proposition. Only women show a statistically more negative response than the population as a whole, however.

Table 16
Attitudes Toward Forms of Gambling

	Lottery to Help Finance State Programs		Lottery to Help Finance Education
Strongly Agree	43.9%	Strongly Agree	56.1%
Agree	21.9	Agree	16.2
Disagree	7.6	Disagree	4.6
Strongly Disagree	19.8	Strongly Disagree	18.3
Don't Know	6.7	Don't Know	4.8
N =	524	N =	524

	Continue Bingo Games For Cash		State Run Betting On Horse Races
Strongly Agree	31.9%	Strongly Agree	25.4%
Agree	28.6	Agree	21.9
Disagree	10.1	Disagree	12.4
Strongly Disagree	22.7	Strongly Disagree	31.1
Don't Know	6.5	Don't Know	9.2
N =	524	N =	524

Half of our purpose has been served by this examination of public opinion toward specific issues. We have observed some variation in the attitudes of South Carolinians on a wide variety of national and state-based issues. Departures from full consensus rested on demonstrable, if not consistent, group differences. The other half of our purpose in exploring issues will be served if we can establish a partisan basis to some of these issue or issue-group divisions. Because one of the primary roles of political parties is to translate the socio-economic power of groups in society into political power by forging winning coalitions, these divisions should produce meaningful partisan distinctions on the issues which have been discussed in this section.

Issue Partisanship. Among the educational issues, only disputes over teacher quality separate partisans and independents. Table 17 shows us that Republicans are much less satisfied with the quality of public school teachers than are Democrats. Independents fall between. This ordering makes some political sense, if we recall that those most satisfied were also those most likely to belong to the Democratic coalition, blacks and the less educated, and that educational issues concerned women and blacks generally more than men and whites.

Table 17
Agreement that S.C. Teachers Are Among Nation's Best
within Categories of Party Identification

	Democrat	Republican	Independent
Strongly Agree	31.0%	17.5%	25.0%
Agree	29.8	15.8	24.4
Disagree	17.9	27.2	19.4
Strongly Disagree	21.4	39.5	31.3
N =	168	114	160

Race, gender, and education play important roles in explaining the responses of South Carolinians to crime and punishment issues. Party identification does not play an equivalent role, with the exception of its impact on attitudes toward the death penalty. On capital punishment, the party differences are very plain, Table 18 notes. Democrats stand alone against an alliance of Republicans and Independents in the weakness of their endorsement of the death penalty and on the question of disregarding the convict's age at the time of the capital crime's commission. The contribution of race especially must be underscored in these partisan comparisons.

Party identification appears related to social issues through their economic dimension. Hence we should recall the racial and socio-economic differences between Democrats, Independents and Republicans. Racial minorities and those coming from the lower end of the socio-economic status ladder are more likely to identify themselves as Democrats, not as Republicans or Independents.

Table 18
Attitudes toward Capital Punishment
within Categories of Party Identification

Panel A: Favor or Oppose the Death Penalty

	Democrat	Republican	Independent
Strongly Favor	46.4%	64.6%	67.9%
Favor	16.4	22.9	11.9
Oppose	8.2	3.1	4.6
Strongly Oppose	29.1	9.4	15.6
N =	110	96	109

Panel B: Age and the Death Penalty

	Democrat	Republican	Independent
Minimum Age	36.0%	27.8%	24.6%
No Minimum Age	52.3	71.4	70.8
Don't Know	11.6	.8	4.7
N =	172	126	171

No party-based differences can be uncovered concerning the importance of the national debt, but Table 19 reveals that, although cutting spending is the most frequent response for all categories of identification, Republicans and Independents are much more likely to favor that alternative, than Democrats who are, in turn, comparatively more likely to support the taxing alternative.

This economic alliance between Republicans and Independents appears on issues of indigent medical care as well. There is an evident consensus that those who cannot afford hospital care should receive it. Even so, the strength of one's commitment to this humanitarian value is related to partisan identification. Table 20 indicates that approximately three-quarters of South Carolina's Democrats strongly agree with the proposition. The Democrats' commitment is emphasized further when the method of payment question arises. Both of these positions reflect the particular importance of these issues to minority groups in the population, a fact to which we alluded above.

Table 19
Methods of Reducing the National Debt
and Party Identification

	Democrat	Republican	Independent
Raise Fed. Taxes	19.5%	6.4%	8.4%
Cut Spending	71.4	80.9	78.6
Some of Both	9.0	12.7	13.0
N =	133	110	154

Table 20
Indigent Medical Care and Party Identification

Panel A: Hospital Care Provided Regardless of Ability to Pay

	Democrat	Republican	Independent
Strongly Agree	77.2%	54.7%	57.3%
Agree	12.2	35.8	31.8
Disagree	2.4	3.2	4.5
Strongly Disagree	8.1	6.3	6.4
N =	123	95	110

Panel B: Raise Taxes to Pay for Indigent Medical Care

	Democrat	Republican	Independent
Yes	87.0%	77.8%	69.7%
No	13.0	22.2	30.3
N =	115	90	109

Finally, opposition to maintenance of the Sunday blue-laws was strongest among those most likely to identify as Republicans or Independents: the young, the better educated, and the financially better off. If parties do "translate" group interests into political power then clear partisan differences should occur. In Table 21, we note some of the expected differences. While a majority of Democrats favor some modification, among the remainder a two-to-one plurality favors retention. Among Republicans, there appears more polarization. Less than a majority favor modification and the remainder are fairly closely split between the extremes of retention and elimination. Thus the partisan "translation" is not always direct or complete.

Table 21
Party Identification and Attitudes toward Sunday Blue Laws

	Democrat	Republican	Independent
Eliminate	15.1%	23.2%	27.4%
Modify	53.2	47.5	57.5
Retain	31.7	29.3	15.0
N =	126	99	113

It is worth emphasizing this point that parties and issues are related complexly. Let us recall what issues party identification did not organize neatly: abortion, school prayer, lotteries, wagering, crime rates, incarceration, general responses to problems of education, etc. That is a formidable list that challenges any simple conclusions about the role of parties. What, then, is the bottom line?

Conclusion

One important variable that helps explain the distribution of attitudes among South Carolinians is one that we have not addressed directly, ideology. The data available give us no precise distributional characteristics. Nevertheless, we can proceed on the assumption that most respondents would identify themselves as conservatives, regardless of their party identification.

That conservatism pervades both political parties, especially at the state level, is important to keep in mind when we encounter what appears to be a consensual approach to problems that transcend group or party affiliations. The consensus is neither fragile nor artificial. It is bred in a culture which shares certain fundamental values that find political expression in both the issues selected as important and the solutions offered for the problems those issues pose. Political parties cannot long survive without recognizing regional culture as a significant feature of any state's political character.

Conservatism has many features, however. To some it means states' rights, especially in matters of social choice. To others it means a market approach to economic allocations that precludes a strong governmental presence. To still others it entails a foreign and military posture that brooks no compromise with adversaries. To these characteristics, that have no necessary relationship with one another, we must add a dimension of conservatism that reflects positive and negative feelings toward particular groups. Thus to identify something as conservative is to evoke a set of symbols in the minds of South Carolinians to which they are favorably disposed for any one of a number of very different reasons.

It is conceivable that when the conservative symbol is invoked to justify a policy or a candidacy that people react as much to the symbol as to the substance of the policy or the candidacy. Use of conservatism in this way may obscure substantive disagreements in the formation of political coalitions. Thus the issue reponses which we have uncovered and their linkage to political parties depend, to some degree, on their symbolic presentation or articulation by parties through elected and appointed leaders, as further refracted by the media.

Another complication upsetting the direct linkage of issues to parties or vice versa is the important distinction between global and dual identifiers (Maggiotto, 1986; Maggiotto and Wekkin, 1987). This distinction suggests that people may identify with different political parties at different levels of government, that federalism, in short may play an important role in organizing party identification among South Carolinians. The issues with which this paper deals combine elements associated with national parties and those more closely associated with state-based parties or decisions. If one's party identification reflects a focus on national issues and their ramifications, then one set of attitudinal outcomes would be predicted. Quite another set of outcomes might be predicted if the focus were on the state. The easiest way of seeing how this complication operates is to consider the number of Democratic identifiers who vote regularly for national Republicans and state and local Democrats. At bottom, the combination of outcomes militates against consistency within any partisan grouping.

These theoretical and technical considerations should not obscure totally what this chapter has revealed, however. A range of opinion on a series of important domestic issues exists that contains somewhat more consensus than disagreement. The roots of this consensus may feed on the common soil of conservatism as both ideology and symbol. An unmistakable trend toward the Republican party also emerges from the data. Whether one examines cohort development in light of national tides or socio-economic and demographic changes, the conclusion remains: a realignment of substantial proportions is underway. This conclusion is bolstered by the frequent issue isolation of Democrats from Republicans and, significantly, Independents alike. One should not conclude from this observation that the Democratic party is doomed. It would be more appropriate to suggest that these findings support the notion that effective two party competition is emerging as a regular state of affairs in South Carolina.

South Carolina in the mid-1980s stands at a political crossroads. Long pictured as a member of an outcast minority of states, it may now be in the process of shedding that identity for one more recognizably mainstream. The state's new identity may simply signal that the mainstream itself has shifted course. If so, then those who have defended their fidelity to traditional values and purposes will enjoy final vindication.

Notes

[1] The data in Table 1 come from a variety of sources. The national and Florida figures are from Parker (1985). The 1985 figures for South Carolina are taken from the October, 1985 poll described below. All other figures in the Table are derived from state summaries compiled by the National Network of State Polls.

Three polls of South Carolinians form the basis for the empirical results that this paper reports. These polls were conducted using random digit dialing and targeting a non-institutionalized population of eligible voters. The polls were conducted in January and October, 1985 and again in January, 1986. The January, 1986 poll reports results for registered voters only.

[2] The literature on the disjunction between agreement with abstract principles and their concrete application is very large and generally linked to political tolerance, equality, and civil liberties in American studies. See, for example: Prothro and Grigg (1960); Sniderman (1975); Sniderman and Hagen (1985); Samuel A. Stouffer (1955); and Sullivan et al. (1982).

References

Beck, P. A. (1976). "A Socialization Theory of Partisan Realignment," pp. 396- 411 in R. G. Niemi and H. F. Weisberg (eds.) *Controversies in American Voting Behavior*. San Francisco: Freeman.

Campbell, A., P. E. Converse, W. E. Miller, and D. E. Stokes (1960). *The American Voter*. New York: Wiley.

Cotter, C. P., J. L. Gibson, J. F. Bibby, and R. J. Huckshorn (1984). *Party Organizations in American Politics*. New York: Praeger.

Crotty, W. (1983). *Party Reform*. New York: Longman.

Franklin, C. H. (1983). "Issue Preferences, Socialization, and the Evolution of Party Identification." *American Journal of Political Science* 28 (August): 459-478.

Edelman, M. (1964). *The Symbolic Uses of Politics*. Urban, Ill.: University of Illinois Press.

Franklin, C. H. and J. E. Jackson (1983). "The Dynamics of Party Identification." *American Political Science Review* 77 (December): 957- 973.

Jennings, M. K. and R. G. Niemi (1974). *The Political Character of Adolescence: The Influence of Family and Schools*. Princeton: Princeton University Press.

(1981). *Generations and Politics. A Panel Study of Young Adults and Their Parents.* Princeton: Princeton University Press.

Ladd, E.C. and C. D. Hadley (1978). *Transformations of the American Party System: Political Coalitions from the New Deal to the 1970s.* New York: Norton.

Luttbeg, N. R. ed. (1981). *Public Opinion and Public Policy: Models of Political Linkage.* Itasca, Ill.: F. E. Peacock.

Maggiotto, M. A. (1986). "Party Identification in the Federal System." Paper presented at the annual meeting of the American Political Science Association, Washington, D.C., August.

Maggiotto, M. A. and G. D. Wekkin (1987). "Global Concepts and Segmented Partisans: Rejoining Theory and Data." Paper presented at the annual meeting of the Southwestern Political Science Association, Dallas, Texas, March.

Nie, N. H., S. Verba, and J. R. Petrocik (1979). *The Changing American Voter.* Cambridge: Harvard University Press.

Parker, S. L. (1985). "Are Party Loyalties Shifting in Florida?" *Florida Public Opinion* 1 (Winter): 16-20.

Polsby, N. W. (1983). *The Consequences of Party Reform.* New York: Oxford.

Prothro, J. W. and C. W. Grigg (1960). "Fundamental Principles of Democracy: Bases of Agreement and Disagreement." *Journal of Politics* 22 (May): 276- 294.

Ranney, A. (1975). *Curing the Mischief of Faction: Party Reform in America.* Berkeley: University of California Press.

Sniderman, P. M. (1975). *Personality and Democratic Politics.* Berkeley: University of California Press.

Sniderman, P. M. and M. G. Hagen (1985). *Race and Inequality: A Study in American Values.* Chatham, N.J.: Chatham House.

Stouffer, S. A. (1955). *Communism, Conformity, and Civil Liberties: A Cross Section of the Nation Speaks Its Mind.* Garden City, N. Y.: Doubleday.

Sundquist, James L. (1973). *Dynamics of the Party System: Alignment and Realignment of Political Parties in the United States.* Washington: Brookings.

10

The Evolving Executive in South Carolina

Cole Blease Graham, Jr.

Introduction

Strong executive institutions often use budgeting and financial management techniques in order to bargain executive preferences with the legislature and with agencies. Exploration of evolving executive influences on the traditional legislative dominance of budgeting and management of South Carolina government is the focus of this chapter. The chapter's central theme is that strong executive direction of state budgeting and state agencies has emerged through the development of a state board that is in the position to centralize state fiscal and operating policies.

The first section of the chapter gives a brief sketch of the historical circumstances and events that underlie institutions now responsible for South Carolina budgeting and agency management. Next follows an overview of the contemporary structure and operations of the state's central budgeting and management agency — the South Carolina State Budget and Control Board (SBCB). A concluding section focuses on the impact of more powerful, executive-type staff direction of traditional legislative efforts to control state agency budgets and operations.

Although SBCB does not fit the ideal model of a gubernatorially-dominated executive or of a governor and cabinet structure, the overall discussion demonstrates that South Carolina has an executive base to its budget decisions and, through centralized administrative services, to agency operations. The SBCB is a broad institutional context in which decisional preferences of the governor and fiscal executives are compared and weighed against the preferences of legislators and agency governing bodies. Coupled with today's budgeting practices and the wide-ranging responsibilities of the SBCB, South Carolina's hybrid "gubernatorial-executive-legislative" structure has resulted

---

Cole Blease Graham, Jr. is a faculty member in the Department of Government and International Studies at the University of South Carolina.

in a decline in the exclusive and longstanding legislative dominance of state agencies and their budgets.

Origins of South Carolina's Budget Board

The Need for a Budget System. South Carolina's use of a hybrid legislative-executive budget board builds on political antecedents that reach as far back as 1870 with the creation of a sinking fund commission to manage repayment of the state debt and interest (Rogers, 1987: 103). The Sinking Fund Commission was composed of executive and legislative branch members: the Governor, the Attorney General, the Comptroller General, the Chair of the Senate Finance Committee, and the Chair of the House Ways and Means Committee. Later, in 1883, the State Treasurer was added as a member. Government by small commissions or committees often reflects established tradition through dominance by a small and cohesive social elite. Through such a governing device, designated members are able to assemble to sort out preferences or problems. Many commissions have been created in South Carolina, often one per problem. As noted in Chart 1, the conflict that immediately led to the formal creation of a separate budget commission stemmed from concerns about administration of the property tax during the time of industrial change and development in the state surrounding World War I.

When the Comptroller General prepared the budget for 1919, he reported to the legislature that the various state institutions and departments requested appropriations that exceeded estimated revenues by over ten percent. Since the 1895 state constitution (Section 2, Article X) required that the property tax levy be sufficient to cover all of the regular state expenses plus any deficiency from the year before, that translated into a three-fourths mill increase (8.8 percent) in the existing eight and one-half mills property tax. The Comptroller General's report observed:

> The accumulation of apparent balances from year to year and their use in meeting the current expenses of the following year is due to our system of tax collections, the expenditures being made every year before the taxes levied therefor are collected . . . we are rapidly going into debt, decreasing the apparent reserve or accumulations, and increasing the amount necessary to be borrowed in order to meet the appropriations (*The State*, 1918a: 9).

The "borrowing" refers to tax anticipation notes by which the state borrowed the cash it needed to operate until all of the levied taxes could be collected.

In addition to expenditure control, there was also a problem with revenues. At this time, about 90 percent of state expenditures was financed by a tax on

Chart 1
Milestones in South Carolina Budget Organization

- Longstanding tradition of committee government in South Carolina — a reflection of a small, cohesive, permanent elite with no specific preferences dividing their perceptions of public order.

- 1916 — creation of a State Tax Commission to oversee state revenues.

- After World War I, emerging problems in coordinating state property tax revenue, state agency expenditures, and budget management.

- 1919 — creation of a State Budget Commission to coordinate spending proposals. The governor took the lead in consultation with two legislative committee chairs.

- 1920s — general move away from sole dependence on property tax as state revenue source.

- 1920-1950 — relatively smooth functioning of State Budget Commission. A big battle between the governor and the legislature over the state highway commission (1935-1937) raised questions about the exercise of the executive powers by the governor.

- 1950 — reorganization of State Budget Commission into a State Budget and Control Board. The new Board was composed of more members of the executive branch (3) than legislators (2). The Board also assumed wider responsibilities for some staff operations of state government.

- 1950-1978 — Board operated by State Auditor largely through informal arrangements and agreements with executives, legislators, and the Board's Finance Division.

- 1978 — Formal establishment by the Board of an Executive Director position to administer the various Board Divisions.

- 1986 — Internal reorganization to improve the span of executive control by the director through appointment of three deputy executive directors to manage specific clusters of Board functions.

property. The Comptroller General went on:

> It therefore seems that appropriations should not be increased more than absolutely necessary until the system for the assessment of property has been so reformed as to equalize the burden (*The State*, 1918a: 9).

The "burden equalization" problem referred to unequal assessment ratios used by counties across the state. The local tax assessor (the county auditor) was in a position to influence how much revenue the state could actually collect in each county. County auditors used a variety of methods to determine the tax base, possibly in response to the impact of the property tax on politically sensitive interests. Even so, some banks and cotton mills had begun to pay their property taxes under protest. The resulting insecurity shook the credibility of state revenue policies and demanded a more controlling influence at the state level.

One attempt to solve the revenue equalization problem was in the creation by the legislature in 1916 of a state tax commission. Soon, both the House and Senate had tried to abolish it with replacement agencies because of its "dictatorial" powers over local officials (*The State*, 1918b: 2). But, the governor's role was not clear in the legislative proposals and no changes were passed. The reform of the revenue system did not really begin until a "luxury tax" was placed on tobacco, cigars, cigarettes, and soft drinks in the late 1920s. The collection of these taxes was administered successfully by the state tax commission and the revenues from them began to replace the property tax as the main source of state revenue. The real focus of changes in the budget system was a more direct movement to enlarge executive control over state agency expenditures, rather than to reform revenues.

Controlling Expenditures and Corruption with Boards. Much attention was given by government officials in 1918 to the escalating requests for public school expenditures by the state superintendent of education. The costs of the office and the state share of local public schools amounted to almost $570,000 or 16.8 percent of agency requests. The other two large items in the state's budget were for the state hospital for the insane ($616,496 or 17.9 percent) and for Confederate survivor pensions ($300,000 or 8.7 percent).

Questions about the administration of some state agencies also emphasized the need for more centralized direction. A particular outrage in state agency conduct was focused on the state game warden. He overspent his travel account. If this was not bad enough, he also appeared to arrange his appointment by turning out his supporters at the society meeting that nominated him. In reaction, the legislature tried to make the office an elected position, but the governor vetoed the legislation. Much attention was also given in the legislative debates to removal of the game warden's office from politics altogether through creation of an independent board with staggered terms to make the appointment.

The board idea was broadly advanced by political leaders as a way to get control and direction over other, diverse state activities. Alleged corruption was not always the motivator for a proposed change to central board administration. A bill in 1919 sought to place all the state higher education institutions under a central board. It seemed a practical way to develop a great university like the Western states that typically used a single board. The bill's sponsor observed that state institutions like the University of South Carolina and the Citadel had been founded before the great, modern, central state university came into existence. Without a single, unifying board, South Carolina's numerous universities and colleges could not rank with the state universities of the West. The debate also mentioned that without private contributions they could not rank with Harvard and Princeton (*The State*, 1919a: 4).

The Adoption of Commissions, Including one for Budgeting. While a single higher education board was not adopted, the idea for commissions or boards as a political reform continued with executive support. The governor defended the state tax commission as a "businesslike" way to control the county auditors on revenue matters. He also advocated the proposal for the central state college board, a central board for the state's charitable and penal institutions, and, in a reaction to the death of five prisoners from influenza, a reform board to oversee the state's chain gang system. Also, the Farmers' Union called on the governor and the legislature to devise a board to govern the state agriculture department.

Still, there was no system for preparing a budget beyond the work done by the finance committees of the two legislative houses and the accounting made by the Comptroller General and the State Treasurer. Perhaps building on "the South Carolina tradition of conducting its public business in small groups rather than through powerful individuals or direct plebicite" (Underwood, 1986: 131), Advocates won legislative approval of a budgeting board — the state budget commission — in 1919. The new commission established consultation between the two branches as one basis on which a more formal, but combination legislative-executive budget system grew. Supporters hoped for more regularized attempts to prepare and review expenditure and revenue estimates and to establish a centralized system for state budget making. The commission was composed of the Governor, the Chair of the Senate Finance Committee, and the Chair of the House Ways and Means Committee. It was required to meet after November 1 and make a report to the session of the General Assembly in January of each year after hearing "all interested parties as to appropriations" (*The State*, 1919b: 5).

171

Advocates of the new budget commission argued that it would reduce the concentration of power in the legislators who made up the conference committee that negotiated the differences between House and Senate in the annual appropriations bill. In their opinion, the conference committee had become a "bottleneck" that made far-reaching decisions under the pressure of time late in the session with little public discussion. Under the commission approach, all of the General Assembly as well as the public would be aware of the original budget proposals and there would be a focused starting point for budget deliberations. A single report would, it was hoped, take the pressure for budget preparation off the House Ways and Means and Senate Finance committees and relieve them of "the tedious methods now in force and which were out of date" (*The State*, 1919b: 5). The 1920 budget was the first to be prepared under the governor's leadership by the new commission system.

Reorganizing the SBCB. Despite transfer of the duties of the State Bank Examiner and its authorization to appoint a State Auditor by a 1933 law, the State Budget Commission worked without significant structural changes through World War II. For the most part, the commission's recommendations may have been more suggestive than directing. The legislative budget logjam remained largely unbrokened and commission work "exercise[d] less influence than it deserve[d]" (Wallace, 1961: 683). The monumental battle in the mid-1930s between the governor, the legislature, and the Highway Commission over the control of that department (Huss, 1961: 64-72), raised new and divisive questions about possible gubernatorial excesses. It became clear that the two legislative finance committee chairs and a "cooperative" governor were to recommend general fund appropriations, but also that they were to steer clear of controversies such as the Highway Commission's recommendations for "earmarked" revenues. Provisos to the annual appropriations bill attest to the need for legislative acceptability of the specific recommendations in the process. Focus on the functions of the budget commission did not occur until assessment of state general fund activities by reorganization studies in the 1940s (See especially *Report, Preparedness for Peace Commission*, 1945: 5-77).

In a major reorganization in 1950, the state's budget commission was reorganized as an enlarged State Budget and Control Board (SBCB). Two new executive members, the state treasurer and the comptroller general, were added to the original three member commission. These two with the governor represented the executive branch and made the executives "dominant" over the two legislative members. The governor was designated by the new law as the chair of the revamped executive-legislative board. Ten smaller state agencies, including the state sinking fund commission — the debt management body originating in 1870 — as well as selected other financial and technical support service bodies, were abolished as separate entities and their responsibilities came under the board's supervision (South Carolina Budget and Control Board, 1984: 6). The highway department kept its structural and operating independence from this new state general fund budget agency.

Through 1978, the sections of the SBCB operated separately and were coordinated informally, but with some authority, by the State Auditor who also served as board secretary. The State Auditor had been selected by the state budget commission members since 1933. Among the SBCB sections were a general services division and a finance division. The finance division was formally headed by the State Auditor. The auditor was responsible for development of the annual state budget through the finance division. Under the auditor's direct supervision, the division also monitored and approved federal funds received by the various state agencies, reviewed construction projects, supervised the installation of data processing equipment, and audited the financial records of all state government agencies. The State Auditor today is once again literally an auditor and no longer has responsibility for the entire budget as the office did under the more informal division structure before 1978. In September 1978, an executive directorship was established as formal SBCB head.

Under the executive director, the divisions of today's SBCB engage in a variety of activities. As illustrated in Figure 1, the Board's individual units are grouped somewhat hierarchically under the supervision of three deputies who assist the executive director. These units manage the state's budgeting (expenditure analysis and estimation); local government grant liaison and rural development; the fire marshal's office; research and statistical services (including revenue estimation); personnel or human resource management — a compensation plan, a fringe benefits system, and other state agency personnel services; general services such as purchasing and insurance; the state's telephone service; and its motor vehicle management policies.

In addition to its major units and divisions, the state's retirement system is coordinated by the Board. The Board membership also makes up the State Education Assistance Authority which issues revenue bonds to finance loans to students pursuing a post-secondary school education at certified institutions. The Board acts as the State Educational Facilities Authority in order to assist construction and financing of facilities at private, nonprofit educational institutions. The legislature has also established an independent Board of Economic Advisors to assist SBCB in preparing economic forecasts and general fund revenue projections.

The State Budget and Control Board today is a multipurpose executive-functioning agency that engages in a wide variety of management pursuits for

FIGURE 1

STATE BUDGET AND CONTROL BOARD ORGANIZATION

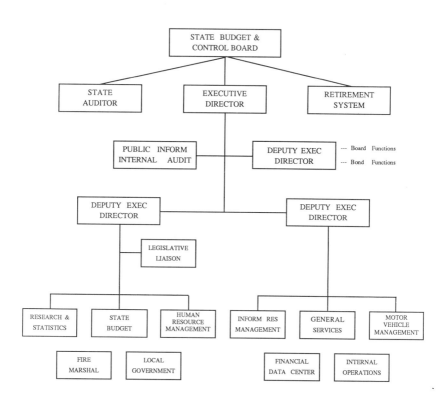

The State Budget and Control Board today is a multipurpose executive-functioning agency that engages in a wide variety of management pursuits for state government. In the midst of such variety, it is still the source of budget recommendations for the legislature. It is to a more detailed discussion of the SBCB units and their involvement in the general processes of South Carolina government and budgetmaking that the chapter now turns.

South Carolina's SBCB Units

Executive Director. The SBCB executive director is responsible for all the activities of SBCB, except for the retirement systems and the State Auditor's office. All three of these offices report directly to the five-member SBCB. However, the executive director is much more involved in the routines and operations of the Board. The office represents the Board to the legislature and to the general public and also develops Board meeting agendas and follows

174

up on duties that emerge from Board meetings.

It may be fair to describe the SBCB executive director as a "chief of staff" who coordinates Board affairs, the retirement systems, and the State Auditor; oversees preparation of the state budget; manages through deputies the operations of the other staff functions such as personnel and various administrative services; and maintains liaison with important bodies or groups such as federal agencies or local governments.

Some details describing the functions of the major SBCB divisions follow. More emphasis is given to the budget division, since budgeting is the focus of the closing section of this chapter. Sketches are provided of selected other SBCB units to illustrate just how expansive the control function of the Board is. The centralized executive force for budgeting and control of the traditional staff functions in administration — among them are personnel, planning, administrative services, and community relations — in South Carolina government is actually quite pervasive.

State Budget Division. This unit proposes the annual budget through a process that it designs and supervises. The critical initial step in budget development is the SBCB allocations for each program in each agency of state government. With these allocations as a base, each agency then generates detailed budget requests by program. Through a more executive controlled process, agency budget requests are not "pie-in-the-sky" and the SBCB through the budget division is able to take the initiative in consulting and advising agencies on priorities and cost-effectiveness of the particular elements of their operations. The budget division, not the individual agencies, sets the tone for consideration of overall, statewide needs and plans rather than individual agency funding alone.

As before, the SBCB recommended operating budget goes to the legislature in January. But, communications about budgetary issues between the SBCB and the General Assembly are year-round. Issue papers that analyze major funding problems in order to inform legislative discussions are a relatively new occurrence. Fiscal impact statements on pending legislation may also be prepared for legislative committees.

In general, the budget division monitors the expenditure of funds as a management auditor. It generally validates the implementation of legislative intent, statutory requirements, and constitutional principles. Good management practices in the allocation and utilization of funds are an additional object. Fund transfers are monitored and recommended as are changes in an agency's full-time-equivalent position authorizations with respect to funding source. The division also administers the state's capital budgeting or permanent improvements program. Supervision comes from the SBCB executive director who coordinates the capital expenditure program with the bond authorization process.

Research and Statistical Services. This SBCB unit has grown rapidly from its initiation in 1966 as a general source for budget data and general fund revenue analysis. It has expanded into demographic statistics, economic research, census information, mapping, health statistics, geological and geodetic surveys, and information technology and management. Many of these requirements have been added through the years by specific legislative act. Other duties are based in executive orders or SBCB directives that implement specific policies or federal requirements.

Human Resource Management. Originally called the State Personnel Division, this unit began in 1968 with the specific purpose of developing a statewide classification and compensation system. Its name was changed in 1984 to reflect more emphasis on comprehensive development and management of state employees as a resource for state government. Human Resource Management has individual sections that study developing conditions in the labor market to see that employees are classified properly and paid fairly; that keep track of all the information needed for the system; that improve relations between state government and its workers by advancing performance appraisal, dealing with discipline, and promoting training; that recruit new employees; and that extend the administration of a merit system into all state agencies.

Information Resource Management. With technological advancements in data processing, telephone communications, and office systems, this unit was spun out of the general services division in 1983. It manages the state's telecommunications system, its microwave network, and its information processing center for computing and programming services. Office automation is also a part of the information resource management effort. The services range from publishing 26,000 state telephone directories to providing high-tech solutions to the information needs of state agencies. The definition and coordination of services by this SBCB unit requires extensive contact and visits with all state agencies.

Local Government. Through this division, the SBCB acts as a liaison for financial grants among local governments, the governor's office, and the General Assembly. Its primary objective is to provide state level support for economic development and its progress is self-measured by the number of jobs created or retained through promotion of water and sewer development or improvement. The unit is a source of advice and guidance for local units who may be puzzled by the maze of regulations and funding requirements in municipal infrastructure management.

General Services. This SBCB unit manages five major activities: agency services; building codes and regulatory services; the insurance reserve fund; materials management (purchasing) office; and property management. By tradition, general services is at the heart of the SBCB activities. Especially before specialization and frequency of use demanded creation of new and separate divisions during the 1980s, general services was the most frequent SBCB "face" for state agency operations.

Agency services includes a state engineer who is the state's chief procurement officer for construction, a planning and construction office for state facilities' development and design, and a building services section for maintenance and renovation of state office buildings.

Building codes and regulatory services coordinates and supports five boards created by statute: the Board for Barrier Free Design — a program of minimum standards for access to public buildings for the aged, disabled, or physically handicapped; the Building Codes Council — approves county and municipal building and construction codes; the Manufactured Housing Board — regulates manufactured housing; a Modular Appeals Board — hears appeals disputing the Building Codes Council's regulation of modular housing; and the State Board of Pyrotechnic Safety — regulates fireworks.

The *insurance reserve fund* is a general service that manages the claims for damages from the state that may be brought in a legal proceeding against a state agency. It includes insurance coverage for medical professional liabilities, automobile liabilities, and general tort liabilities.

Materials management refers to operations that centralize the purchase of goods, services, and equipment. Agency needs are tracked by a system that is used to identify initial requirements and then to follow utilization of an item or service contract through completion. This unit actually buys the data processing, telecommunications, or office systems that state agencies use. Even if it does not provide purchasing services directly, the materials management division audits the procurement activities of all state government agencies and some of the larger public school districts. This division runs a central supplies store to reduce duplicate inventories, it runs a mail service for state agencies to save on postage, it auctions off wornout state equipment, it trains personnel of other agencies in procurement, and it even helps state agencies purchase sophisticated office, telecommunications, or data processing equipment on the installment plan.

The *office of property management* is the state's real estate agent. It negotiates leases for commercial space and leases out state-owned building or land. It also buys and sells state land and buildings and the unit manages state leases and the state's real property. For example, in 1986-87, it bought 6,750

177

acres of land and had over 350 leases to arrange over 2 million square feet of office space for state agencies in commercial, non-state-owned buildings.

Motor Vehicle Management. The SBCB created this division in 1975 to supervise the state motor vehicle fleet, except for school buses and service vehicles of the department of education and all highway department vehicles. Motor vehicle management draws up specifications for the purchase of state vehicles, maintenance of the vehicles while they are in service, and then their disposal. The operation is statewide and many of vehicles are leased to state agencies. The division runs an extensive safety program and its fleet travels more than 17,000,000 miles per year.

Some Units That Serve The SBCB Itself: SBCB is large enough that some internal units are necessary to serve its needs. It has a section for financial data systems to perform computing work for the Comptroller General, the State Treasurer, and the state retirement system as well as other SBCB divisions like Human Resource Management. Internal operations manages the financial and personnel services for SBCB and most of its divisions. In a typical year, its personnel department processes over 3,000 job applications. There are also units for internal audit and public information.

The litany of SBCB divisions and activities illustrates that it is more than just the budgeting conference identified in 1919; it is the executive department of state government. Although many of the state agencies have a separate board or commission with legislative authority to act on general matters of policy, the SBCB has authority to allocate state agency budget requests; to build agency buildings; to design their financial, personnel, informational, and telephone systems; and to control their vehicles and the equipment or service contracts they use. The cross-cutting effects of centralized, executive controls are extensive enough to characterize South Carolina as an executive state in every respect but name.

In the following section is a discussion of how executive dominance has supplanted legislative supervision of budgeting in South Carolina.

A Focus on State Budgeting Activities

Executive and Legislative Staff Resources. The twenty-three full time management, analyst, and clerical positions in the SBCB budget division approximately double the size of the legislative budgeting committee staffs even when committee clerks are included in the count. If the eight to ten positions on the governor's staff that are devoted to budget recommendations are counted along with other executive resource staff, it is easy to identify up to fifty executive branch positions devoted to budget analysis and proposals. An important future consideration is whether SBCB budget staff will have the same general preferences as an individual governor's budget assistants.

In order not to underestimate legislative budgeting clout, it is also possible to expand the "count" of legislative budgetmaking staff. Based on the practices of consultation in a "legislative state," it is possible to make the case that the additional budgeting staff for the legislature is actually drawn from the agencies. Legislators "call and see what the agencies can do for them" in constituency service, facility development, or program changes. Agency budget staffers often deliver an estimate of "what it will cost to do what the legislator wants." These "estimates" become woven into the work of committee and legislature as completed legislative staff work. Legislative staff overlaps with agency staff in flexible activities that vary from problem to problem.

The reflexive nature of much legislative staff input into budgeting contrasts with the more regularized approach of the SBCB. SBCB has a budget preparation manual that lays out the format and procedures for new agency budget requests each year. The agencies routinely comply. The preparation process gives SBCB the initiative to preview and recommend agency requests to the legislature. The advantages of centralized information, of direct access to SBCB members, and of legislative or executive authority to prescribe systems to which agencies much conform restrict legislative budget committee staff to exploration of marginal adjustments or special agency needs.

Staff Orientations. The SBCB staff has a reputation among agencies and legislators of being "task-oriented;" they do "lots of work, use statistics." When they make presentations they are "longwinded." These perceptions are no doubt due to the presence of professional staff in the SBCB. Earlier State Auditors have been forceful, good government oriented personalities; the last three have been university-trained accountants. Two of them had extensive experience in education finance administration before being appointed to the office. The current Executive Director has an earned doctorate as do two of the three deputies. The third one, the deputy for SBCB functions and bond activity, is a senior certified planner who came to the state two decades ago to direct the state's early efforts to comply with Circular A-95 under the Intergovernmental Cooperation Act of 1968. It is a thoroughly professional group, large in number, and remote from daily political battles.

If the SBCB professionals are "cool" to agency politics, then the directors of research for the legislative committees have to deal with all of the "hot" issues between agencies and legislators. Legislative staffers tend to want "no bruised heads;" so, they have to avoid many controversial issues in order to keep favor from the particular legislators they serve. Legislative staffers have a tendency to "let it lie, defer to legislators." While personally competent and in one case a former employee of the SBCB budget staff, legislative committee staffers are required to have a clear political orientation and sensitivity in their role perceptions.

Legislative-Executive Fit. The functional relation between SBCB budgetary recommendations and legislative consideration of them suggests the classic reform orthodoxy of executive control of the budget function (Seidman and Gilmour, 1986: 3-36). The only problem in South Carolina is that major decisions are made by a single board of three executives with separate functions and two legislators. But, one of the board members and its chair is the governor. If the governor persuades the SBCB in its recommendations, then the board's proposals have the same force as if they were the governor's.

The main struggle for the General Assembly today may be to stay competitive rather than to worry about dominance. While there is no state equivalent of the Congressional Budget Office as a separate legislative source of budget information, the legislative staff, particularly House Ways and Means, collects data independently to counteract or enhance executive recommendations on very specific matters. The legislature also has a management audit agency, the Legislative Audit Council, that writes critical reports of specific agencies much like the federal General Accounting Office. The legislature is generally supportive of its management auditor, but an individual legislator may become an open opponent if the Council is too harsh in its criticism of an agency that a legislator wants to protect.

Probably the most significant recent change that may affect executive-legislative relations is the possible second four-year term for the governor, beginning with the 1982 election. It enhances the governor's ability to influence both SBCB and legislative decisions. Richard Riley (1979-1987), the first eight-year governor, was able over time to take a hand in the appointments to agency boards and commissions in virtually all instances.

The current governor, Carroll Campbell (1987-), has advocated budgeting staff positions for political executives in a more straightforward, gubernatorially-directed, executive budget process. Campbell wants each agency to provide the governor's office with program objectives for their budget recommendations and for them to organize their budgets by program. So far, Campbell's process changes have not been formally adopted by the SBCB, but his staff has lobbied for them directly with the legislature. Campbell continues attempts for more direct gubernatorial influence on agency funding. He vetoed more than 200 items in the 1987-1988 budget and the legislature did not override any.

Interrelation between Policy and Control. The executive control elements for budgetary accounting are well organized. The Comptroller General uses a computerized state accounting and reporting system (STARS) and the office preaches use of generally accepted accounting principles (GAAP) for state agencies. This part of the executive has restrictive, institutionalized accounting control.

The legislature has informally recognized veto over SBCB transfers from one line item to another during the implementation phase. Legislators have repeatedly voiced concern over the SBCB determining priorities through transfers. What this may mean is that the SBCB professionals may change a line item for a pet project of the legislators without a formal vote of the five Board members. In fact, there is a kind of "collusion or invisible handshake" — the pet projects are fairly clear when the budget is passed; then, the SBCB and its staff tacitly agree to leave them alone.

The legislature also has some policy control through a joint committee for reviewing and advising on appropriations necessary for federal funds. There is also a Bond Review Committee for permanent improvements. From them, the legislature gets improved information for decision making. When constituents and legislators join, some "agencies do not have to lobby" for budget increases. Agency administrators are fond of telling stories of items that appear in their budgets that they did not know about or request. These legislative initiatives are nonetheless generally small and inconsequential. The larger ones, especially if capital expenditure is involved, are usually public knowledge before any final legislative action.

The agencies are at their best when they help a legislator "understand the consequences" of a budget proposal or decision. One of the currently popular tactics is "if we don't spend here, we will get a lawsuit there." Corrections, mental health, and regulatory agencies may be examples. In the past, the SBCB separated its deliberations from the agencies, except for directly negotiated recommendations with agencies that had a political point. Now, the SBCB interaction with the agencies is more "textured" and some agency staff claim that they have to convince SBCB staff to keep them from contradicting the agency position with the legislature. As one agency observer put it, "It is not as easy to misinterpret facts for the legislative testimony [as it used to be]. [The state budget] people are there taking notes to see if you are lying." The implication is increased centralized executive budget clearance.

All in all, the policy initiative is clearly in the hands of the SBCB. It is the "Big Board" that represents the collective wisdom of the elected officials of the state. Even if the Ways and Means Committee starts a new budget in January, it gets its policy ideas from the SBCB preparations. The Ways and Means Chair is forced to "zero-out a board recommendation in public forum." The lack of legislative power is consistent with the South Carolina idea of government by small groups that represent major interests but that watch each other intently to forestall potential abuses of power.

Summary

Today, almost all states prepare the budget in the governor's office as part of the duty of the executive and the budget is one of the governor's strongest sources of power (Dye, 1985: 193). South Carolina may be the most noteworthy exception; in a national survey of state agency administrators to ascertain the importance of governors as chief administrators, not a single respondent from South Carolina ranked the governor as most influential (Abney and Lauth, 1983). The state's governor is actually a member of a separate administrative board composed of three executives and two legislators that proposes the budget and administers it through all phases of the budget cycle.

South Carolina's budgetmakers still use a line-item format, despite the fact that budget makers across the country gradually moved on to program budgets by the 1950's (Wanat, 1978: 98-104). The line-item budget is consistent with the state's fiscally conservative views. The legislature gives the SBCB recommendations a "thorough scouring" to make sure they fit political needs and realities. Yet, the legislature gives wide deference to executive-type preparation, implementation, and audit of state taxing and spending policies once they are made. The legislative "window" on administration is the two legislators who sit on the SBCB. It allows the legislature to keep a position of "first refusal" on administrative decisions that may alter the specific elements of the approved spending plan in which a legislator may have an interest. Since they are a minority, the refusal must take the form of loud public disapproval so that other legislators are alarmed.

The discussion of the involvement and roles of the respective budget staffs suggests that they largely stay out of each other's way in attending to the details of their respective responsibilities. While the outward form is not streamlined like a governor's budget or consensus-based like a cabinet model and even though there is much legislative noise during the process, underneath, executives and legislators with their staffs play their roles more and more in keeping with the larger principles of a more powerful executive.

Future approaches to designing centralized budgeting and management processes in South Carolina may follow two general tracks. One is refinement of the existing, hybridized system; another is to place greater reliance on the governor. Each approach has merits as well as drawbacks. A governor may be just as partisan and narrowly focused as the present system is multilayered, informal, and vulnerable to the demands of specific political actors. The overall purpose of any reform, following traditions of democratic theory, is to maintain a consistent eye on statewide concerns and, if necessary, to raise the level of the budgetary and administrative dialogue above narrow partisan, functional, or geographic interests.

References

Abney, Glenn and Thomas P. Lauth (1983). "The Governor as Chief Administrator." *Public Administration Review*, 43 (January/February): 40-49.

Dye, Thomas (1985). *Politics in States and Communities* 5th ed. Englewood Cliffs, New Jersey: Prentice-Hall.

Huss, John E. (1961). *Senator for the South: A Biography of Olin D. Johnston.* Garden City, New York: Doubleday & Company.

Report, *South Carolina Preparedness for Peace Commission* (1945). Columbia: South Carolina, January.

Rogers, George C., Jr. (1987). Review of J. L. Underwood, *The Constitution of South Carolina*, Vol. I, in *South Carolina Historical Magazine*, 88 (April), No. 2: 102-104.

Seidman, Harold and Robert Gilmour (1986). *Position, Power, and Politics: From the Positive to the Regulatory State.* New York: Oxford.

South Carolina Budget and Control Board (1984). *Annual Report, 1984-1985.* Columbia.

The (Columbia, S.C.) State (1918a). "Financial Status of State Shown" (January 13): 9.

———(1918b). "Wish To Abolish Tax Commission" (January 24): 2.

———(1919a). "To Coordinate Higher Education" (January 2): 4.

———(1919b). "Senate Provides a Budget System" (February 21): 5.

Underwood, James L. (1986). *The Constitution of South Carolina. Volume I: The Relationship of the Legislative, Executive, and Judicial Branches.* Columbia: The University of South Carolina Press.

Wallace, David D. (1961). *South Carolina: A Short History.* Columbia: The University of South Carolina Press.

Wanat, John (1978). *Introduction to Budgeting.* Belmont, California: Wadsworth Publishing Company.

11

Budget Reform in S. C.: A Historical Perspective

Philip G. Grose Jr.

Introduction

During the 1980s, budget reform has occupied considerable attention from governors, legislators and others concerned about the state's financial well-being. Issues such as reserve funds, capital bonds, revenue-estimating, and — with increasing persistence — the format of the budget itself have given budget reform center stage in many debates within the halls of the State House.

While each of the issues has a relevance and currency immediately pertinent to the State's present financial status, there is nothing new about the zeal for budget reform. The seeds of many of the current issues, in fact, were planted decades ago, early in the 20th century, when government in this state — and elsewhere — began taking on the kind of size and permanence which required more than casual public attention.

This chapter is an account of budget reform over the last 70 years in South Carolina — an examination of some of the major stages in the development of the budget process in South Carolina — with particular attention being paid to organizational changes and the modification and development of the format of the state's budget document.

Early Reform

Budget reform in South Carolina, Washington, and elsewhere in the nation was born in the wake of the rough-and-tumble political days of the late 19th and early 20th century. The concept of public budgeting, in fact, was one of the early expressions of governmental reform by which advocates sought to restore public confidence in government and the political process in general.

Philip G. Grose, Jr. is assistant executive director of the South Carolina Budget and Control Board. Formerly he was director of the State Reorganization Commission. He has been a newspaper man and was on the staff of Governors Robert E. McNair and John C. West.

". . . it will have a wonderful moral effect on the present state of mind of all the American people," said one supporter of legislation which led to the first federal government executive budget in 1921, and another said, "(it will) . . . save much duplication in work and much waste and extravagance of expenditure" (Senators Edge (N.J.) and Swanson (Va.) quoted in Pitsvada, 1988: 87).

Those expressions were both a political acknowledgment of the low public opinion of governmental management at the time and an optimistic belief that remedies could be found through the institution of the type of business practices already in place in the private sector. Ten years earlier, a report developed by a special Commission appointed by President William Howard Taft (1911) had planted many of the seeds for governmental reform at the federal and state level. That report, one of the earliest management efficiency studies conducted for government, made sweeping recommendations dealing largely with organizational issues. It also addressed significantly the concept of public budgeting, and defined its three basic functions as planning, management and control.

While the Taft Commission's 1911 recommendations on public budgeting did not have direct results until Congress adopted the Budget and Accounting Act of 1921, its indirect impact was considerable. According to the 1987 work, *Reforming Bureaucracy*, by Jack C. Knott and Gary J. Miller, "Budget reform swept through state capitols and city halls" (Knott and Miller, 1987: 210).

Among those state capitols ripe for reform was Columbia, just emerging from the bitter factionalism and turmoil of the Ben Tillman (1890-1894) and Cole Blease (1911-1915) gubernatorial administrations and still reeling from the post-Reconstruction fiscal disorder.

Blease's successor as Governor, Richard I. Manning (1915-1919), undertook a number of reform measures in an effort to stabilize state government, including a bold step to strengthen the state's financial operation with the creation of the State Tax Commission. Historian David D. Wallace called it "the most important fiscal legislation for years," and wrote, "the Commission became the chief tax advisory and superintending agency of the government . . ." (Wallace, 1951: 666-667).

Budget reform was the next step for South Carolina, and it came in 1919 with the passage of Act No. 130, establishing the state's first formal budget process. Coming in an atmosphere of warm relations between Governor Manning and the legislature, the Governor — for the only period in the state's history — was vested with the authority of submitting an executive budget to the legislature. "No South Carolina Governor ever secured better cooperation with the legislature or saw more of his recommendations adopted," wrote Wallace of Manning's administration.

First State Budget

The Budget Act was adopted in the last year of Manning's two terms, and it was his successor, Robert A. Cooper (1919-1922), who submitted the state's first budget to the General Assembly in 1920. The budget was a 208-page document which requested appropriations of $5,466,631.65 for some 55 agencies covering a fiscal year which ended December 31, 1920. (Prior to 1934, the fiscal year coincided with the calendar year.)

As had been the case at the federal level, Cooper's first budget was both an acknowledgment of a woeful management condition in the state, and an expression of optimism about the curative powers of organized budgeting.

Writing in the Foreword of the 1920 budget, Cooper said his examination of the state's finances "reveal a condition and practice in the State government which are fraught with the possibilities of financial danger . . ." (S.C. State Budget, 1920). Citing a deficit from the previous year of some $2 million (almost 40 percent of all state expenditures at the time), he called such overspending "unregulated, uncontrolled and unappropriated" (S.C. State Budget, 1920: Foreword).

In that atmosphere, early budget reform was viewed as a means of policing governmental spending through the imposition of strict control and accounting procedures. ". . . the focus of attention," write Knott and Miller (1987:210) about the federal reform effort, "was on the control function through improved accounting procedures." Accountants devoted their efforts to improving methods of control through line-item objects of expenditure. Economist Allan Schick described the period as one in which "technique triumphed over purpose" (Knott and Miller, 1987: 210).

Similarly, the Cooper budget was essentially an accounting document. A recent analysis describes the first South Carolina budget as follows:

> The format . . . was stringently laid out as an itemized plan of all expenditures for each state department, institution or agency. . . . Also, specific financial information was required . . . such as a statement of current assets, liabilities and reserves, an estimate of the condition of the treasury, and a complete financial balance sheet (South Carolina State Reorganization Commission, 1985a: A-44).

Governor Cooper wrote that the budget encompassed "recognized practices in budget-making," establishing the principle that expenditures should be classified and itemized by five categories:

1. by funds charged,
2. by organization units,
3. by functions or activities,
4. by character, and
5. by object (S. C. State Budget, 1920: Foreword).

Cooper's budget was not only the first of its kind; it also became the prototype for the state. Writing 65 years later, an analyst observed that "these classifications form the basis for the chart of accounts still used in the budget and the Statewide Accounting and Reporting System (STARS) used today" (South Carolina State Reorganization Commission, 1985a: A-44).

Expenditure-oriented budgeting thus became something of a legacy of the early efforts at budget reform in South Carolina. Sometimes overlooked, however, is the fact that the seeds of later interest in "program budgeting" were also planted in those days. The Taft Commission had, in fact, in what Knott and Miller call "a remarkable foretaste of the planning and budgeting movements of the 1960s and 1970s," envisioned program-oriented budgeting. The Commission "rejected line-item or 'object-of-expense' classifications for the budget (such as supplies, salaries, travel, capital purchases, and so forth) in favor of activity or functional classifications according to class of work" (Knott and Miller, 1987: 210).

As early as 1913, Dr. F. A. Cleveland had condemned the practice of detailed, line-item budgeting at the national level, saying:

> The best that may be said for the detailed appropriations of the past is that they are a part of a system that has operated to prevent administrative action premised on infidelity and ignorance; that legislative control over administration through detailed appropriations is a device adapted for use of a political institution, in which all the elements essential to administrative efficiency are lacking. Given a responsible government and a real executive, the restrictions which go with detailed appropriations are the first obstacle to efficiency to be removed (quoted in Coleman, 1935: 38).

Governor Cooper himself, also anticipating such later budgetary devices as "units of service" and "program measures," wrote in the Foreword to his 1920 budget, "It was unanimously agreed by those entrusted with the determination of the procedure that the unit of recommendation, as well as the appropriation, should be the activity, but certain problems make it impractical the first year" (S. C. State Budget, 1920: Foreword).

Despite such clear articulation of broader budgetary purpose, however, only the accounting-oriented function received serious attention. Of the three functions of budgeting laid out by the Taft Commission, planning, management and control, only one of the three — the control function — gained the immediate attention of lawmakers. Public budgeting thus became identified in its infancy with accounting, detailed line-item and expenditure reporting, and its broader purposes were laid aside, and eventually obscured in strategic in-fighting over organization and authority. In Washington, efforts to continue the development of a broadly-based budget process became bogged down in reorganization struggles, and President Hoover's bid to strengthen the hand of the executive went down to defeat by a Congress he said was the victim of "vested officials, vested habits, (and) organized propaganda" (Knott and Miller, 1987: 84).

Governor Cooper's ideas of more sophisticated budgeting fell victim to the harsh realities of South Carolina's economy in the 1920s, and to what a 1930s analyst said "were not so much the inevitable result of adverse conditions as the outcome of an absence of legislative policy and administrative control" (Coleman, 1935: 40-41).

For whatever the reason, the momentum for budget reform was lost in the 1920s and 1930s, and with it went the opportunity for early attention to broadening the budget function beyond its narrow early interpretation as a control mechanism. Disenchantment over the curative powers of public budgeting set in, and within 13 years after the development of its first budget, the state's "experiment" with executive budgeting was abandoned. The job of carrying on budget reform was, in essence, left to later generations.

Early Studies. Beginning with the 1920 study by Griffenhagen and Associates, South Carolina government was the subject of a series of management studies which accompanied, and sometimes paralleled, the state's efforts in management and budget reform. Support for the state's early emphasis on accounting systems, for example, was found in Griffenhagen's finding that "(t)he great weakness under present conditions is the absence of any systematic executive or other central control after the money has been appropriated" (Griffenhagen and Associates, 1920: 47).

Subsequent studies by James Karl Coleman (1935), and the Preparedness for Peace Commission (1945) set the stage for a revival of budget and management reform in post-war South Carolina.

In his mid-Depression report, Coleman recorded some of the financial woes the state had endured in the 1920s, noting that South Carolina ran up operating deficits for five consecutive years (1925-1930), and ended 1931 with a total deficit of almost $5 million. The resultant deterioration of the state's financial standing, he wrote, created conditions in which:

> . . . there was no market for state bonds and credit was not available until the deficit was refinanced. Governor Blackwood (Ibra C., 1931-1935) was quoted as having described the situation in these words: "Every time the State goes to borrow money at present, the deficit looms in its face like a penalty to be added for its financial status" (Coleman, 1935: 40-41).

While the deficit was erased by the 1933 General Assembly by the extraordinary measure of reducing total appropriations by 35 percent, the state's rocky financial experience cost the Governor whatever direct authority he had over the state's budget. A 1933 Act of the General Assembly instituted formally the State Budget Commission, revoking the exclusive budget power granted Governors since the days of Governor Cooper, and vesting budget preparation authority in the hands of a legislative-executive hybrid composed of the Governor, the Chairman of the Senate Finance Committee and the Chairman of the House Ways and Means Committee (Coleman, 1935: 52). Coleman was, in fact, dubious about the Governor's budgetary powers even under the earlier system. "The Governor," he wrote, "is the 'chief budgeting officer' in name only, for the legislative committees actually handle the details of constructing the so-called budget" (Coleman, 1935: 53).

Obscured again in the organizational changes of the 1930s were the embryonic notions expressed a decade earlier of program budgeting and units of service, as envisioned by the framers of the Taft report and the Cooper budget. The South Carolina budget remained a highly-detailed, accounting-type document, and Coleman wrote:

A satisfactory work program cannot be formulated when the appropriations are highly itemized. Considering . . . the appropriating function of legislative bodies, we note the three methods of revising budget requests, viz: (1) percentage cuts; (2) study of probable needs; (3) authorization of maximum expenditures. The second method is found in the majority of the states. The third method of fixing the maximum amount and allowing the spending officers to perform the task, assures that the cuts will be made where they least interfere with administrative work.

Obviously, the first method of cutting on a percentage basis is the simplest and most unsatisfactory method. It is the most unintelligent and generally results from an insufficient budgetary procedure. Without sustaining information, the legislative body practically has no other choice. Such is the case in South Carolina (Coleman, 1935: 58).

Fifty-two years later, a South Carolina governor grappling with a $3 billion budget would have a similar lament. Governor Carroll A. Campbell (1987-present), in his first State-of-the-State address, said: ". . . the most urgent challenge confronting us is to develop a responsible budget process which frees us from the shackles of mid-year budget cuts. . . . We've had mid-year budget cuts for five of the last seven years. . . . These cuts disrupt the entire operation of state government.

"Our inability to discern good programs from bad forces blind cuts for everyone. We therefore are locked into a cycle where priorities are disrupted and programs thrown into confusion" (Campbell, 1987: 2).

The Coleman report, as were the Taft and Griffenhagen reports before it, was tied to organizational change, dealing largely with a restructuring of the executive branch and granting additional authority to the Governor. Coming only two years after the legislature had formally weakened the Governor's budgetary authority, it provoked no immediate action.

One of Coleman's proposals involved the merging of eight financially-related entities into a single Cabinet position of Commissioner of Finance. Abolished in the merger would have been the offices of the Comptroller General and the Treasurer, as well as the State Finance Committee, the Sinking Fund Commission, the Joint Committee on Printing, the Contingent Fund Committee and the Board of Claims. Taking their place would have been five Bureaus: accounting, treasury, personnel, purchasing and local government finance. Although the proposal was unaddressed, elements of it resurfaced 11 years later in recommendations which ultimately led to the creation in 1950 of the Budget and Control Board.

Wartime intervened, and with it came fiscal prosperity for state government in South Carolina. General Fund Revenues increased by more than 46 percent between 1940-41 and 1944-45 (from $18.1 million to $27.1 million). The State was not only able to operate in the black, it was able to convert the 1944-45 operating surplus into a post-war Reserve Fund of $5.5 million (Dennis, 1982: 6).

Preparedness for Peace Commission

Preparation for the conclusion of the war revived interest in management and budgetary reform with the creation in 1942 of the Preparedness for Peace Commission. The Commission, designed to provide orderly transition from wartime to peacetime footing for the state and its government, based its findings on "a detailed study of the State's administrative and economic structure by a professional group of public administration consultants" (Stoudemire, 1977: 1).

The recommendations conformed to "such standards (of) . . . governmental reorganization as strengthening the Office of the Governor; centralizing budgetary, financial and personnel administration under his control . . . establishing a strong post-audit procedure controlled by the legislature; and revamping state services and financial resources based on anticipated needs and priorities" (Stoudemire, 1977: 1).

The Preparedness for Peace Commission was chaired by Greenville business executive Roger C. Peace, and included in its 32 members a cross-section of private and governmental leadership in the State, including Speaker of the House Solomon Blatt and Senator Edgar A. Brown. Its product was a three-section 682-page volume submitted to the 1945 General Assembly which addressed governmental operations, the state's tax structure and peacetime economic possibilities and potential in South Carolina.

191

Like Griffenhagen and Coleman before it, the Peace Commission found major flaws in the state's budget system. Unlike Coleman, however, it tended to focus on the mechanics of the state's financial operation, rather than the budget process. Among its observations was the following:

Although total expenditures and revenues are given by departments in the departmental detail of the budget document, most of the budget summaries deal only with the appropriation expenditures and with net revenues "available for appropriation" for general State purposes. Departmental expenditures and revenues are apparently not reconciled in every case with the annual report of the Comptroller General.

In many cases amounts listed as expenditures seem to be the amount of the appropriation and not the actual expenditure. There is no encumbrance system, and very little expenditure control. There are few current reports made to the Governor, legislature and public on budget operations. The annual financial reports are made to serve this purpose, and these are inadequate. Operation of the budget system is further complicated by a relatively complicated fund structure, necessitating the accounting for many funds, and for dedicated or restricted revenues with funds (South Carolina Preparedness for Peace Commission, 1945: 22).

To remedy what it deemed confusion and disorder in the state's fiscal house, the Peace Commission called for restructuring of the financial entities, but in a somewhat less drastic method than Coleman had envisioned ten years earlier. Peace proposed creation of a centralized Finance Department under the Governor whose functions — somewhat more limited than those proposed by Coleman — would oversee accounting, budgeting and purchasing. An additional five departments would be created: (1) A Finance Committee (composed of the Governor, House Ways and Means and Finance Chairmen) to replace the Budget Commission created in 1933, (2) a Department of the Treasury (headed by the Treasurer), (3) a Department of State Audits (headed by the Comptroller General), (4) a Department of Local Government and (5) a Commission on Local Government Finance.

The Peace Commission also recognized that governmental inertia could doom its recommendations, as had been the fate of Griffenhagen and Coleman in the past. It included in its proposals the appointment by the legislature of a committee "to digest and analyze the facts, findings, and recommendations and submit to the General Assembly proposed legislation to enact as much of the report as it deems feasible at this session of the legislature" (South Carolina Preparedness for Peace Commission, 1945: xviii-xix).

While such a committee was not created that year, it did come along three years later under Governor Strom Thurmond (1947-51), whose proposal to the General Assembly led to the establishment of the State Reorganization Commission. The Commission, created by Act No. 621 of 1948, was comprised of three senators, three House members and three gubernatorial appointees, and was chaired by industrialist A. L. M. Wiggins of Hartsville.

While traces of Griffenhagen, Coleman and Peace can be found in its work, the Reorganization Commission set its own course for the most part. Significantly, it did not increase the Governor's authority, as Coleman had proposed, nor did it maintain — at least from a governance perspective — the strict separation of budgeting functions from the control functions as Peace had suggested.

Instead, it came up with a recommendation which brought all functions — budgeting and control included — together under the same organizational roof, merging the members of the 1933 Budget Commission (Governor, Chairmen of Senate Finance and House Ways and Means) with the two constitutional officers primarily involved in the control functions, the State Treasurer and the Comptroller General.

Creation of Budget and Control Board

The result was the State Budget and Control Board, established by Act 46 of the 1950 General Assembly, and creating what would become the state's third budget-making entity in 30 years.

Creation of the Board abolished eight existing entities variously mentioned in the organizational recommendations by both Coleman and Peace: the State Budget Commission, the Sinking Fund Commission, the Board of Phosphate Commissioners, the State Finance Committee, the Board of Claims, the Commission on the State House and State House Grounds, the Joint Committee on Printing, and the South Carolina Retirement System. The eight boards were absorbed into the operation of three Budget and Control Board Divisions: Finance, Purchasing and Property, and Personnel Administration (Journal of the Senate, January 10, 1950).

The first budget submitted by the new Budget and Control Board was for fiscal year 1952-53. It retained a standard budget classification only slightly modified from the 1920 Cooper budget, and was divided into two sections: (1) operation and maintenance of state government and (2) permanent improvements. It was 498 pages long, contained information on 63 state agencies, and requested appropriations of $139 million (State Reorganization Commission, 1985a: A-47).

Establishment of the Board was accomplished by Reorganization Plan No. 2. It, and the earlier consolidation of state purchasing accomplished under Reorganization Plan No. 1, were hailed later by Governor Thurmond as steps "to reorganize and streamline the state government in the interest of economy and efficiency . . . (they) will save the taxpayers millions of dollars annually" (Thurmond, 1954: 10).

Creation of the Budget and Control Board did, in fact, address many of the concerns about organizational fragmentation of the state's budget and financial system expressed during the previous 30 years. It was, however, essentially an organizational step designed to correct mechanical flaws, and, in Governor Thurmond's words, to "streamline government."

As had been the case 20 years earlier, flaws in the state's budgetary process were addressed with structural changes. Left relatively untouched was the long-obscured notion articulated decades earlier, namely, that budgeting should evolve from a dependence on line-item expenditure data of an accounting nature into an activity-related document whose use could be broadened to include management and planning for policy-making purposes. While structures changed, the state's reliance on detailed, line-item, expenditure-oriented budget information and format did not.

Budget Reform, 1960-80s

It would be the late 1960s and early 1970s before budget reform surfaced seriously again as an issue in South Carolina, and governmental growth was the major motivation. Passage of the state's first sales tax (three percent) to support public education in 1951 under Governor James F. Byrnes (1951-1955), and subsequent modifications under the impetus of the "Moody Report" in the administration of Governor Robert E. McNair (1965-1971) created a four percent sales tax which would become the state's largest revenue source. Those additional educational funds, along with expansion of the traditional fund sources through the state's economic expansion, caused governmental revenues to grow significantly. From $139 million in FY 1952-1953, general fund expenditures rose to $263.8 million in FY 1965-66, and to $650.1 million in FY 1972-73.

It was the "Moody Report," which also articulated something of a clean bill of health for the state's once lamentable credit position. Recovering from the deficit days of 1930s, South Carolina — under the leadership of its Treasurers Jeff B. Bates (1940-1967), and Grady L. Patterson Jr. (1967-present), had gone from being a state of "no credit" in the days of Governor Blackwood, to a state whose credit rating — AAA — was the best on Wall Street. Its fiscal strength was such, in fact, that Moodys proclaimed in its 1968 recommendations to Governor McNair, that the State could withstand comfortably the incurring of some $320 of general obligation debt for capital improvements over a 12-year period (Moody's Investors Service, Campus Facilities Associates, 1968: 399-422).

A major initiative to strengthen the budget process in the face of governmental growth came from Governor McNair, who moved to stabilize revenue-estimating by creating informally a Board of Economic Advisers, comprised of Tax Commission Chairman Robert Wasson, Thomas P. Evans, Director of the Budget and Control Board's fledgling Division of Research and Statistical Services, and chaired by Dr. James A. Morris of the University of South Carolina.

The Board, later modified and established formally by the Budget and Control Board in 1973, became a statutory entity in 1982, and, though sometimes embattled, has remained the state's sole source of official revenue estimates for more than two decades. In stark contrast to the bitter battles on Capitol Hill over revenue (and deficit) projections, South Carolina's insistence on a single source of official revenue estimates has remained a relatively stable part of its budget process.

In 1972, the most comprehensive review of state government management since the Peace Commission was undertaken by Governor John C. West (1971-1975), who created — with executives "loaned" by private corporations in the state — an entity known as the Governor's Management Review Commission. The Commission's report in 1972 made the first major recommendations for structural change in the Budget and Control Board since its creation 22 years earlier. It proposed that the Board's divisions, which had by then grown to six, be consolidated back to three, and — most significantly, — it recommended the creation of the Office of Executive Director to oversee the entire operation (Governor's Management Review Commission, 1972: 12). The Management Review Commission also sounded one of the early alarms over what would later become a major issue in budget reform of the 1980s: incrementalism in budgeting. The report observed:

> There is an awareness of the need to improve the budget process, and a Director of Budget Planning has been employed in an initial step of recognizing the necessity for a formalized approach to budget planning. However, the traditional budgeting process continues to be followed. Decisions concerning next year's appropriation are largely based on the level of current expenditures and increases in appropriations are primarily based on anticipated increases in revenues (Management Review Commission, 1972: 14).

There ensued a series of management reports which focused primarily on structural and procedural issues, notably dealing with control and accounting mechanisms. Creation of an Executive Director of the Board got a boost from a 1976 report of consultant, Louis Bofferding, submitted to long-time State Auditor Patrick C. Smith. Bofferding envisioned an "Administrative Officer" of the Board who would provide policy support to the Board itself and would supervise all the Board's units.

The Executive Director's job was created in 1978, and was filled by Smith's successor, State Auditor William T. Putnam. Five years later, in 1983, the Board was given the authority by statute to "organize its staff as it deems most appropriate" (*S.C. Code of Laws*, Revised 1986, 1-11-22). Upon his retirement, Putnam was succeeded by Dr. Jesse A. Coles Jr., an early advocate of program budgeting in his roles as Planning Director and Budget Director of the Board. During the internal organizational changes, the State Auditor — who had traditionally been viewed as the senior staff officer of the Board — was separated from the jurisdiction of the Executive Director and given independent reporting status directly to the Board. The move made incumbent Edgar A. Vaughn Jr. the state's auditor in fact as well as in name, and significantly strengthened the state's post-audit function.

It was the Bofferding survey, and subsequent studies by Haskins & Sells (1977), and Peat Marwick, Mitchell & Co. (1979), which also helped to re-introduce the issue of program budgeting in South Carolina. Bofferding called for "a completely revised system of budget management," and wrote, "This means the development of a program system of budgeting that measures program costs rather than objects of expenditure — it should also be started by using the justification principle of 'Zero' budgeting, as a means of starting on reorienting the State's priorities" (Bofferding, 1976: 11, unnumbered).

A year later, Haskins & Sells, in conducting a study to determine the state's financial management information needs, reported among its findings: "Information concerning object expenditures is usually available, but it is difficult to obtain program expenditure information" (Haskins & Sells, 1977: 2). The report's findings were supported by a survey of Budget and Control Board members, who complained also about "too much detail," and cited a need for "relevance, brevity, clarity, consistency and accuracy" (Haskins & Sells, 1977: 10).

In its study of the state's budget preparation process a year later, Peat Marwick found the state immersed in a virtual data overload. "As the budget preparation process has become more sophisticated, the volume of data processed during the budget cycle has increased dramatically. However, the existing accounting system and budget preparation system have been unable to support the agencies' budget preparation process . . ." (Peat, Marwick, Mitchell & Co., 1979: III.4).

The purpose of most of the consultants' work was to define the state's accounting needs, and on July 1, 1981, South Carolina instituted under the leadership of Comptroller General Earle E. Morris Jr. its Statewide Accounting and Reporting System (STARS). Two years later, in fiscal 1983-84, the Comptroller initiated efforts to establish Generally Accepted Accounting Principles (GAAP), a process for which the state is scheduled to become certified in August, 1989.

It was in the process of addressing such system needs that the concept program budgeting surfaced again, coming to the attention of a generation of budget-makers who were too young to remember the Coleman report or the Taft Commission recommendations. Their textbooks, in essence, were popular management techniques such as Planning, Programming and Budgeting System (PPBS), Zero-Based Budgeting (ZBB), and Management by Objective (MBO), programs which were making the rounds in the 1960s and 1970s in business and government circles.

The combination of the influence of these programs, along with the state's internal studies of the time, left a remarkable impact on the state's budgeting in the 1970s and 1980s. Most of the expenditure-oriented data collected under the state's traditional budgeting system could not be translated into information useful for program budgeting or its alphabetical partners, PPBS, ZBB, or MBO. That meant that as each new wave of budget "reform" swept through the state, its attempted implementation usually led to an informational "add-on" to the already-detailed budget document the state produced. As a result, the sheer bulk of the state's detailed-oriented budget documents grew not only in proportion to the size of the budget, but also in relationship to the new information requirements.

By 1969-70, with appropriations at $474 million, the budget document had swelled to 1,014 pages. Subsequent additions of new statistical data, reporting requirements and an increase in standard budget classifications sent the size of the budget up to 2,753 pages in 1978-79, and the addition of "effectiveness measures" two years later caused the bulk to grow to 3,659 pages (State Reorganization Commission, 1985a: A-47-48).

The sheer size of the budget documents, by now dubbed the "bricks" by users, leveled off at around 3,000 pages in the mid-1980s, with the addition and subsequent deletion of "five-year" plans, and the increase in expenditure classifications from 102 to 175.

Legislative Initiatives. At least part of the stirring for budget reform was also coming from the General Assembly. The mid-1970s had seen a wave of initiatives designed to strengthen the legislative branch, leading to the creation of the Legislative Audit Council (LAC), the passage of the Administrative Procedures Act giving legislators' oversight of rules and regulations, the staffing of standing committees with professional research staffs, and the creation and staffing of certain powerful joint committees with specific statutory responsibilities such as the Joint Bond Review Committee, the Joint Appropriation Review Committee and the Joint Committee on Health Care Planning and Oversight.

The Reorganization Commission, once the instrument of management-minded governors, had become more oriented to the legislature in the mid-

1970s. In response to a request from Governor James B. Edwards (1975-79), it authorized a study of the organization of the state's executive branch, and submitted a report to the Governor which explored several organizational options and models. The report, developed by Dr. Charlie B. Tyer of the University of South Carolina and Joyce Prokop, also addressed budget process needs, noting that the state must update its budget process to provide more than just uninformative detail to managers, executives, and legislators" (Tyer and Prokop, 1976: v). Governor Edwards subsequently submitted recommendations to establish a cabinet form of government in the state, but the legislative influence on the Reorganization Commission, namely senior Senator L. Marion Gressette, scuttled the effort before it reached the General Assembly.

Legislative interest in budget reform persisted, however. In one of its first reports in 1977, the Legislative Audit Council cited deficiencies in the state's ability to cope with the impact new federal programs were having on the state's finances, and it stated:

> Due to the rapid increase of Federal and other funds and the limitations of the current budgetary process, the General Assembly is not able to control completely the rate and direction of growth of state government. Legislative priorities were found to be hindered and altered in many cases by the influence of programs funded from Federal and other sources. In essence, the current budgetary process is "open-ended . . ." (Legislative Audit Council, 1977: 10).

The Audit Council report set off alarms within state government, and while it cited needs for both planning and control mechanisms elsewhere in its report, most of the response was in the form of stronger controls, leading generally to additional reporting and procedural requirements.

Three years later, the LAC followed up its initial work by noting the addition of "program budgeting" in 1978, and the establishment of the Joint Appropriation Review Committee (JARC) to strengthen the General Assembly's hand in overseeing federal funds coming into the state. The LAC also began probing the flaws in the state's efforts at "program" budgeting, noting that "the budget format needs further refinement . . ." (Legislative Audit Council, 1980: 27). It observed further: "The primary purpose of the traditional (budget) format was to impose accounting and administrative responsibility upon department or division heads who expend the State's funds. Without modification it does not show total expenditures for specific services, functions or activities which are components of the program concept" (Legislative Audit Council, 1980: 28).

After 60 years of relative neglect, the concept of program budgeting thus gained some new respectability, picked up some new advocates, and became a major item for budget reform consideration in the 1980s. It was, in essence, an old idea which was resurfacing as what many believed to be a new and innovative approach to public budgeting. On the heels of the Audit Council reports, and amid increasing grumbling about various aspects of the state's budgeting process, the State Reorganization Commission re-entered the picture. In June, 1983, Senator Rembert C. Dennis, then Chairman of the Senate Finance Committee, formally asked the Commission, chaired by Senator John Drummond, to undertake a comprehensive study of the state's budget process and to report its findings and recommendations back to the General Assembly.

By then, a growing list of issues had arisen to fuel the budget reform efforts, including the following (Dennis, 1982):

Governmental Growth. Driven by the influx of federal funding for Great Society and other programs, as well as significant state revenue growth from economic growth and new taxes, state expenditures leaped from $365 million in 1965 to $3.5 billion in state and federal funds in 1980.

Debt Service. Once considered an almost incidental part of the budget, funds needed to make payment on the state's capital debt reached $119 million by 1982-83, 5.7 percent of the budget.

"Built-in" Funding. Establishment of "formula-funding" for public education and higher education programs, along with federal matching funds, debt service, and — more recently — funding required to meet court-imposed orders in such areas as Corrections and Mental Health — narrowed the margin of "new moneys" available for which legislative discretion could be applied in a policy-making sense.

Incrementalism. The traditional practice of providing each agency its "base" of the previous year, plus an "allocation" or "fair share" of new funding further eroded funds available for new or expanded initiatives in priority areas.

New voices were also being heard from within the budget process itself. In 1985, a report from the House Ways and Means Committee complained that "the budget process has become self-executing, and there are no decisions or choices left for the legislature. Formulas and other requirements are self-perpetuating . . ." (quoted in State Reorganization Commission, 1985b: 2).

Reorganization Commission Report

It was in that atmosphere that the Reorganization Commission produced its report. Submitted in June, 1985, it addressed a number of issues, including revenue analysis, revenue estimating, the shared nature of the budget sequence, and — most significantly — it reinforced the new interest in reshaping the state's unwieldy budget document to address planning and management — as well as control — functions.

It was the latter consideration which led to the most immediate legislative reaction. The Ways and Means Committee, trying to find ways to break out what many of its members felt was a budgetary strait-jacket, took the first step.

A proviso in the 1984-85 General Appropriation Bill, initiated by Rep. Jennings G. McAbee and supported actively by Reps. Herbert Kirsh and future chairman Rep. Robert N. McLellan, called on the Reorganization Commission to develop efficiency and effectiveness measures for each state agency (Section 167, S.C. General Appropriation Bill, 1984-85).

While the provision seemed to some to be a tiresome repeat of the 1978 requirement for the development of effectiveness measures (abandoned two years later), the Commission chose to use it as an opportunity to reopen the entire issue of program budgeting and the format of the budget document.

Through lengthy orientation meetings with each agency, the Reorganization Commission separated itself from the 1978 effort by requiring that performance indicators not be established on the basis of organizational units of the agency; they would instead be based on "program" as tied to the statutory missions of the agency. For each statutorily-defined "program," a mission statement, goals and objectives would then be developed, on which performance indicators would be based.

The process required a great deal of simulation of data, because the indicators did not, in many instances, correspond to the organizational structure of the agency; they instead corresponded to the program as defined by statutory mission. Similarly, cost data was not readily available to support the program-oriented indicators because the state's traditional data requirements were expenditure-based and oriented only to the agency's organizational structure.

The result was a clear departure from past efforts. While its assignment had not primarily been the development of a new budget format, the Commission's presentations clearly pointed in that direction. Its reports stimulated enough support (and curiosity) not only to continue refining the development of its indicators, but to give its proposed budget format a "test run."

The first "pilot" of the format involved eight agencies who volunteered for the assignment, and gave legislators their first look at a format which was radically different from the traditional control document. It carried "program data," based on statutory mission, goals, objectives and indicators, side-by-side with rolled-up expenditure and fund source data for the same program. Legislators were thus given an opportunity to compare funding input (expenditures) with program output (service delivery costs). Because the programs as defined in the Reorganization project did not always conform to agency organization, and because only expenditure data was available for many of the programs, much of the data represented estimates and simulations. But the exercise nonetheless constituted a serious — if somewhat primitive — effort to fulfill the elusive goal articulated by Governor Cooper in the state's first budget in 1920, to define and quantify the "unit of activity" on which budgeting could be based.

The "pilot" provoked mixed reactions, but sustained enough interest among its supporters to lead to a second year of effort, and an expansion of the project to 15 agencies. Subsequently, a third year of piloting was added, reflecting a strategy of increasing participation gradually so as to gain support and add to the learning experience, without straining either the political or manpower tolerances of the existing system.

The third year of the pilot effort brought a growing level of interest and participation from Ways and Means members and staff, as well as budget analysts from the Budget and Control Board. The strategy of gradualism began to pay dividends as reform of the state's budget format and document began to gain converts and stimulate the belief among many that change was in the wind.

Ways and Means Leadership. It was thus of particular significance that the report of the third year of piloting with the new format carried the imprimatur not of the Reorganization Commission, but of the House Ways and Means Committee. Building even more credibility for the seriousness with which legislators greeted the 1988 effort was a cover letter by Chairman McLellan which stated:

> The pilot project was initiated to find an alternative approach to the current budgeting process. The format being recommended addresses four specific areas of the budget document.
>
> 1. Condensing and simplifying much of the line-item expenditure detail in the present document.
>
> 2. Establishing statutorily authorized programs as the basis of agency budgets.
>
> 3. Requiring definitions of missions and objectives for each program.
>
> 4. Providing performance indicators by which effectiveness and cost of agency services may be identified and measured (S.C. House of Representatives, Program Budget, Progress Report, 1988: 1).

McLellan's letter represents what may be the strongest statement of support yet registered by the state's budget leaders for a specific form of "program budgeting." Coming in the context of Governor Campbell's earlier statements of support, it helps create what some believe may be the best conditions yet for change in the format and information base on which the state has

201

essentially based its budget decisions for 65 years.

The target date as set by law for the full implementation of the new program format is the 1989-90 fiscal year, but Chairman McLellan, in his submittal letter, wrote:

> The Committee recommends that the program budget be implemented in an orderly and careful transition, rather than . . . all at once as the law would require.
>
> Because of the problems and difficulties in developing the programs, missions and objectives and performance measures for the pilot agencies, the Committee feels that it is important to work out these problems before the new budget format replaces the current format.
>
> The Committee intends to expand the numbers of participating agencies each year and use the program budget for reviewing these agencies' funding requests. Eventually, all of the agencies would be done in the program budget format (Ways and Means, 1988: 2).

McLellan's restraint is viewed as evidence of his interest the development of a quality product which can stand the test of political scrutiny and the rigors of budget development. But even as McLellan's letter was beginning its circulation through the legislative halls, there was evidence that legislative ardor for line item details was not diminishing in some camps. Scarcely six weeks after McLellan's letter appeared, legislative debate erupted in the Senate over that most provocative of line-items: staff salaries.

The fight came in the waning days of consideration of the 1988-89 Appropriation Bill, and provoked from newsman Trip DuBard this tongue-in-cheek lead sentence: "Though it may not look it, the 5-inch thick 1988-89 state budget being reviewed by the Senate is missing a few things."

Finance Committee Chairman James M. Waddell defended the roll-up of legislative salaries, and was quoted as saying he thought "the budget is too bulky already and the information is extraneous to the central debate."

"I think the bill is awfully detailed," he said, but before the controversy had cooled, attorney Jay Bender had entered the fray to suggest that roll-ups of salaries "seem at odds with last year's strengthening of the state Freedom of Information Act" (Associated Press story carried in *The Charlotte Observer,* May 17, 1988: 1-B).

Thus the old debate over program budgeting vs. line-item expenditure detail continued through its seventh decade in South Carolina. There are a few new wrinkles, but the essential issues remain the same. The new format, with its program information and roll-up of expenditure detail, seems destined for a head-on collision with traditionalists who view line-item detail as the essence of responsible budgeting controls. As now projected, that day may come some time early in the 1990s, and while some claim that "legislators will never give up their line-item detail," others believe that new leadership in both the executive and legislative branches may carry the day.

Whatever the outcome, it may well be a pivotal point in the 68-year long development of South Carolina's budget process. If nothing else, it may settle a question which has remained unanswered since those earliest days, a question as to whether the State views budgeting as essentially an exercise in expenditure control, or whether it is prepared to extend the role of budgeting into more formal planning and management functions.

Conclusion

The development of South Carolina's current budget process has been evolutionary, rather than revolutionary. Unlike most other states, it has resisted the extension of budgetary authority to the Governor, just as it has rejected major organizational change of governmental agencies to accommodate centralized governmental budgeting. There have been a series of compromises between legislative and executive branches, retaining the characteristically strong legislative influence, and creating joint or shared authority where centralization or consolidation has occurred.

Only twice since direct budgetary authority was taken from the Governor in 1933 has a Governor undertaken to submit budget recommendations of his own. Once, in 1973, Governor West submitted budget recommendations to the General Assembly for usage of a "windfall" of federal moneys, above and beyond those of the Budget and Control Board, and most recently, Governor Campbell submitted his own budgetary recommendations to the Budget and Control Board for fiscal 1988-89 prior to the Board's own budgetary deliberations.

For the most part, however, the state's budget has been something of a composite of agency requests, built on early consensus of legislative and executive leadership. Such composite and consensual characteristics, in fact, have recently received some critical support from academician Bernard T. Pitsvada, who wrote that South Carolina's (and Mississippi's) "budget practices demonstrate rather ingenious methods to defuse budgetary conflict before it begins" (Pitsvada, 1988: 90).

In that kind of atmosphere, the development of South Carolina's current budget process has been slow and gradual, ever since its inception in 1920. Major changes have been structural (passage of the Budget Act, 1920, statutory establishment of the Budget Commission, 1933, and creation of the Budget and Control Board, 1950), and priority attention has been focused on developing accounting and reporting mechanisms to strengthen the state's ability to control expenditures.

Not until governmental growth swelled its budgeting documents to an enormous and unwieldy size in the late 1970s and 1980s did the state turn its attention seriously to the changing of a budget format which had traditionally been characterized by exceptionally detailed line-item expenditure data.

Experimentation with a new budget format, which rolls up the line-item detail into summaries, and presents new budget information in the context of program and service costs, promises to force the next major decision in the state's seven-decade-old pursuit of budget reform.

In its earliest days, budgeting provoked optimism and high expectations that it could somehow become a mechanically perfectible process. Times have changed, and rather than perfectibility, reformers now seek a budgeting process with the characteristics of adaptability and accommodation to changing times.

For that reason, budget reform itself will never be complete, but will continue to be a reliable measure of the fiscal mood and condition of the state, and of the overall political climate in which a state makes its budgetary and financial decisions.

References

Accomplishments and Record of Strom Thurmond (1954). Campaign Literature, 23 pp.

Bofferding, Louis (1976). *Limited Reconnaissance Review of Functions under the Budget and Control Board.* Campobello, S.C.: EJB Associates.

Campbell, Carroll A., Jr. (1987). *The State of the State.* Columbia, S.C.: Office of the Governor.

Coleman, James Karl (1935). *State Administration in South Carolina.* New York: Columbia University Studies in the Social Sciences.

Dennis, Rembert C. (1982). "South Carolina at the Crossroads," *Business and Economic Review.* Vol. No. 28, no. 6: 4-12.

Governor's Management Review Commission (1972). *Survey Report and Recommendations.* Columbia, S.C.: Governor's Management Review Commission Inc.

Griffenhagen and Associates Ltd. (1924). *Extracts from Report to the South Carolina Budget Commission of 1920.* Columbia, S.C.: South Carolina General Assembly, Joint Committee on Printing.

Grose, Philip G. Jr. (1987). "Budget Blues." *Business and Economic Review.* Vol. 33, No. 3: 27-31.

Haskins & Sells (1977). *Report of Findings Resulting from a General Survey of Financial Management Information Needs of the Executive Branch.* Columbia, S.C.: Haskins & Sells.

Knott, Jack H. and Gary J. Miller (1987). *Reforming Bureaucracy.* Englewood Cliffs, N. J. Prentice-Hall, Inc.

Moody's Investors Service, Inc. and Campus Facilities Associates (1968). *Opportunity and Growth in South Carolina, 1968-1985.* Moody's Investors Service Inc. and Campus Facilities Associates.

Peat, Marwick, Mitchell & Co. (1979). *State of South Carolina Budget Preparation System Requirements.* Prepared for the Comptroller General's Office, State of South Carolina. Columbia, S.C.: Peat, Marwick, Mitchell & Co.

Pitsvada, Bernard T. (1988). "The Executive Budget — An Idea Whose Time Has Passed." *Public Budgeting and Finance* 8 (Spring): 85-94.

South Carolina Budget and Control Board, (1987). *Annual Report (1986-87)*. Columbia, S.C. Budget and Control Board.

South Carolina General Appropriation Bill, 1984-85. Columbia, S.C.: South Carolina General Assembly.

South Carolina House of Representatives, Ways and Means Committee (1988). *Program Budget: Progress Report, FY 88-89*. Columbia, S.C.: South Carolina House of Representatives, Ways and Means Committee.

South Carolina Legislative Audit Council (1976). *The Problem of Dual Funding in State Government in South Carolina*. Columbia, S.C.: South Carolina General Assembly.

South Carolina Legislative Audit Council (1977). *A Study of the Impact of Federal and Other Funding on Legislative Oversight*. Columbia, S.C.: South Carolina General Assembly.

South Carolina Legislative Audit Council (1980). *A Review of Legislative Oversight in the State Budget Process*. Columbia, S.C.: South Carolina General Assembly.

South Carolina Preparedness for Peace Commission (1945). *Report to the Governor and Members of the General Assembly*. Columbia, S.C.: South Carolina Preparedness for Peace Commission.

South Carolina Senate, (1950). *Journal*. Columbia, S.C.: South Carolina Senate

South Carolina State Budget, (1920). Submitted to the General Assembly of South Carolina by Governor Robert A. Cooper.

South Carolina State Reorganization Commission (1985a). *The Budget Process in South Carolina: A Management Study*. Columbia, S.C.: State Reorganization Commission.

South Carolina State Reorganization Commission, (1985b). *The Budget Process in South Carolina: A Management Study, Report Summary*. Columbia, S.C.: State Reorganization Commission.

South Carolina State Reorganization Commission (1986). *Annual Report, 1985-86*. Columbia, S.C.: State Reorganization Commission.

Stoudemire, Robert H. (1977). "State Government Structure in South Carolina Since 1945." *University of South Carolina Governmental Review*. Vol. 19, No. 2: 1-4.

Tyer, Charlie B. and Joyce F. Prokop (1977). *A Framework and Policy Options for State Government Modernization*. Prepared for the Governor and the State Reorganization Commission, State of South Carolina. Columbia, S.C.: State Reorganization Commission.

Wallace, David W. (1951). *South Carolina: A Short History, 1520-1948*. Columbia, S.C.: University of South Carolina Press.

12

Managing South Carolina's Workforce: Policies for the Future

Steven W. Hays and Edwin Thomas

Introduction

Within a political environment dominated by truly controversial and foreboding policy dilemmas, the efficiency of governmental administration has only occasionally surfaced as a major public concern. Compared to the emotion-packed debates surrounding such topics as economic development, hazardous waste disposal and prison over-crowding, government's management performance is not an especially gripping issue.

In recent years, however, the administrative practices of public agencies have increasingly attracted the interest and scrutiny of politicians and a concerned citizenry. Among the factors that have contributed to this phenomenon are citizen frustration with prevalent taxing policies (the so-called "taxpayer revolt"), corresponding pressures upon politicians to reduce the tax burden, and the related belief that government is less efficient than the private sector. And, while purely mercenary considerations have served as the primary catalyst for changing public perceptions, there is also a growing realization among all elements of the political community that government's ability to respond to the challenges of contemporary society will be largely dependent upon the managerial capabilities of public institutions.

No public program — no matter how well conceived, designed or planned — can hope to succeed if it is ineffectively implemented or managed. This reality becomes increasingly important as state governments scramble for an

Steven W. Hays is a professor in the Department of Government and International Studies at the University of South Carolina. Edwin Thomas is a research associate in the Bureau of Governmental Research and Service at the University of South Carolina.

advantage in an intensely competitive environment. The ability of the State to acquire scarce federal dollars, to attract industry, and to upgrade its residents' quality of life directly depend upon the efficiency and effectiveness of governmental administration.

These widespread sentiments have generated unprecedented pressure upon politicians and public managers alike to make government perform more expeditiously, economically, and effectively. The term that has recently become the watchword of this movement in the public policy arena is *productivity*. Simply stated, the emphasis upon productivity improvement is an attempt "to do more with less," to increase output during a time of steady-state or even diminishing resources. Understandably, it is a time of great ferment in public management circles. Traditional methods of operation are being re-examined, orthodox approaches are being questioned, and the willingness to innovate is becoming more pervasive.

The purpose of this chapter is to detail the ways in which South Carolina's administrative machinery is responding to the productivity age. More specifically, it examines the steps that are being taken to enhance the morale, capability, and management tools of the State's civil servants. After a brief historical overview of the State's underlying managerial framework, several ongoing administrative innovations and reforms are catalogued and assessed. Although not an exhaustive treatment of such measures, the chapter provides insights into how a variety of disparate techniques can be brought to bear to promote a common objective — improving the performance of the State's public workforce.

The Managerial Framework: Historical Antecedents

Bluntly stated, South Carolina does not have an especially proud nor progressive public management history. Until very recently, the State generally followed a pattern that was characteristic of almost all of the states of the Old Confederacy — it was slow to adopt management innovations, electing to permit traditional administrative arrangements and practices to run their course. This traditionalistic management style is best exemplified in the way that the State responded to one of the most significant developments in the contemporary history of professional public administration, the emergence of merit systems.

Modern principles of public management first gained official recognition in 1883, with the passage of the federal Civil Service Act (the Pendleton Act). By introducing a merit system into the federal civil service, the Pendleton Act represented an immensely important victory for reformers who were intent upon wresting control of the civil service system from politicians. The concept of *neutral competence* gradually began to supplant party loyalty and political pay-offs as the chief currency of the public personnel system. Among the public management ideals that were embraced by this revolution were the following: (a) all public jobs are to be distributed on the basis of the *abilities* of the candidates, as determined through competitive examinations; (b) the personnel system is *open*, in that all citizens have a right to compete for public jobs on an impartial basis; and (c) employee retention and other job benefits are allocated on the basis of objective standards of *performance*.

Obviously, the adoption of a merit system by any governmental jurisdiction involves a number of significant trade-offs. The competence and professionalism of the workforce is presumably enhanced, thereby contributing to a more effective brand of public management. Additionally, the jurisdiction gains corresponding measures of continuity (offices don't change hands at each election) and objectivity (officials who do not owe their offices to a political patron or party are more likely to apply relevant laws and procedures in a strictly neutral fashion). In exchange, however, the jurisdiction surrenders large portions of two important management commodities, flexibility and accountability. Public employees who are insulated by an array of merit system protections are not necessarily responsive to political directives. And, since they do not directly rely upon political or public approval for raises and promotions, they may become somewhat "distant" and insensitive to demands arising from outside of the bureaucracy.

Despite the inherent tension between the competing needs for both competence and accountability, modern public administration firmly embraces the belief that merit systems are preferable to less formal approaches to staffing government agencies. Thus, the extent to which merit practices have penetrated a state's personnel system is a widely used measure of that jurisdiction's progressiveness, professionalism, and presumed managerial competence.

By this standard, South Carolina historically has been one of the least developed states in the nation. Most states long ago turned a deaf ear to the seductive siren calls of patronage,[1] opting instead for modern personnel systems grounded in the merit principle. By 1939, for example, twelve states had adopted merit selection systems for *all*[2] their employees. This trend was hastened in that same year due to the federal government's requirement that only merit-selected personnel could administer certain grant-in-aid programs. By the mid-1980s, thirty-six states utilized comprehensive merit systems (Greene, 1982: 53). The remaining states operated dual systems in which only a portion of the state workforce was recruited, selected, promoted, and evaluated within a formal merit framework (Birch, 1983: 117). South Carolina is a member of this latter group, in that its merit system coverage continues to be restricted to those employees who *must* be included pursuant to federal law.

In the absence of a comprehensive merit system, the staffing practices that predominated in South Carolina until recent times were anachronistic. As late as 1968, each agency functioned more or less independently in all personnel management spheres. There were no uniform classification or compensation plans, no systematic testing or recruitment activities, no centralized records management systems, and no standardized procedures for the adjudication of employee grievances against management.

This situation generated a plethora of administrative problems, not the least of which was a severe problem in internal pay equity. Due to the lack of a centralized compensation and classification system, employees performing essentially the same functions in different agencies often received widely disparate salaries. Moreover, many discrepancies existed in such "terms of employment" areas as holiday observance, annual leave requirements, transfer policies, sick leave, and other employee benefits. Likewise, many state employees were required to work a six-day week, as most public agencies remained open on Saturdays even though a number of surveys had demonstrated that "nothing meaningful was taking place on Saturday" (Ellis, 1980: 35). Raise and promotion decisions were often made according to the most idiosyncratic and/or arbitrary criteria, and the intrepid employee who sought to challenge such decisions was not provided with any recognized means to do so. Given this depressing state of affairs, it is not surprising that the state experienced serious difficulties in attracting and retaining qualified workers (Ellis, 1980: 14).

Substantial changes in the State's personnel management system finally began to appear in 1968, with the election of Governor Robert McNair. One of his chief administrative objectives was to "modernize" the civil service and to eliminate the internal equity problem that had grown to near-crisis proportions. Pursuant to that objective, by Executive Order he created the State Personnel Division (SPD) within the Budget and Control Board, and appointed F. Earl Ellis as the Division's first director.

Soon thereafter, a series of important "innovations" found their belated way into the public personnel system in South Carolina. Foremost among these was the adoption by the General Assembly of the Classification Act of 1968, by which a standardized pay plan was introduced into state government. The pay plan was necessarily preceded by a comprehensive classification study through which the state's more than 25,000 jobs were analyzed, allocated to graded compensation levels, and assigned (more or less) uniform titles and qualifications. Then, in 1971, medical support workers at the Medical University of South Carolina engaged in a work stoppage to protest the arbitrary dismissal of some fellow employees. When this dispute appeared to be the leading edge of a public unionization movement in the State, the General Assembly promptly passed the State Employee Grievance Act to defuse the crisis. As will be discussed more thoroughly later, this Act provides due process protections for employees who feel that they have been treated unfairly by state managers.

Other improvements in the state personnel system during this rapid process of reform included the initiation of the Employee Training and Development Section of the SPD in 1972, the creation of a much more generous health plan than had been in effect earlier (the Group Health and Medical Insurance Plan of 1972)[3], and the promulgation of a uniform Merit System Rule in 1974 to regularize personnel practices and procedures throughout merit system agencies. In 1975 the State Personnel Act elaborated the statutory foundation of the SPD by articulating the various staffing functions that are to be provided by the unit for the merit system agencies (e.g., Classification, Compensation, Employee/ Employer Relations, Recruitment, Testing, and Training). It is important to note in this regard that these functions are not necessarily performed centrally. For the most part, individual agencies are permitted wide discretion in many staffing areas, while the Division takes primary responsibility in only a few areas (e.g., testing for merit system positions, handling employee/employer relations problems that cannot be settled at the agency level). The proliferation of sections and units within SPD culminated in 1979 with the creation of the Data Management and Research Section, which was established to provide centralized personnel records retrieval.

Thus, by the mid-1980s, South Carolina's staffing apparatus had progressed to the point that it could justifiably be termed a "modern" personnel management system. Despite only limited coverage, the merit system management structure provided up-to-date staffing services to its member agencies, and also to non-member agencies that requested special assistance. In recognition of this fact, the name of the SPD was changed in 1984 to the Division of Human Resource Management (DHRM). The new title reflects the Division's expansive statutory charge to improve the quality and performance of state government by providing a multi-faceted array of employee development services. The following section brings the discussion up to date by providing an overview of how the state's personnel system functions today.

The Managerial Framework: The Current Management System

Despite the immense progress that has been made during the past two decades in modernizing the State's management infrastructure, the coverage of the merit system did not expand at all during this period. The personnel system remains a dual structure in which merit agencies are far outnumbered by those that are not formally contained within its provisions.

At present, approximately 10,500 of the State's 55,000 employees (including school system workers) are employed in merit agencies. This represents about 20% of the workforce, which is a very low proportion relative to the merit system coverage that exists in most other states. Among the many large state agencies (out of almost 200 agencies, boards and commissions) that are outside of the system are the Department of Wildlife and Marine Resources, the Department of Highways and Public Transportation (the largest state agency), the Department of Corrections, the university and technical college system (including the University of South Carolina, Clemson, the Citadel, and all other colleges and universities), the Department of Education, the Department of Mental Health, and the Department of Youth Services. As noted previously, the system's membership is limited to those agencies that are *required* by federal law to belong to a formal merit system. The ten agencies that are subject to this requirement are as follows:

S.C. Department of Social Services [Full Coverage]
S.C. Department of Health and Environmental Control [Full Coverage]
S.C. Employment Security Commission [Full Coverage]
S.C. Adjutant General's Office, Divison of Emergency Preparedness
S.C. Commission on Aging [Full Coverage]
S.C. Department of Labor [Data Management, OSHA, and Administration]
S.C. Commission on Alcohol and Drug Abuse [Partial Coverage]
S.C. State Budget and Control Board, Division of HRM
The Governor's Office, Health and Human Services Division
S.C. Health and Human Services Finance Commission [Full Coverage]

Given the unwillingness of other state agencies to join the merit system, it is tempting to imagine the worst when one speculates as to the conditions that prevail in non-merit agencies. Sweatshop style exploitation of employees and rampant politicization of the workforce through patronage appointments and party assessments (i.e., requiring civil servants to contribute to political parties) are the consequences that we have been taught to expect where merit requirements are absent. Thankfully, however, the management and staffing practices that exist in non-merit agencies are not significantly different from those in the ten merit units. In effect, the influence of modern human resource management practices extends far beyond the confines of the formal merit system.

Although state merit requirements constitute the strictest and most explicit staffing procedures in South Carolina, they are by no means the only source of standards governing the conduct of the public personnel function. Obviously, all state agencies are required to adhere to federal guidelines covering recruitment practices (Civil Rights Act of 1964, Equal Employment Opportunity Act), wages and salaries (Equal Pay Act, Fair Labor Standards Act), and the treatment of aged and handicapped workers (Age Discrimination Act, Vocational Rehabilitation Act).

Closer to home, the coverage of the state's Classification Act extends to over 85% of the workforce, thereby ensuring that a (more or less) uniform set of requirements controls entry qualifications, pay, and job titles throughout government agencies. All classified employees, regardless of their agencies' merit status, are treated equally by the General Assembly in the allocation of salary increases and benefits. Similarly, all classified employees are entitled to utilize the legal machinery provided by the State Employee Grievance Act. Unclassified employees, meanwhile, are generally able to avail themselves of grievance rights within adjudicatory procedures established by their employing agencies (which, for the most part, are the state's colleges and universities).

While it is difficult to generalize about the specific staffing practices that exist in non-merit agencies, a few truisms can be identified. Large state agencies have established, by necessity, elaborate internal personnel offices which are generally operated in a highly professional manner. These units supply line managers with a full range of staffing services, including recruitment and selection (advertising positions, testing, interview referrals), employee orientation and training, and employee/employer relations (i.e, counseling managers and workers concerning their rights and obligations in labor/management disputes). As will be discussed below, a number of agency personnel offices have also branched out into such innovative areas as employee assistance programs and health styles management.

Smaller state agencies exhibit a far greater variation in their approaches to staffing and human resource management. Because it does not become cost-effective to create a specialized personnel office until an agency reaches a critical mass of about 150 employees, a number of small agencies make do with part-time and/or under-staffed personnel units. An obvious consequence of this arrangement is that the range of services that is provided probably declines in direct proportion to the size of the operation. It must be assumed that the bulk of personnel activity in these agencies is devoted to ensuring compliance with state and federal staffing guidelines. The seriousness of this potential shortcoming is minimized by the fact that most smaller agencies recruit on a "vacancy basis." That is, they only recruit and select when a vacancy occurs, in contrast to the merit system practice of continually recruiting and testing applicants, maintaining registers of qualified candidates, and referring candidates to the managers who will make the ultimate appointment decisions. Due to the small scale of vacancy-by-vacancy recruitment, agencies do not need to maintain an aggressive staffing infrastructure in order to meet their immediate personnel needs. Their ability to deliver any services beyond the bare essentials, however, is seriously compromised in such a setting.

A strategy that a few agencies have followed to upgrade their staffing efforts is to *contract* with the Division of Human Resource Management for some of the services that they are unwilling or unable to provide internally. Five agencies, for example, contract with DHRM for recruitment services. DHRM advertises positions, tests applicants, and refers candidates to the relevant unit in exchange for a flat fee based on the total number of employees within the contracting agency. More specialized arrangements have also been devised to accommodate unusual circumstances. The Department of Corrections, for example, must annually screen a huge number of prospective candidates for the position of Correctional Officer Trainee. To expedite this ongoing task, the Department negotiated a special arrangement at an extremely low cost; DHRM tests all applicants for that one job classification, and charges only $4 for each test that is administered.

An obvious question at this point in the discussion is: "Why don't more agencies enter the merit system, or at least contract with DHRM for recruitment services?" Although each agency could probably offer a different explanation for going it alone, three factors impede the expansion of merit system coverage. First, most agencies simply do not need the level of services that DHRM is prepared to provide. Because their recruitment and selection needs are minimal, vacancy based hiring is a suitable (if not optimal) staffing strategy. Moreover, recruitment and testing services can be prohibitively expensive. DHRM bases its fee for recruitment services on the total number of employees in the using agency; the figure currently is $65 per employee. For many agencies, this is too heavy a burden for a service that can often be provided internally (albeit, with varying levels of effectiveness).

The final impediment is probably the most troublesome for purists who wish to promote blanket merit coverage. Stated simply, most non-merit agencies are reluctant to join the system because membership carries with it a number of additional staffing restrictions. Under the merit appointment rule, for example, the hiring authority must select a candidate from among the top twenty "eligibles" on the placement register.[4] This contrasts with the virtually unrestrained discretion that can be exercised by managers making appointments outside of the merit system requirements. Moreover, the managers' freedom of action is further constrained by similar types of restrictions in the various functional staffing areas, most especially in regard to classification and compensation. To the practicing manager, then, the merit system almost surely is perceived as another layer of bureaucracy that ought to be avoided. Consequently, it would be naive to anticipate any pronounced increase in the scope of merit system coverage.

In effect, then, South Carolina's political establishment has elected to employ a hybrid management system that combines elements of both traditional and modern staffing formats. An unusually high level of managerial flexibility is maintained, owing in large part to the absence of any pervasive set of exceptionally prohibitive merit requirements. Additionally, the decentralized nature of the personnel system provides individual state agencies with extraordinarily wide latitude in the operation of their staffing activities. Compared to the situation in most other governmental settings, South Carolina's public managers truly enjoy a high level of discretion in hiring and related personnel decisions. Although widespread politicization has not surfaced in recent times as the price for this flexibility, it remains a potential threat merely because of the limited number of protections that exist outside of the formal merit system.

Within recent decades, a number of important buffers have evolved between the State's management infrastructure and the more intrusive influences of partisan politics. Thanks largely to the impact of the personnel system changes that are detailed above, the quality of the public workforce has increased substantially over the years. This increase in the employees' level of technical competence has been coupled with a heightened sense of professionalism, which undoubtedly inhibits the politicization of management. And, notably, the State's administrative and political leaders have encouraged the modernization of managerial practices through a variety of innovative programs. In the following section, a representative sample of these managerial initiatives is described and assessed.

Policies For The Future

Having been a managerial backwater for much of contemporary history, South Carolina's journey into the administrative mainstream has been unexpectedly smooth and rapid. Although the process of modernization has only recently begun, the State's public managers have made enormous strides in refining and perfecting their administrative machinery. Over the past two decades, innovations and reforms have touched almost every facet of management practice. One way to gain a partial appreciation for the transformation that has taken place is to survey the management programs that are currently in operation, as well as some that are now being planned and/or implemented within state government. To structure the discussion, the various administrative initiatives are divided into three broad and overlapping groups: Staffing Innovations, Productivity Enhancement Activities, and Employee Development Efforts.

Staffing Innovations

Like almost all central personnel offices, the State Division of Human Resource Management (DHRM) once seemed more concerned with *policing* the merit system than with serving as a resource and aid for line managers. In recent years, however, the pressure for increased governmental efficiency has altered the underlying philosophy of the staffing function. The current emphasis is on easing the restrictions that apply to various personnel management activities, and on working together with operational managers in enhancing their effectiveness. For this reason, a number of activities that were traditionally handled in the central office have been delegated to the agencies. DHRM, meanwhile, has begun to concentrate upon fine-tuning the staffing functions that it shares with the agency personnel offices.

Some of the most significant refinements have occurred in DHRM's recruitment and selection programs. A simple example serves to illustrate how the agency is striving to abandon its role as *regulator* in preference to that of *facilitator*. Under the old staffing format, applicants who were on a register for particular classes of jobs (i.e., those who had passed the relevant merit exam and been certified as eligible for placement) were required to *reapply each year* if they were not immediately selected for employment. For obvious reasons, this requirement tended to discourage applicants. In response, it — and a large number of similar impediments — has been eliminated from merit system procedures.

In addition to cleansing the personnel system of unreasonable staffing constraints, many imaginative selection strategies have recently been introduced. A special effort is being made to tailor tests to the peculiar needs of individual state agencies. The Department of Education, for example, uses an *assessment center* format for the selection of school principals. This device is based on the widely accepted premise that multiple evaluation methods are necessary to judge abstract traits such as leadership, initiative, resistance to stress, and judgment. Applicants are consequently exposed to a battery of evaluation strategies, including group exercises, management games, written exams, oral presentations, and in-basket simulations (Ross, 1979).

Relatedly, the Alcoholic Beverage Control Commission, Department of Youth Services, and Parole and Community Corrections Department have all contracted with DHRM to design performance-based tests for a number of jobs that require specific types of physical ability and/or agility. Wildlife officers, for instance, are subjected to an obstacle course that contains swimming as one of its components. DHRM has also developed a sign language test for applicants interested in working for the South Carolina School for the Deaf and Blind. In order to provide greater access to state jobs for all of South Carolina's citizens, many merit examinations are available in braille, and special provisions (such as regularly scheduled and assisted test administrations) are made for handicapped persons who wish to apply for civil service positions.

Another interesting trend in the staffing arena is the increasing application of videotape technology to the selection process. Examinations for some classes of workers are administered on videotape, a technique that reduces costs and which ensures that all applicants receive a standardized set of instructions. Additionally, a videotaped message is used by the Department of Corrections to provide applicants with a realistic sense of what the job of Correctional Officer actually entails. The 30-minute tape — which provides a brutally frank overview of prison life — is intended to encourage attrition among Correctional Officer aspirants who were not fully aware of the demanding nature of the jobs they were considering. In so doing, the tape may save the State the considerable expense of selecting and training employees whose tenure within the Department would have been short lived.

The State's managers are equally interested in improving the quality of the applicant pool upon which selection decisions depend. Three major initiatives are ongoing in this area. The state's first manpower forecasting study commenced in 1988, with the introduction of a semi-annual personnel needs assessment survey. This program is intended to identify hard-to-fill positions so that the State's recruitment energies can be targeted on the areas of greatest need. The survey instrument requires agencies to predict attrition rates by job category, and to identify any positions that may need special Affirmative Action/Equal Employment Opportunity efforts to fill. Once the results of this survey are compiled, state recruiters can make better informed decisions concerning visitations to educational institutions, attendance at "career days," and related "advertising" efforts. Moreover, the state's ongoing career counseling program, by which applicants for state positions receive free advice concerning professional opportunities, can also be used more effectively to channel workers into high-need job categories.

An important supplement to the forecasting effort is CASIS, the Centralized Applicant Skills Inventory System. CASIS is a computerized, on-line recruitment system which links applicant credentials to the vacancy notices provided by agencies from throughout state government. Upon becoming operational in the Summer of 1988, CASIS replaced an antiquated and cumbersome file-card system. It is expected to expedite the retrieval of personnel files, and to greatly enhance DHRM's ability to match qualified applicants with available openings.

For upper-level positions, DHRM operates a relatively sophisticated Executive Search Program (ESP) that provides agencies with the full range of recruitment services. Boards and commissions that elect to use ESP need only to define their broad recruitment priorities; DHRM then coordinates all related activities. It advertises the vacancy, pre-screens applicants, develops a tailored selection format (structured interviews, assessment center, etc.), conducts a thorough background check, makes an appropriate salary recommendation, and arranges candidate interviews and visits (Middleton, 1988). To date, fifteen executive searches have been successfully concluded through

217

the ESP. Of these, ten involved agency directors and the remainder dealt with deputy directors and other upper-level workers.

Productivity Enhancement Activities

The second set of management innovations focuses less on people than it does on the work processes and procedures that are utilized within state government. Virtually all state agencies are currently engaged in aggressive efforts to improve their management capacities. Among the many types of administrative changes that are being implemented and/or considered are: *structural improvements* involving the reconfiguration of functional and programmatic departments; *staffing analyses,* which are designed to evaluate the efficacy of existing supervisory patterns, reporting relationships, and manning ratios;[5] *social audits,* which are intended to inventory the skills and abilities of agency personnel with an eye toward making better use of the available human resource pool; and *organizational development efforts,* the majority of which are used to identify and remedy organizational factors (e.g., poor communication networks, inappropriate structural framework, interpersonal dilemmas) that inhibit work performance.

Obviously, activities of this nature are difficult to examine thoroughly because they are so varied and diffuse. For this reason, only broad generalities can be offered to characterize the many efforts that are occurring in the area of productivity improvement. As one nationally recognized expert on the topic expresses it, organizational efforts to enhance productivity inevitably occur in one of three spheres: "working smarter" [rearranging the timing or flow of work]; "working harder" [increasing individual or group effort]; and "working better" [the use of new technology or materials] (Balk, 1976: 177).

While state agencies have probably made strides in all three areas, the greatest progress has most certainly occurred in the technological arena. A lion's share of any increased efficiency that may have been gained in recent years is undoubtedly attributable to the automation of routine work. According to most productivity studies, however, most of the gains that we can hope to extract from automation have *already* accrued, and the point of diminishing returns may be upon us. Therefore, the two alternative strategies for productivity improvement will represent more attractive targets of opportunity for the foreseeable future.

Not surprisingly, this is where the bulk of the State's productivity enhancement energies are being devoted today. Improvements in the timing and flow of work ["working smarter"] are the intended target of the structural and work process changes that are mentioned above, while social audits, organizational development efforts, and staffing analyses are expected to increase individual and group efforts ["working harder"]. Common examples of how these concepts are translated into workplace reality abound. Many state agencies, for instance, make widespread use of flexible employee work schedules ("flextime") as a means to improve worker morale while gaining the advantage of better office "coverage." The State's Employee Suggestion Program has similar objectives, in that it provides financial rewards to workers who propose cost-saving and/or safety-enhancing alterations in state policies and procedures (*ESP Manual*, 1988). And, notably, increasing numbers of agencies are using the services of professional consultants to orchestrate and direct management reforms, mostly in the "working smarter" vein. An important precursor to this development has been the tendency on the part of many agencies to abandon much of their traditional reluctance to engage in self-examination and criticism. Although large bureaucracies have a notorious reputation for being secretive and defensive, an amazing degree of openness and responsiveness to change seems to be evolving in much of the state's labor force.

A noteworthy indication of the state government's commitment to productivity enhancement can be found in the recent creation of the Productivity Management Section within DHRM. Established in 1984 to "promote the efficient and effective use of human resources in State government" (Budget and Control Board, 1987: 102), the Section offers consultative services on a contractual basis to any requesting public agency. In so doing, it uses intervention and evaluation methodologies that are similar to those employed by the U.S. General Accounting Office, the federal government's primary management assessment agency. Although it was originally intended to review agency personnel practices, the Section's mission quickly expanded to include a full range of management consulting activities. Its professional staff offers low-cost assistance in such areas as (Productivity Management Section, 1988):

- Analyzing work load and staffing levels and recommending the reallocation of resources to objectives of higher priority;
- Identifying cost savings by detailed analysis of program operations;
- Surveying employees and clients to determine obstacles to increased productivity and goal accomplishment;
- Establishing systems to ensure the achievement of goals and objectives; and
- Identifying outdated laws, regulations, and procedures to eliminate unnecessary work.

Employee Development Efforts

The "working harder" approach to productivity improvement is especially evident in a number of programmatic initiatives that are intended to increase employee competence, motivation and morale. Those that are aimed at developing worker skills and abilities occur primarily under the rubric of "training," and include a diverse array of educational opportunities that are sponsored either by individual agencies or the DHRM. Since 1972 the state personnel department has operated the Staff Development and Training Section, which offers a curriculum focusing largely on management development and supervisory skills. Both open enrollment and in-house training programs are available on such varied topics as employee evaluation strategies, fundamentals of supervision, interviewing, labor-management relations, word processing, and secretarial skills. The scale of such efforts is impressive. During the 1986-1987 fiscal year, for example, the Section conducted 183 training programs that were attended by nearly 4500 public workers. When one considers the fact that most of the larger state agencies also operate their own training programs for their workers — with many employing full-time trainers — it becomes obvious that employee development is now a much higher priority than once was the case.

In addition to providing educational opportunities to its workers, state government has recently begun to pay more attention to other factors that promise both to stimulate greater employee effort and to generate better morale among the workforce. Progress has been made in a number of specific areas, including employee evaluation, compensation, and the resolution of labor-management disputes.

Employee Evaluation: The search for a fair and effective means of evaluating worker performance has preoccupied managers for decades. In addition to providing critical information on which most major staffing decisions are based (raises, promotions, transfers), performance evaluations furnish workers with a formal measure of their worth to the organization. For these reasons, few aspects of organizational life are as threatening and potentially troublesome as is the appraisal process.

Over the years, virtually all performance evaluation strategies have been criticized for their vulnerability to a number of potentially fatal pitfalls. The most serious of these is simply the fact that evaluations do not measure true *performance*, but instead merely assess personality characteristics and other subjective factors that should not be relevant to the staffing decisions. Negative by-products that result include perceptions of supervisory favoritism among workers, reduced motivation due to the inability of the organization to recognize superior performance, and a corresponding reduction in the authority that managers are able to wield over their subordinates. For obvious reasons, reduction or elimination of such problems has assumed immense importance as public managers strive to improve worker productivity.

Many of the common failings of performance evaluation have been ameliorated in the appraisal format adopted in South Carolina state government in 1982. A major advantage of the the Employee Performance Management System (EPMS) is that it offers public managers a great deal of *flexibility* in tailoring the evaluation instrument to each employee's particular work situation. Instead of evaluating all workers on an identical set of traits — a characteristic of many evaluation instruments — EPMS requires that the supervisor and evaluatee engage in a planning session at the beginning of the review cycle. During this session, the two agree on the specific job duties, performance characteristics, and work objectives that will be assessed at the end of the one year cycle (Appendix). The process ensures that the evaluation is based on relevant job factors that are performance-based. These advantages are further promoted by the availability of extensive training programs that supervisors are encouraged to undergo before they use the EPMS in evaluating subordinates. Although the system is by no means perfect,[6] it is far superior to past evaluation techniques, and compares very favorably with the most progressive appraisal techniques in use in other states.

Another encouraging advance in the general area of employee evaluation and development is the recent appearance of *employee assistance programs* in a few of the larger agencies. These programs offer supervisors a welcome helping hand in dealing with workers who are troubled by stress-related illnesses, alcohol or drug addiction, or other types of personal problems that require the intervention of trained health professionals. Employees who suffer from such problems can either be referred by their supervisors or, more commonly, seek help independently. In addition to providing counseling services, most employee assistance programs sponsor workshops and seminars on many self-improvement topics, including stress management, weight control, and the elimination of the smoking habit. Programs of this type are quickly becoming a fixture in public and private organizations throughout the country because they have been shown both to enhance employee performance *and* to increase workforce morale.

Compensation: Considerable effort has also been invested in the design and study of compensation systems that reduce employee turnover and foster motivation. Consistent with trends in compensation reform throughout the nation (Perry, 1988), the State has emphasized *pay for performance*. This involves the linking of salary levels and raises to objective measures of performance, rather than to longevity or other non-merit factors.

Of particular note in this regard is the pay for performance plan that is applied to all agency heads. Prior to its establishment, agency head salaries were determined through the political process as items in the line-item budget. There was no formal evaluation process, a factor which contributed to wide disparities and inequities among agency heads. In addition to damaging the executives' morale, the situation resulted in unusually high turnover at the highest level of state government.

Implemented in 1983, the agency head pay plan is truly unique (Johnson, 1988). As an initial step, a private consulting firm was retained to recommend equitable and competitive salary ranges for all of the state's agency heads. These recommendations were subsequently adopted by the General Assembly. Once a measure of equity had been introduced to the agency head salary scheme, a plan was devised to ensure that future increases be allocated on a fair and reasonable basis.

The plan calls for members of state boards and commissions to receive training concerning the purposes and methodologies of modern compensation practices, as well as in devising appropriate evaluation standards. With that background, planning sessions are conducted between the commission or board and the relevant agency head. The agency directors are ultimately evaluated according to the standards that are identified during the planning stage. The boards and commissions make their ultimate salary recommendations to a newly created Agency Head Salary Commission. Composed of seven legislators and three laypersons appointed by the Governor, the Salary Commission has final responsibility for allocating the raise pool among all the state's agency heads. Through this novel mechanism, political factors have largely been excised from salary determinations, while both equity and merit considerations have been introduced.

Although much discussion has also taken place concerning the application of a true merit pay system to rank and file public employees, final legislative approval has thus far proven to be elusive. Under present compensation practices, annual salary increases are usually allocated on an across-the-board basis. If merit increments are provided for in the enabling legislation, they usually comprise only a small portion (perhaps 20%) of the pay package. This probably has a minimal effect on worker motivation, and may even serve as an irritant because it requires supervisors to make difficult choices when the rewards that they are distributing are embarrassingly inadequate.

In an attempt to address this problem, the State has commissioned several exploratory examinations of alternative pay plans. The most recent study occurred in 1986, when a committee of employees was appointed to formulate a pay for performance plan for all of state government. The committee's proposal would have essentially eliminated automatic salary increases by putting all available funds in a raise pool. Supervisors would have complete control over the allocation of the merit raises, within legislatively mandated ranges. For example, if the pool consisted of an average four percent raise, then supervisors might be able to assign raises from 0% to 8%. Such decisions would be based on the results of EPMS reviews, and would all occur at the same time each year in order to simplify administration of the plan.

Although this proposal is consistent with the way that merit pay plans generally operate in other jurisdictions, it did not generate much enthusiasm among state workers. Opposition arose on a number of fronts. Employees based outside of Columbia expressed concern that "they may not get a fair shake" in salary allocations because preference would be given to those working near the agency headquarters, almost all of which are in the state capital (Johnson, 1987). Also, many employees were apparently fearful that bias and favoritism would intrude into the process and distort its results. The study committee attempted to alleviate some of these concerns by including an extensive supervisory training component in the proposal, but were unsuccessful in establishing even a pilot project. The plan passed the House, but was defeated in the Senate due partly to a lobbying effort mounted by the State Employees' Association. Despite this momentary setback, however, merit pay continues to be a frequently mentioned priority of important decisionmakers in state government. Given this fact, it is likely to stay on the policy agenda until a more acceptable approach to pay for performance is devised.

Protection of Employee Rights: A seldom-mentioned prerequisite to a dedicated and motivated workforce is the need for managers to respect their employees' legal and professional rights. Workers who are free from arbitrary and capricious supervisory actions can, for obvious reasons, be expected to exhibit more organizational loyalty and commitment than those who do not enjoy such a labor-management environment.

As was discussed earlier in this chapter, a reliable means of redressing grievances against management did not exist in South Carolina until 1971, when the State Employee Grievance Act was passed. That Act created a procedure which enables employees to present their side of labor-management disputes to an impartial authority.[7] Under provisions of the Act, employees are permitted to grieve demotions, dismissals, suspensions, transfers in excess of fifteen miles, involuntary reassignments, and certain other "adverse actions." They are expressly precluded from filing grievances over pay and classification issues.

The grievance system currently operates as follows. Employees who believe that their procedural or constitutional rights have been infringed must first attempt to resolve the dispute internally. Although situations in different agencies vary, the first avenue of appeal is usually to the employee's supervisor. From there, the appeal is carried to the supervisor's own superior, and ultimately to the agency head.

In the event that no mutually agreeable resolution can be found within the agency, the Act requires that the two parties mediate the dispute. This process is handled by the DHRM's Employee/Employer Relations Section, which interprets relevant legal requirements and assigns a mediator who attempts to resolve the dispute informally. If mediation fails, then the grievance is submitted to the State Employee Grievance Committee. Composed of state employees who are appointed by the Budget and Control Board, the Committee conducts a formal adjudicatory hearing and issues a final and binding decision.

Data from the Employee/Employer Relations Section indicate that about 100 grievances are litigated annually. Of these, more than 50% are usually resolved during mediation, while the remainder are forwarded to the Grievance Committee. In general, about 40% of the employees who have their cases heard by the Committee are successful, meaning that agencies ("the State") win about 60%.

The mere existence of a formalized adjudicatory process ensures that managers and supervisors will be less inclined to treat employees arbitrarily. This reality is reinforced by a number of related developments. To sensitize supervisors concerning the need for fair treatment of all workers, the State sponsors numerous training programs on the legal environment of management. Moreover, state agencies are required to compile personnel manuals that specify the rights and obligations of employees and supervisors alike. An important component of these manuals is the *progressive discipline* procedure, which identifies various punishable offenses and prescribes the appropriate remedies. Notably, recent judicial decisions have concluded that these personnel manuals constitute legal contracts which cannot be violated by either party (management or labor) without invading a contractual guarantee. In effect, then, public managers are contractually obligated to honor the due process rights of their subordinates. Since failure to do so can result in agency liability, there is a strong incentive to abide by all relevant procedural requirements.

Conclusion

As this discussion hopefully has demonstrated, South Carolina has made enormous progress over the past two decades in upgrading its administrative infrastructure. Although much work remains to be done in areas such as merit system coverage, that fact does not detract from the reality of what has been accomplished. One of the most traditional and archaic management systems in the nation has been transformed to the point that it compares favorably with those of the most advanced states in the region. And, perhaps more importantly, the State has demonstrated a willingness to continue the experiment. New and better ways of managing the State's workforce are continually sought and eagerly awaited. Given this state of affairs, further improvements will certainly follow.

Notes

[1]Although patronage is no longer a generalized phenomenon in public personnel systems, a portion of *every* state's workforce consists of patronage appointees. Governors and other influential political figures ordinarily may appoint a significant number of policymaking personnel, as well as "confidential" employees (primarily secretaries), without having to follow merit procedures.

[2]The term "all" applies to the classified civil service system. It does not relate to the political and confidential appointees mentioned in Note 1.

[3]Prior to the adoption of this plan, the State's health plan consisted of little more than a group insurance policy which offered only a small discount over private, individual coverage.

[4]This so-called "rule of 20" provides public managers with much more discretion than comparable rules in many jurisdictions. For example, the most common appointing procedure is to require that a candidate be selected from among the top *three* finishers on the merit exam (the "rule of 3"). Other variations include rules of five and ten, but seldom is a rule of 20 utilized.

[5]Manning ratios are determined by assessing the "usual" or "standard" mix of employees within a given unit or service area. For example, agencies attempting to determine if they are over-staffed in a particular field office may perform a study to ascertain the staffing pattern in comparable offices in other jurisdictions. In this manner, general staffing "ranges" or ratios (of managers to workers, workers to clients, and the like) are determined.

[6]No method of performance evaluation is ever universally applauded by managers and workers. The EPMS is sometimes criticized for being unwieldy, difficult to complete, time-consuming, and the like. More frequently, managers complain that the actual evaluation that is given has no effect on an employee's salary (because of the absence of merit money in the pay package), thereby making the evaluation process somewhat vacuous.

[7]Members of the Grievance Committee are appointed by the Budget and Control Board from among the state workforce. Thus, it is composed entirely of state employees. According to some managers, this gives the Committee a decidedly pro-labor orientation. This accusation is not supported by the Committee's decision patterns, however.

References

Balk, Walter (1976). "Decision Constructs and the Politics of Productivity," in Marc Holzer (ed.) *Productivity in Public Organizations*. Port Washington, New York: Kennikat Press.

Birch, Harold (1983). "South Carolina State Government Administrative Organization: The Orthodox Theory of Administration Reexamined," in Luther F. Carter and David S. Mann (eds.) *Government in the Palmetto State*. Columbia, South Carolina: University of South Carolina Bureau of Governmental Research and Service: 115-135.

Corley, Charlene (1987). Interview conducted by Edwin Thomas; Employee Performance Management System, Division of Human Resource Management, Columbia, South Carolina, March 13.

Ellis, F. Earl (1980). Interview conducted by C. Blease Graham as part of the Governor Robert McNair Oral History Project, Columbia, South Carolina, March 21.

Greene, L. D. (1982). "Federal Merit Requirements: A Retrospective Look," *Public Personnel Management* 11 (Spring): 39-54.

Johnson, Paul (1987). Interview conducted by Edwin Thomas; Classification Section, Division of Human Resource Management, Columbia, South Carolina, February 24. Updated by Steven W. Hays, February 25, 1988.

Klimonski, R. and W. Strickland (1977). "Assessment Centers — Valid or Merely Prescient?" *Personnel Psychology* 30: 353-361.

Mason, Geoffrey (1987). Interview conducted by Edwin Thomas; Productivity Management Section, Division of Human Resource Management, Columbia, South Carolina, March 4. Updated by Steven W. Hays, February 23, 1988.

Middleton, Ernestine (1987). Interview conducted by Edwin Thomas, Recruitment Section, Division of Human Resource Management, Columbia, South Carolina, March 4. Updated by Steven W. Hays, February 24, 1988.

Pope, Sara (1987). Interview conducted by Edwin Thomas; Test Development Section, Division of Human Resource Management, Columbia, South Carolina, March 3. Updated by Steven W. Hays, March 1, 1988.

Productivity Management Section, South Carolina Division of Human Resource Management (1988). *Advertisement Circular — Productivity Services*. Columbia, South Carolina.

Pylant, Jill and Henry S. Domeracki (1980). "Personnel Administration in South Carolina Local Government — An Exploratory Study of Policies and Procedures." Columbia, South Carolina: University of South Carolina Bureau of Governmental Research and Service.

Ray, Jim (1984). "Assessing and Developing Leadership Potential: The South Carolina Assessment Center Program." *South Carolina School Board Association Journal* 5 (January): 29-32.

South Carolina Budget and Control Board (1987). *Annual Report 1986-1987*. Columbia, South Carolina: Budget and Control Board (July).

South Carolina State Personnel Division (1974). *Rule of the State of South Carolina Interagency Merit System*, Regulation No. 97-50.

Wallace, David (1961). *South Carolina: A Short History*. Columbia, South Carolina: University of South Carolina Press.

13

The Changing South Carolina Economy From 1950 To The Present

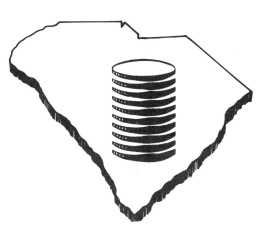

Richard W. Ellson

Introduction

Prior to World War II, the South Carolina economy was dominated by three factors. First, approximately 75 percent of the industrial work force was employed in textile mill products. The crucial role of the textile industry during this period is highlighted by the fact that one-fourth of the country's cloth and yarn was produced in South Carolina during the 1920 to 1941 period.

At the same time agriculture continued to be extremely important. Despite several setbacks cotton production was still reasonably strong, the tobacco industry had quadrupled its output in the past 30 years, and corn production was also significant. In terms of acreage, three-fourths of the agricultural land was in cotton or corn.

A third major factor of the period was the outmigration of the black population. Beginning in 1890 around 10 percent of the black population moved out of the state each year. Between 1890 and 1940 the percentage of blacks in South Carolina's total population fell from 60 percent to 43 percent.

Following World War II these conditions began to change, albeit slowly. More dramatic shifts in economic trends would not really occur until the 1960s. At this point a process of industrial diversification began, abetted by an inflow of foreign (mostly European) capital.

Richard W. Ellson is vice-president for Mortgage Systems Research with Bear, Stearns and Co., Inc., New York, New York. He was formerly associate professor of economics and associate director of the Division of Research, College of Business Administration, The University of South Carolina.

This period of industrial diversification continued through most of the 1970s, when for various reasons, the manufacturing sectors became increasingly vulnerable. At the same time, the service and tourism sectors began to exhibit very strong growth, and this period to the present could be characterized as one of economic diversification.

Although sweeping generalizations can often be hazardous, what follows will be a discussion of the postwar South Carolina economy defined in terms of the periods described above. An economic profile for each period will be presented, and key economic trends will be identified. Following this, some comments will be made regarding the South Carolina economy in the future.

The Postwar Period: 1950-1960

The period from the end of World War II to 1960 did not bring substantial changes to the South Carolina economy. Rather, it remained an economy dependent on textiles and agriculture, as it was prior to the war.

In 1950 total personal income in South Carolina was $1.93 billion, which represented 5.5 percent of the Southeast total and 0.86 percent of the national total. Per capita income was $914, and this was only 61.3 percent of the national average, which was about the same level as in 1860 prior to the Civil War. It had taken nearly a century to return to this level, and further advances toward the national norm remained years away.

Table 1
Personal Income
(millions of dollars)

	S.C	SE.	U.S.
1950	1,932	34,931	225,684
1955	2,654	47,982	307,601
1960	3,358	63,478	398,843
1965	4,774	89,246	536,152
1970	7,730	142,269	803,922
1975	13,140	241,996	1,258,643
1980	23,786	448,445	2,252,021
1985	35,434	677,970	3,310,545

Source: U.S. Department of Commerce, Bureau of Economic Analysis.

The manufacturing sector dominated state employment in 1950. Out of a total of 461,400 nonagricultural jobs, 210,400 jobs were in manufacturing.

Table 2
Per Capita Personal Income
(dollars)

	S.C	SE.	U.S.
1950	914	1,032	1,492
1955	1,206	1,355	1,872
1960	1,404	1,632	2,216
1965	1,914	2,132	2,772
1970	3,001	3,301	4,051
1975	4,631	5,112	6,069
1980	7,585	8,478	9,910
1985	10,586	11,989	13,867

Of course, textiles and apparel employment accounted for 32 percent of total nonfarm employment and 70 percent of all manufacturing jobs. Wholesale and retail trade (18 percent) and government (14 percent) were the next two largest employment sectors. Nothing else exceeded 10 percent.

Between 1950-1955, total nonagricultural employment increased by 15.5 percent. Note that this interval includes the recessionary period from the third quarter of 1953 to the second quarter of 1954. However, the manufacturing sector underperformed relative to the economy as a whole. Manufacturing employment rose 10 percent in the period, but textile and apparel employment only increased 8.1 percent. The largest gainers in percentage terms were finance, insurance, and real estate (60 percent), government (28 percent), and construction (21 percent).

Per capita income rose a sharp 32 percent during the period. After adjusting for inflation, this amounted to a gain of 15.5 percent. Compared to the national average, per capita income in South Carolina increased to 64.4 percent.

Nationally, the 1955-1960 period was characterized by fairly moderate economic growth. Another recession occurred from the fourth quarter of 1957 through the second quarter of 1958. By the fall of 1960, the economy was again falling into recession, and this no doubt aided the election of John F. Kennedy over Richard M. Nixon.

Accordingly, the South Carolina economy expanded at a modest rate during this period. Total nonagricultural employment rose by only 9.3 percent. Manufacturing and textile employment were even more sluggish with growth rates of 5.8 percent and 2.1 percent. The leading sectors were again finance, insurance and real estate, up 31 percent, government, and construction, both

Table 3
Nonagricultural Employment, Selected Industries
(thousands)

	Total	Manuf.	Textile Mill Product & App.	Trade	Gov't	Serv.	Const.	Trans., Comm. & Pub. Util.	Fin., Ins. & Real Est.
1950	461.4	210.4	146.7	81.9	64.2	42.7	24.3	26.5	10.2
1955	533.0	231.4	158.6	97.6	82.4	48.2	29.5	26.3	16.3
1960	582.5	244.8	162.0	103.1	96.1	55.5	34.6	25.5	21.3
1965	686.1	293.3	180.8	115.4	111.1	69.9	42.9	28.0	23.8
1970	842.0	340.3	193.0	141.8	149.9	89.2	51.5	37.5	29.7
1975	982.6	339.9	179.1	175.6	199.8	123.9	61.8	40.5	39.1
1980	1,188.8	391.9	183.3	225.1	236.4	159.3	73.4	53.0	47.7
1985	1,299.1	365.1	148.8	278.9	245.8	210.2	83.9	56.4	57.1

230

Table 4
The Structure Of Nonagricultural Employment, 1950-1985
(percentages)

	Total	Manuf.	Textile Mill Product & App.	Trade	Serv.	Const.	Trans., Comm. & Pub. Utl.	Fin., Ins., & Real Est.	Gov't
1950	100	46	(32)	18	9	5	6	2	14
1955	100	43	(30)	18	9	6	5	3	15
1960	100	42	(28)	18	10	6	4	4	16
1965	100	43	(26)	17	10	6	4	3	16
1970	100	40	(23)	17	11	6	4	4	18
1975	100	35	(18)	18	13	6	4	4	20
1980	100	33	(15)	19	13	6	4	4	20
1985	100	28	(11)	21	16	6	4	4	19

NOTE: The numbers on column 4 overstate the decline of textile employment, as some of the losses of Textile Mill Products and Apparel employment were covered by other textile-related industries (Synthetic Fibers, and Textile Machinery, e.g.).

231

up 17 percent. Per capita income adjusted for inflation grew at an annual rate of only 0.8 percent. South Carolina per capita income as a percentage of the Southeast and the U.S. fell from 89 percent and 64.4 percent in 1955 to 86 percent and 63.4 percent respectively in 1960.

In general then, the decade of the 1950s brought few significant changes to the structure of the South Carolina economy. Our relative position in the Southeast declined in per capita income terms from 88.6 percent to 86 percent. Conversely, there was marginal improvement compared to the national average (61.3 percent to 63.4 percent).

The nonagricultural economy was still dominated by the manufacturing sector, and particularly textile and apparel employment. In 1950 manufacturing accounted for 46 percent of all nonfarm employment, and by 1960, this had declined only to 42 percent. Comparable figures for textile and apparel employment were 32 percent and 28 percent.

It is interesting to note that a total of $1.23 billion in investment for new plants and plant expansions was announced during the period. This investment was supposed to generate 84,285 new jobs in the manufacturing sector. However, manufacturing employment increased by only 34,400 jobs in the decade. The disparity between announcements and actual jobs became more pronounced in later years.

While the nonfarm economy in South Carolina did not change rapidly in the period up through 1960, the agricultural sector was undergoing an interesting shift. Between 1950 and 1959 the number of farms in the state declined 44 percent from 139,000 to 78,000. In contrast the number of farms nationally dropped by 31 percent. Land for farming in South Carolina fell from 11.9 million acres to 9.1 million acres, a decline of 24 percent. For the nation as a whole, land in farming fell only 3 percent. The average size of a farm in the state rose from 85 acres to 117 acres versus 215 acres to 303 acres nationally.

Therefore, farm consolidations were quite severe in the state during this decade. However, there were not only fewer farms, but the total amount of land under cultivation dropped significantly as well. Yet, the average farm size remained well below the national average.

Total cash receipts from farm marketings ranged from $308 million in 1950, to $364 million in 1955, and dropping to $349 million in 1960. One can infer from this that it was the subsistence farmers who left the industry.

Moreover, this also reflects heavy outmigration of Blacks from the state in search of job opportunities in the expanding northern economies. From 1945-1960, the state's population rose only 13.2 percent versus 14.8 percent for the Southeast and 19 percent for the nation. It would be another decade until this trend was reversed.

Table 5
Five-Year Percent Change In Employment, Selected Industries
(percent)

	Total	Manuf.	Textile Mill Product & App.	Trade	Serv.	Const.	Trans., Comm. & Pub. Util.	Fin., Ins., & Real Est.	Gov't
1950-1955	+15.5	+10.0	+8.1	+19.2	+12.9	+21.4	−0.8	+59.8	+28.3
1955-1960	+9.3	+5.8	+2.1	+7.3	+15.1	+17.3	−3.0	+30.7	+16.6
1960-1965	+17.8	+19.8	+11.6	+11.9	+25.9	+24.0	+9.8	+11.7	+15.6
1965-1970	+22.7	+16.0	+6.7	+22.9	+27.6	+20.0	+33.9	+24.8	+34.9
1970-1975	+16.7	−0.1	−7.2	+23.8	+38.9	+20.0	+8.0	+31.6	+33.3
1975-1980	+21.0	+15.3	+2.3	+28.2	+28.6	+18.8	+30.9	+22.0	+18.3
1980-1985	+9.3	−6.8	−18.8	+23.9	+32.0	+14.3	+6.4	+19.7	+4.0

Table 6
S. C. Per Capita Personal Income as a Percentage
Of Per Capita Personal Income in the SE. and
the U.S.

	% of SE.	% of U.S.
1950	88.6	61.3
1955	89.0	64.4
1960	86.0	63.4
1965	89.8	69.0
1970	90.9	74.1
1975	90.6	76.3
1980	89.5	76.5
1985	88.3	76.3

Table 7
Number of Farms, Land in Farms, and
Average Farm Size

	Number of farms (thousands)		Land in farms (1,000,000 acres)		Average farm size (acres)	
	S.C.	U.S.	S.C.	U.S.	S.C.	U.S.
1950	139	5382	11.9	1158.6	85	215
1954	124	4782	11.1	1158.2	89	242
1959	78	3711	9.1	1123.5	117	303
1964	56	3158	8.1	1110.0	144	352
1970	52	2949	8.3	1102.4	160	374
1975	36	2491	6.8	1062.7	189	427
1980	34	2433	6.4	1038.9	188	427
1985	27	2285	5.5	1015.6	200	445

Source: U. S. Department of Agriculture, South Carolina Crop and Livestock Reporting Service;
County and City Data Book, several issues.

Table 8
Cash Receipts From Farm Marketings
(millions of dollars)

	From Livestock and Livestock Products	From Crops	Total Cash Receipts
1950	N/A	N/A	308
1955	N/A	N/A	364
1960	106	243	349
1965	119	276	395
1970	172	277	449
1975	257	550	807
1980	414	695	1,109
1985p	388	619	1,007

a: Government payments not included.
p: Preliminary.

Industrial Diversification: 1961-1975

The period from 1961 to 1975 was a particularly important one for the South Carolina economy. It was a time when the state's textile industry began to be exposed to Asian competition, initially the Japanese. Employment in the textile industry would peak during this period and begin what has become a sharp slide over the last 10 years.

However, it was during this time that the industrial sector of the South Carolina economy diversified, and accordingly, it was a period of rapid growth for the state. Not surprisingly, the state also had significant gains in terms of relative measures such as per capita income. Some have argued that much of the diversification was in fact textile related. Examples would include growth in the chemicals sector, some of which represented dyes used in textiles. However, although this argument is correct in a limited sense, it does not reflect the tremendous strides made during the period.

Between 1960-1965, South Carolina's population increased by only 4.3 percent compared to 7.6 percent for the Southeast and 7.5 percent for the nation. Similarly, in the 1965-1970 period the equivalent percentage increases were 4.2 percent, 5.1 percent, and 5.3 percent respectively. However, in the 1970-1975 period, these trends were reversed. South Carolina's population jumped by 11.6 percent, exceeding the Southeast growth rate of 10.9 percent and doubling the national rate of 5.7 percent. At this latter stage, South Carolina had clearly become a full-fledged participant in the so-called "sunbelt" population surge.

Table 9
Population
(thousands)

	S.C	SE.	U.S.
1950	2,113	33,860	151,235
1955	2,200	35,399	164,308
1960	2,392	38,885	179,954
1965	2,494	41,857	193,451
1970	2,598	43,974	203,799
1975	2,900	48,788	215,457
1980	3,136	52,894	227,255
1985	3,347	56,457	238,740

Source: BEA

Perhaps the best indicator of economic growth during this period was personal income. After adjusting for inflation personal income in South Carolina rose at annual rates of 5.8 percent in 1960-1965, 6.2 percent in 1965-1970, and 4.6 percent in 1970-1975. The latter figure of course includes the 1973-1975 recession which depressed that period's growth rate.

Table 10
Five-Year Percent Increase
In Population

	S.C	SE.	U.S.
1945-1950	10.0	9.9	13.4
1950-1955	4.1	4.5	8.6
1955-1960	8.7	9.8	9.5
1960-1965	4.3	7.6	7.5
1965-1970	4.2	5.1	5.3
1970-1975	11.6	10.9	5.7
1975-1980	8.1	8.4	5.5
1980-1985	6.7	6.7	5.1

Compared to the Southeast with annual growth rates of 5.5 percent, 5.9 percent, and 4.7 percent respectively, the state more than held its own. However, state growth far exceeded national gains of 4.6 percent, 4.6

Table 11
Annual Rates Of Growth, Real Personal Income
(percent)

	S.C	SE.	U.S.
1950-1955	4.0	3.9	3.8
1955-1960	2.5	3.5	3.0
1960-1965	5.8	5.5	4.6
1965-1970	6.2	5.9	4.6
1970-1975	4.6	4.7	2.9
1975-1980	4.8	5.3	4.6
1980-1985	3.2	3.5	2.9

Table 12
Real Personal Income
(millions of 1972 dollars)

	S.C	SE.	U.S.
1950	3,395	61,390	396,633
1955	4,121	74,506	477,641
1960	4,670	88,287	554,719
1965	6,184	115,604	694,497
1970	8,357	153,804	869,105
1975	10,487	193,133	1,004,504
1980	13,288	250,528	1,258,112
1985	15,534	297,225	1,451,357

NOTE: Series deflated by the implicit deflator for personal consumption expenditures.

percent, and 2.9 percent respectively.

Despite much faster population growth in the 1970-1975 period, stronger income gains enabled the state to improve dramatically relative to national norms in terms of per capita income. In 1960 per capita income in South Carolina was only 63.4 percent of the national average. By 1965 it had reached 69 percent, and this was followed by gains to 74.1 percent in 1970 and 76.3 percent in 1975. In 15 years the state had improved its relative position by 13 percent, in a period of unprecedented economic growth nationally. It is noteworthy that 10 years later the ranking of the state was unchanged at 76.3 percent of the national average. Therefore, the 1960-1975 period was clearly unique in South Carolina's economic history.

Beginning in the 1960s, it has become clear that a consensus had developed among many private and public sector leaders that diversification was a prudent economic development goal. Activities by the State Development Board were focused along the lines of industrial recruitment. This was reinforced by other public initiatives such as the development of the vocational and technical education system, other job training programs, and transportation improvements. Therefore, many of the economic gains from the period resulted from an explicit program to attract more manufacturing jobs to the state. The state's economic base accordingly began to diversify away from its extreme reliance on the textile sector, which by now had become threatened by imports from Asian countries.

Reliance on the manufacturing sector to spur economic development and diversification remained the central theme of state economic policy until just recently. Some have argued that this policy inhibited our ability to move to the information/service based economy of the future, thereby guaranteeing our status as a state which picks up "economic leftovers." Such criticism benefits greatly from hindsight because in the 1960-1975 period, the policy worked.

A look at the employment statistics bears this out. Between 1960-1965 total nonagricultural employment grew 18 percent. This growth rate improved to 23 percent in the 1965-1970 period, before falling to 17 percent in 1970-1975. Again, the slower growth rate in the latter period reflects the rather severe recession of 1973-1975.

Ignoring the effects of the recession, manufacturing employment rose by 20 percent in 1960-1965 and 16 percent in 1965-1970. This mirrored the gains in total employment.

In contrast employment in the textile and apparel sectors increased 12 percent in 1960-1965 and 7 percent in 1965-1970, but it declined 7 percent in the 1970-1975 period. Looking at it from a different perspective, textile and apparel employment was the same in 1975 as it was in 1965.

As expected the shares of total employment changed substantially as the South Carolina economy diversified. Between 1960-1970 manufacturing employment fell only from 42 percent to 40 percent of the total. By 1975, the manufacturing share was 35 percent. Much more striking were the textile related sectors. From a 28 percent share of total employment in 1960, textile and apparel employment fell only to a 26 percent share in 1965 and 23 percent in 1970 before plummeting to an 18 percent share during the 1975 recession year. Therefore, one could conclude that the modest weakening of the manufacturing sector in South Carolina during 1960-1975 more precisely reflected a declining growth rate in textiles and related employment, which ultimately resulted in absolute declines by the end of this period. This means of course that the durable goods manufacturing sector (i. e., lumber products, machinery, electronic equipment and instruments) experienced rapid growth because the relative shares of the nonmanufacturing sectors were only slightly changed. Between 1960-1975, the 7 percent decline in manufacturing's share of total employment went strictly to services (3 percent) and government (4 percent). This reinforces the view that this was a period of industrial diversification rather than economic diversification. Since the new jobs that were created were in relatively high wage industries such as metalworking, machinery, and equipment, improvement in per capita income was a natural outcome of this diversification process.

A look at the investment figures during this period clearly illustrates the transformation of the industrial economy away from textiles. In 1964 announced investment in the textile sector amounted to 38 percent of the total. This included both new plants and expansions. Over the next 11 years to 1975, in only one other year (1971) did the textile share exceed 30 percent (31 percent). In the late 1960s the share had fallen well below the 20 percent level (12 percent in 1969), whereas in the 1972-1975 period, its share ranged from only 5 to 10 percent.

Part of the reason for the diminished role of the textile sector was the investment surge in other sectors such as the capital intensive chemicals industry, which in some cases is closely linked to textiles (dyes for example). Major chemical plants were announced in 1965, 1968, 1969, 1973, and 1974. In each of these years, announced investment in the chemicals sector exceeded 50 percent of the total.

Moreover, investment growth in other industries such as primary and fabricated metals, machinery, and equipment was also strong. The shares for these sectors combined ranged from a high of 61 percent in 1967 to a low of 9 percent in the 1973 recession year. Generally, these industries accounted for around 20 percent of total announced investment during the 1964-1975 period.

A common interpretation of these capital flows to South Carolina relates to the image of manufacturers abandoning northern production sites and their labor unions for the cheap labor and pro-business environment of South Carolina. Although this scenario is undoubtedly true to some degree, it is probably overstated for two primary reasons. First the state's industrial recruitment efforts mainly attracted branch plants, not the primary manufacturing facilities and home office operations of the corporation. With industry becoming more land intensive and more "footloose" with the development of the interstate highway system, establishing branch plants in the South made considerable sense even without labor cost advantages and tax incentives. Recruitment efforts reflected the state's determination to get our

Table 13
Employment Announcements — New and Expanded
Plants For The Last Two Decades By Industry

Industry	1960-69 Number	% of Total	1970-79 Number	% of Total
Food	4,927	2.9	3,303	2.5
Textiles	44,054	26.1	22,484	16.8
Apparel	32,069	19.0	17,519	13.1
Wood and Furniture	6,580	3.9	6,030	4.5
Paper and Printing	4,555	2.7	2,464	1.9
Chemical	25,055	14.8	15,528	11.6
Metalworking	44,308	26.2	49,048	36.8
All others	7,258	4.3	17,116	12.8
Total Jobs	168,806	100.0	113,492	100.0
Average Jobs Per Year	16,881		13,349	

"share" of the plants that were coming South anyway.

A second major flaw in the traditional industrial recruitment scenario relates to the role of foreign direct investment during this period. Between 1960-1965 foreign direct investment totaled around $150 million, representing 9.5 percent of the total investments announced in the period. This increased to $476 million and 19 percent in 1966-1970, and it jumped to $779 million and 23 percent of the total in 1971-1975.

Table 14
Announced Foreign Manufacturing Investment,
Five-Year Averages

	Average Foreign Investment (millions of dollars)	Percent of Average Total Industrial Investments
1951-1955	N/A	N/A
1956-1960	N/A	N/A
1961-1965	30.0	9.5
1966-1970	95.2	19.2
1971-1975	155.8	23.0
1976-1980	308.8	27.4
1981-1985	279.7	14.9

This foreign direct investment resulted from a number of factors. First and foremost was the attraction of the U.S. market. In the later 1960s and into the 1970s, it became quite clear that the European economic boom was tapering off with a worsening growth rate relative to the U.S. The oil shocks of the early 1970s exacerbated this trend. Another factor was the declining value of the dollar relative to European currencies during the latter part of this period. Because the inflation rate in the U.S. was substantially greater than several European countries, it became more profitable to invest in U.S. facilities than export as the currencies adjusted. Other factors such as political stability and fewer regulatory impediments were also important.

Foreign direct investment in South Carolina is dominated by the Western European nations, primarily West Germany (32 percent), Britain (25 percent), France (14 percent), and Switzerland (9 percent). This investment played an important role in the state's industrial diversification. By industrial sector, the leading industries are chemicals, primary and fabricated metals, rubber and plastics, machinery, textiles, and paper products.

Foreign direct investment in the state has several interesting characteristics. First, many of the plants that were built initially catered to the textile industry in one form or another, but this has diminished over time. Second, sectoral specialization exists with West Germany (metals, machinery, and chemicals), Britain (textiles and paper), and Switzerland (food products). Third, the foreign investment went to build new plants which were wholly-owned subsidiaries rather than entering the market through acquisition. Finally, wages in each of these industries were high compared to the state average. Of course, this at least in part reflects the fact that the foreign investment was concentrated in capital intensive industries.

Another factor to consider is that when asked why they located in South Carolina, foreign producers cited the availability of land and worker characteristics as the primary factors. Incentives such as property tax abatements and other financial incentives were not viewed as having much importance in the location decisions.

Therefore, foreign direct investment has played an important role in the state's economy. It was critical to the establishment of the industrial diversification of the economy during the 1960-1975 period, a time when significant absolute and relative economic gains were made.

If 1960-1975 was the apex of growth for the South Carolina economy and manufacturing in particular, the last 10 years have been a mixed bag overall and extremely difficult for the industrial sector. It is apparent that the South Carolina economy has hit another crossroad.

Economic Diversification: 1975-1985

Following the 1973-1975 recession, the South Carolina economy rebounded strongly, and all of the economic sectors participated in the recovery and expansion which lasted until 1980. The view that the South Carolina economy was worse off than national averages during a recession and better off during an expansion was again reinforced.

However, the basics of the state's economy were rapidly changing in the 1975-1980 period. When the minirecession in 1980 hit and was followed by the more severe 1981-1982 downturn, the South Carolina economy that reemerged in 1983 was vastly different from that of just 4 years before.

Most significant has been the substantial fall-off in manufacturing employment. Textile employment has been in a secular decline for 10 years because of capital-labor substitution and the tremendous surge of imports. However, the durable goods sectors have also been hard hit, and this source of industrial diversification has incurred losses even more severe than textiles in recent years. Perhaps the problem is best illustrated by noting that total manufacturing employment in 1985 was 35,000-40,000 jobs below the 1979 peak after a sustained recovery of 4 years.

Yet, this trend has been evident in the national economy as well. Regions dependent on basic industries and commodities are in serious trouble and have generally not participated in the recovery and expansion. What has emerged instead is the so-called "service based" or "information" economy, which placed South Carolina at somewhat of an economic disadvantage. The attractiveness of the "sun-belt" began to wane — to be replaced by the "brain-belt."

Unfortunately, the drastic turnaround in the international competitiveness of domestic manufacturing industries had serious implications for the South Carolina economy. What had been a steady transition in terms of jobs lost in the textile sector became a rout accompanied by numerous plant closures and consolidations. Rural communities almost solely dependent on the local mills were the worst off and have had the most difficult time trying to cope with the loss of their economic base. Combined with the distressed agricultural sector and its effects on rural South Carolina, the state's economy has become markedly dichotomous. Whereas the major metropolitan areas such as Charleston, Columbia, and Greenville-Spartanburg have expanded and prospered during the current expansion, the rural areas of the state remain distressed for the most part.

The more difficult economic environment in the 1975-1985 period has varied effects on the state. Population growth in the state continued to exceed the national rate while matching the rest of the Southeast. Between 1975-1980, the growth rate in South Carolina was 8.1 percent compared to 5.5 percent for the U.S. and 8.4 percent for the Southeast. The gap narrowed in the 1980-1985 period with South Carolina and the Southeast registering 6.7 percent growth over the 5 years with 5.1 percent growth at the national level.

It is also interesting to note that during the 1975-1980 period (the years for which Census data are available), there were 291,074 immigrants (aged 16 and over) to the state compared to 209,171 outmigrants. In addition to our neighbors, New York, Ohio, Pennsylvania, New Jersey, Maryland, and California were the primary "sending" regions. In contrast the top 10 "receiving" states were dominated by the South and Southeast with the exceptions of New York, Ohio, and California. Moreover, some rough calculations indicate that net migration added between $1.2 billion and $2.9 billion to the South Carolina economy by 1980, without multipliers. Considering the fact that total personal income in South Carolina totaled $237 billion in 1980, the contribution from migration flows was quite important.

Of course, migration to a state is partially determined by economic opportunities, and the South Carolina economy has had a mixed performance in the 1975-1985 period. South Carolina per capita income was 90.6 percent of the Southeast average in 1975, 89.5 percent in 1980, and 88.3 percent in 1985. With respect to the national average, the percentages are 76.3 percent, 76.5 percent, and 76.3 percent respectively. Therefore, significant improvement in the 1960-1975 period has been followed by no change relative to the nation and deterioration with respect to the Southeast as a whole.

A look at growth in real personal income is also important. Between 1975-1980 the average annual growth rate of this measure was 4.8 percent in South Carolina, 5.3 percent in the Southeast, and 4.6 percent for the U.S. In the 1980-1985 period, this growth rate fell to 3.2 percent, 3.5 percent, and 2.9 percent respectively. It is important that the 1980-1985 period represents the slowest rate of growth of real total personal income in the entire postwar period with the exception of 1955-1960.

There are two basic reasons for this general lackluster performance. First was the deterrent to growth presented by two recessions. The downturn in 1981-1982 was the most severe in the postwar era with unemployment in South Carolina reaching 12.3 percent compared to 10.7 percent nationally.

The second major factor responsible for the weak growth in personal income was the deterioration in the manufacturing sector. Again, this was a national as well as a state problem.

In 1975, total employment in South Carolina was 982,600 of which 339,900 jobs were in manufacturing, a 35 percent share, and 179,100 jobs were in the textile and apparel sectors, an 18 percent share. Following the 1973-1975 recession, a typical broad-based recovery and expansion ensued. Total employment had increased over 200,000 jobs to 1,188,800 jobs. The manufacturing sector participated as well with a gain exceeding 50,000 jobs. Despite significant import pressures and rapid plant modernization/consolidation, even textile and apparel jobs grew by 4,200. This is misleading, however, as textile mill products employment peaked in 1976 at 150,000 jobs and had declined by more than 10,000 jobs in 1980. Durable goods sectors more than compensated, expanding by over 20,000 jobs during the period.

Therefore, the 15 percent gain in manufacturing compared to the 21 percent gain in total employment resulted in a modest decline in the manufacturing share to 33 percent in 1980 from 35 percent in 1975. Textile and apparel employment fell 3 percent to 15 percent of total nonagricultural employment. The trade, service, and transportation sectors were the biggest gainers in percentage terms.

Because of the conditions mentioned above, total nonagricultural employment grew by a modest 9.3 percent between 1980-1985. Manufacturing employment suffered a decline of 6.8 percent or 25,000 jobs. However, textile and apparel employment alone lost 35,000 jobs in the period, a loss of nearly 1 of every 5 jobs. The reasons for this are well documented, but the problems have yet to be resolved. After a brief cyclical pickup in 1983, manufacturing employment again deteriorated in 1984-1985.

Reflecting a surge in construction, the service sector, and tourism, the nonmanufacturing sectors performed quite well in the period. Trade employment rose 24 percent, services employment was up 32 percent, construction employment increased 14 percent, and finance, insurance, and real estate employment jumped 20 percent in response to deregulation. Despite the rhetoric, government employment rose by only 4 percent.

By 1985 the manufacturing share of total employment fell 5 percent to 28 percent, with textile and apparel employment down another 4 percent to 11 percent. The trade and service sectors had corresponding increases to 21 percent and 16 percent respectively.

Ironically, the figures on investment announcements remained strong throughout the 10 year period to 1985. Between 1976-1980, over $5.6 billion of investment in new and expanded facilities were announced with an estimated potential job payoff of 77,435 jobs. For the next 5 years, investment announcements totaled nearly $9.4 billion (unadjusted for inflation), good for an estimated 66,230 jobs.

Obviously, the firms' estimates are often overstated due to changing economic conditions and other factors. Moreover, it has been estimated that approximately 20 percent of the announcements do not come to fruition. The major areas of investment, particularly of new plants, continued to be in chemicals, metals, machinery, electronic equipment, tires, and paper products. Investment in the textile sector reflected efforts to modernize and generally resulted in fewer jobs. Foreign investments continued to play an important, but diminishing role. Between 1970-1980 foreign investment was around $1.5 billion, or 27 percent of the total. In the proceeding 5 years, foreign investment fell to $1.4 billion, which was 15 percent of the total.

Like manufacturing, the agricultural sector has been in distress over the last 5 years. The number of farms has declined from 36,000 in 1975 to 27,000 in 1985. All but 2,000 of the loss occurred since 1980. Land in farming dropped to 5.5 million acres, half of the level in 1954. Total cash receipts rose from $807 million in 1975 to $1.109 billion in 1980. However, they declined to $1.007 billion in 1985, and undoubtedly, receipts were considerably lower in 1986 because of the drought.

Therefore, a kind of dichotomy has developed within sectors of the South Carolina economy as well as regions within the state. Since smaller, rural communities are unlikely to have diversified economies, their economic well-being is highly dependent upon their basic industries. The faltering agricultural sector presented one set of problems, as the spin-off effects on local farm equipment dealers and suppliers multiplied through the local economies.

Plant closures presented even greater problems in some communities. The local retail trade and tax base were in some cases devastated as the textile industry consolidated and contracted. The magnitude of the problem was defined above in terms of employment, but it is also appropriate to point out that over 40 major textile manufacturing facilities closed down in 1982 alone.

In contrast, the state's major metropolitan areas with their diversified economies have prospered. Most of the high wage service sectors, such as finance and health care, have located and expanded in Columbia, Charleston, and Greenville-Spartanburg. The so-called high tech industries have followed because of the universities and greater amenities of these areas. It comes as no surprise that their unemployment rates are quite low, with Columbia's around 3-4 percent over the last 2 years.

Thus, the divergence between growth and decline in South Carolina is very real. Although industries such as tourism have picked up the employment slack caused by the decline in some manufacturing sectors such as textiles, there has been somewhat of a substitution between relatively lower wage trade and service jobs for higher wage manufacturing jobs, particularly for the less well educated. This has undoubtedly hurt aggregate income growth, but the substitution has been particularly severe in the isolated, rural communities.

Vigorous efforts have been made to attract new industries to these regions, but their cost advantages are not sufficient to compensate for their locational disadvantages coupled with poor educational systems. In industrial recruitment it is a "buyers'" market, and Greenville is more attractive than a smaller town. South Carolina is not in any position to "direct" investment anywhere.

Thus, we are in the midst of a fundamental economic transition. Some argue that we are moving toward a service-based information economy — whatever it is. Others believe that we should not abandon our manufacturing base, but they often confuse employment for production. Some possible future trends for the South Carolina economy are discussed next.

The Future: 1986-2000

Forecasting future economic trends is part art and part science. Short-term forecasting one to two years out is a difficult task. Going out 15 years with high accuracy is next to impossible. To appreciate this difficulty, simply go back and reread what has happened to the South Carolina economy over the last 15 years.

Nearly all forecasting techniques rest on the assumption that the past is at least some guide to the future. This is known as the "assumption of continuity."

One way to view possible trends is to look at national characteristics. Since South Carolina's economic development tends to lag behind the nation's this can indicate sectors that are likely to grow in South Carolina. The so-called "specialization index" represents the percentage total employment shares of an industry in South Carolina divided by the industry's share as a percentage of total employment nationally. For example, in 1984 manufacturing was 29.8 percent of total employment in South Carolina versus 20.8 percent nationally. The resulting ratio is 143, which means that manufacturing is a much more important employment sector in the state than in the nation. A ratio of 100 indicates parity.

For South Carolina, industries with a specialization index exceeding 100 are construction (139), manufacturing (143), and government (111). Industries with an index below 100 are transportation and public utilities (80); wholesale trade (85); retail trade (95); finance, insurance, and real estate (72); and services (71).

Given the state's status as a resort/tourism center and faster than average population growth, a high construction index is not unexpected, and it is likely to be maintained. Although the trade, service, and financial sectors have all grown rapidly in recent years, these industries should continue to experience above average growth rates.

This also means that manufacturing employment will continue to trend down over time. Again, it is important to draw the distinction between employment and production. In 1910, nearly one-third of all workers were in agriculture compared to the present level of 3 percent. Needless to say, production is much higher now than then.

In the manufacturing sector, import competition will continue to be a problem, particularly with bulk-type commodities which are sensitive to labor cost differentials. However, technological advances will likely result in capital-labor substitution over time. This is typically a "manageable" process as it allows for a transition for workers to adapt to new training and jobs that will develop in the future. The concept that manufacturing workers will only be able to find jobs in fast food restaurants is generally not valid.

Table 15
Economic Structure, South Carolina
And United States, 1984

| | Percentage of Total Nonfarm Wage and Salary Employment | | Specialization |
	S.C.	U.S.	Index
Total Nonagricultural Employment	100.0	100.0	100
Mining	0.1	1.1	9
Construction	6.4	4.6	139
Manufacturing	29.8	20.8	143
Textile Mill Products	8.9	0.8	1,112
Apparel	3.9	1.3	300
Chemicals	2.6	1.1	236
Nonelectrical Machinery	2.4	2.4	100
Transportation & Public Utilities	4.4	5.5	80
Wholesale Trade	4.2	5.9	85
Retail Trade	16.5	17.3	95
Finance, Insurance & Real Estate	4.3	6.0	72
Services	15.5	21.9	71
Government	18.9	17.0	111

Source: South Carolina Employment Security Commission, *South Carolina Labor Market Review*, 1985.

Using an economic model to make projections, the economic characteristics of South Carolina in the year 2000 may be quite different from what they are now given reasonable assumptions about inflation and national economic growth. Real personal income is expected to rise from $31.6 billion in 1985 to $41.6 billion in 2000. This represents an average annual increase of 2.1 percent which is well below any period since World War II with the exception of 1955-1960 at 2.5 percent.

Population growth is expected to moderate to a 1.3 percent annual rate. By 2000, the population in South Carolina will come to 4,093,900 if this rate holds compared to the current figure of 3,358,000. In nominal terms (unadjusted for inflation) per capita income should rise to $23,500 from $10,502 in 1985.

From 1.298 million jobs in 1985, total nonfarm employment could rise to 1.806 million jobs in 2000 under these assumptions. This gain of around 500,000 jobs translates to an average annual increase of 2.2 percent.

The largest employment gains are registered by wholesale and retail trade ($238,000), services (140,000), government (110,000), and finance, insur-

247

ance, and real estate (40,000). However, it is important to note that the growth in government employment is no greater than the growth rate in total employment, which means that its relative share should remain constant over the next 15 years.

Manufacturing employment is expected to decline by around 45,000 jobs during this period. Since 35,000 manufacturing jobs have been lost in the time from 1979 to 1985, such a loss would represent relative stability and a manageable shift in labor resources. Durable goods employment will likely account for 40 percent of the job losses, with the remainder going to the nondurable sectors (i.e., textiles, food products, paper products, and chemicals). However, textile mill products alone will fall by 40,000 jobs under the assumptions to only 63,000 jobs. Yet this may be overstating the decline because the economic model on which this forecast was based is dependent on data from 1965 to 1985, a period that has seen substantial losses in the textile industry.

Therefore, by the year 2000 it is plausible that only 6.4 percent of the state's workers will be in textile mill products employment compared to 32 percent in 1950. For manufacturing as a whole, comparable statistics are 18 percent and 46 percent respectively. Thus, in 2000 a fundamental restructuring of the South Carolina economy will have taken place. This transition will be similar to the early 1900s, which saw a movement of workers from agriculture to the industrial sector. The changes going on today and in the future represent significant economic shifts that will have winners and losers in the state. Some implications are discussed next.

Conclusions

Since 1950, the South Carolina economy has undergone fundamental and mostly beneficial changes. From a very narrowly based economy, it first diversified into a broad-based manufacturing dominated economy. In this period, which was marked by strong public as well as private initiatives, South Carolina made substantial progress toward parity with national norms.

For various reasons, but primarily the emergence of the "global economy," this era came to an end and was replaced by the broader concept of economic diversification. This period is characterized by the emergence of technological advances in manufacturing and information resources, deregulation which has spurred competition in many industries, and severe almost cutthroat competition in many internationally traded goods.

The South Carolina economy has not fared as well in this current time. Our relative status has generally stagnated. However, below the surface one can identify many gainers and some losers. The former would obviously include most of South Carolina's urban areas, the better educated, and the highly skilled. The latter is related to many rural areas of the state that have been hit hard by losses in agriculture and the textile industry. Poorly educated workers and those with job skills that are not easily transferred have suffered greatly.

Therefore, one can conclude that the South Carolina economy has grown more dichotomous in recent years. Urban areas with unemployment rates currently well below 5 percent continue to prosper, whereas rural areas continue to have double digit unemployment. Educational reforms will hopefully ameliorate this divergence in the future, but the disparities will not be easily overcome. However, if South Carolina is going to again progress toward national norms, the rural regions must be a part of this process. This problem is not unique to South Carolina, but in the current economic environment the outlook is not promising. The state's economy has demonstrated great resiliency in the past, and this will be required again. An improving national economy coupled with growing competitiveness should inspire some hope for the future.

Finally, it should be emphasized that this chapter should not be viewed as an economic history of South Carolina. The framework that I chose was useful to identify what I considered to be key trends in the South Carolina economy. The dates that were chosen for each period are admittedly imperfect, but they permitted straightforward comparisons of the data. The chapter solely reflects my own judgments and interpretations.

References

Ellson, Richard W. (1981). "The South Carolina Econometric Model." *Business and Economic Review* Vol. 28, no. 1 (October): 9-15.

Ellson, Richard W. (1983). "The South Carolina Economy: In Transition, But to What?" (with Nancy Grden-Ellson) *Economic Review* Federal Reserve Bank of Atlanta (February): 75-82.

Ellson, Richard W. (1984). "South Carolina: A Strong Recovery but Problems Remain." (with Randolph C. Martin) *Economic Review* Federal Reserve Bank of Atlanta (February): 84-91.

Ellson, Richard W. (1987). "Comings and Goings: Migration and South Carolina." (with Brian Gilley) *Business and Economic Review* Vol. 33, no. 2 (First Quarter): 3-8.

Ellson, Richard W. (n. d.). "The Myth and Reality of Investment Announcements." (with Randolph C. Martin and Sandra Teel) Unpublished Working Paper.

14

The Rural Economy in South Carolina: Prospects and Problems

Mark Henry and Georgann McMullen

Introduction

Rural South Carolina has stalled in its drive to reach the same level of economic well-being as the metropolitan places of the state. Much like the rest of rural America, South Carolina shared in the rural economic renaissance of the early 1970's. However, this rural turnaround proved to be short-lived and there are indications that urban areas are again gaining larger shares of the economic pie.

In the following sections some of the underlying reasons for these trends in South Carolina are considered and some policy options to spread economic development to rural areas are discussed. Our objective is to propose some ways in which government can assist private initiative to improve economic conditions in rural South Carolina.

Rural South Carolina: What Is It?

The U.S. Office of Management and Budget (OMB) has designated 12 counties in South Carolina as Standard Metropolitan Statistical Areas (metro counties).[1] These 12 counties, shown in white in Figure 1, have about 60% of the total state population. About 68% of the population in these metropolitan counties live in urban places (the Census Bureau defines a place as urban if it has at least 2500 people). The remaining 34 counties are predominately rural, although they do include urban areas (communities with a population of 2500

Mark Henry is a professor in the Department of Rural Sociology and Agricultural Economics at Clemson University. Georgann McMullen is a graduate student in the same department at Clemson University.

or more). For the purpose of this analysis, the 34 nonmetropolitan counties will be grouped into three rural regions based on economic characteristics. The three rural regions are: (1) *Nonmetro Upstate*. This region contains 18 counties whose economies are dominated by textile manufacturing, other rural manufacturing sectors, and farming. Only about 31% of the population in the nonmetro upstate area lives in communities of 2500 or more. (2) *Nonmetro Downstate*. This region is composed of 13 counties with a traditional rural economic base and a somewhat smaller manufacturing sector than is found in the upstate. Only about 27% of the nonmetro downstate population live in urban places. (3) *Nonmetro Other*. This region includes three counties, Sumter, Horry, and Beaufort, whose economies are dominated by government and retirement activities. These counties are also more urban than the other 31 nonmetropolitan counties; almost half of these counties' populations live in urban places (47.2%). Each of these rural regions is identified in Figure 1.

FIGURE 1. RURAL REGIONS OF SOUTH CAROLINA

As illustrated in Chart 1, the nonmetropolitan counties are indeed mostly rural counties. However, in South Carolina even the metropolitan counties have substantial numbers of rural residents; about 32% of the metropolitan counties' population (or 600,000 people) live in rural areas of these counties.

The rural residents of the metro counties differ from residents of nonmetro counties because they are often closely linked to the activity of the urban centers and thus can depend on the vitality of these centers for employment opportunities. On the other hand, residents of the nonmetro counties of the state are less affected by the urban growth of metro counties. Therefore, in spite of the fact that even the metro counties in South Carolina retain some rural areas, this chapter will focus on the nonmetropolitan counties since they appear to be most representative of rural South Carolina.

While the majority of South Carolina's population does not live in rural areas of the state, in relation to the United States as a whole, South Carolina could still be classified as a rural state. Rural places in South Carolina have about 46% of the state's population; the corresponding share for the nation is only about 26%[2]. Thus it is important to examine the economies of the rural regions of the state and address some specific questions about those rural economies. In particular: Are there unique rural area characteristics that make economic development less likely than in metro counties? Do basic market trends suggest hard times for rural South Carolina? And, what are the likely socioeconomic consequences of a stagnating rural South Carolina? The following sections will address each of these questions.

Some Characteristics of Rural South Carolina

The first topic to be considered when evaluating the rural economy of South Carolina is the characteristics of rural areas in the state. The economic base, market size and access, and labor force characteristics all impact the present economic health of rural South Carolina and will largely dictate the policies needed to address weaknesses in the rural economy.

Economic Base. Any discussion of the rural economic base immediately brings to mind agricultural activities, but in fact manufacturing is the dominant economic base of rural South Carolina. About three-fourths of the nonmetropolitan county economies are based primarily on manufacturing activity.[3] Nevertheless, farming still plays an important role in the nonmetropolitan economy. The sluggish economic growth of most of rural South Carolina over the 1980's therefore reflects the combination of weak farm income performance and increased foreign competition for low-wage jobs in the manufacturing sector.

The rural employment picture is a reflection of the trends in the low-wage manufacturing sector (e.g., the manufacture of nondurable goods such as apparel). Both the upstate and downstate nonmetropolitan counties experienced a net loss of manufacturing jobs in the period from 1978 to 1985. Because of its concentration of rural manufacturing, the nonmetro upstate

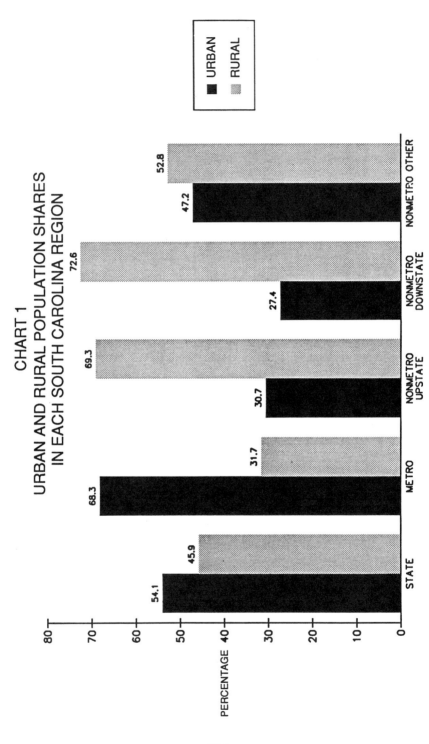

CHART 1
URBAN AND RURAL POPULATION SHARES
IN EACH SOUTH CAROLINA REGION

region had greater employment losses than the downstate nonmetro counties. In terms of total private sector employment losses (manufacturing and service sector jobs), ten of the 14 nonmetropolitan counties which experienced a net loss of jobs were located in the upstate region. The influence of military, retirement and tourist spending in Beaufort, Horry and Sumter counties has been strong enough that these counties are not manufacturing dependent like most of nonmetropolitan South Carolina. These three counties are dominated by service sector activities. All of the metropolitan counties gained employment, except for Anderson County, where there was little change.

FIGURE 2. PRIVATE SECTOR EMPLOYMENT LOSS
1978–1985

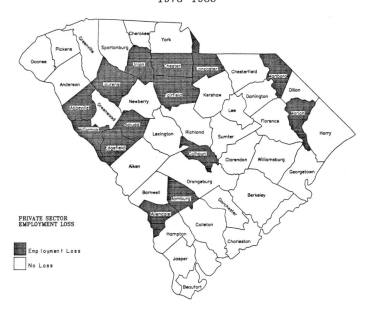

While there were virtually no bright spots for rural upstate employment during the 1978-1985 period, the downstate area provides some interesting contrasts. The coastal nonmetro counties had substantial employment gains. These rural areas have benefited from strong service sector growth as their economic base has shifted from reliance on agriculture and nondurable manufacturing. Much of rural South Carolina, however, does not have the market size or access needed to take advantage of fast growth in the service sectors.

Market Size/Access in Rural South Carolina. One problem for rural counties in terms of potential for economic development is that they generally have low population densities (few people per square mile of land). The nonmetro upstate and downstate counties are grouped by population densities in Figure 3. The least densely populated counties, also tend to be the counties most isolated from the interstate highway systems. A lack of interstate highways limits access to larger markets. The upstate counties of Abbeville, McCormick, Edgefield, and Saluda do not have an interstate highway while the downstate counties of Barnwell, Allendale and Bamberg as well as most of Hampton county are similarly disadvantaged. Not surprisingly, most of these counties lost employment during the 1978-1985 period (see Figure 2). They are not likely to experience growth in service sector employment because of their low population densities. Manufacturing operations may be deterred by the lack of interstate highway access. These counties, in particular, may have to look to a rural growth center strategy within their regions. For example, infrastructure and recruitment efforts might be targeted to places such as Greenwood in the upstate and Orangeburg in the downstate. The contiguous counties would then benefit from jobs created within a short commuting distance.

FIGURE 3.
POPULATION DENSITY FOR SOUTH CAROLINA, 1985

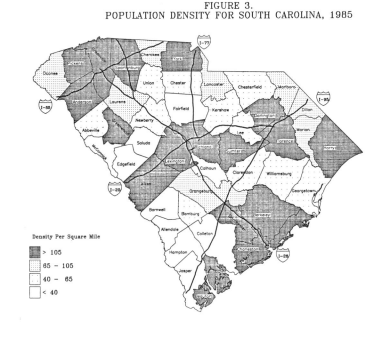

Human Capital Characteristics in Rural South Carolina. Prospects for economic development in the state have traditionally been associated with the comparative costs of doing business in South Carolina relative to other regions of the United States. This perspective emphasizes a low wage labor force, low levels of union activity, infrastructure subsidies to new business, relatively low land costs and low taxes. Indeed, some business climate indices continue to emphasize these characteristics in their evaluation of a state's attractiveness for new business. But South Carolina must increasingly compete internationally with countries in South America, the Carribean, and Asia which offer an even lower cost of doing business. This competition is one reason there is now renewed interest in improving the quality of the labor force. For rural South Carolina, this means both improved basic education and training for the skills required for the industries that will comprise the regional economy of the future.

An alternative view of the state's economic development is based on the widespread belief that endogenous growth at the local level, spawned by local entrepreneurship, will be as important to future economic development as the fortuitous location of branch plants and new large scale manufacturing activities have been in the past (Bergman, 1985). Unfortunately for rural areas, the prospects of generating local entrepreneurship are limited. High levels of entrepreneurship are often indicated by high rates of new business formation, by favorable in-migration patterns, and by a population with more formal education (Malecki, 1986). As shown in Chart 2, in-migration is most pronounced in larger metropolitan counties of South Carolina. Lagging rural counties also tend to have the lowest levels of formal education. The upstate and downstate nonmetro counties have a labor force with about 20% with some college experience. In contrast, college-experienced labor constitutes about 30% of the labor force in the rapidly growing "other" nonmetro counties of Sumter, Horry, and Beaufort and the growing metropolitan counties (see Table 3).

Rural South Carolina: How Well Is It Doing?

The previous section provided a snapshot of a rural South Carolina economy based on low-wage manufacturing and farming, with lower in-migration rates and lower levels of formal education than that found in the metropolitan counties. Most rural counties also have low population densities which may hamper growth of the service sector of the economy. And finally, several South Carolina counties lack ready access to the interstate highway system which in turn limits market access. To complete the picture of the status of rural areas in the state, we will describe the current economic trends in the nonmetropolitan counties.

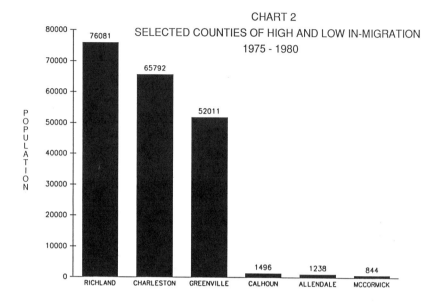

CHART 2
SELECTED COUNTIES OF HIGH AND LOW IN-MIGRATION
1975 - 1980

Employment Change. From 1978 to 1985, about 201,000 people entered the labor force in South Carolina (S.C. Budget and Control Board, 1986). That meant that almost 29,000 new jobs per year were needed to absorb new labor force entrants. During this period, South Carolina was not able to absorb all of the official new entrants to the labor force and estimated unemployment rose from 78,000 (5.7% of the labor force) in 1978 to 107,000 (6.8% of the labor force) in 1985.[4] However, in spite of a higher unemployment rate from 1978 to 1985, South Carolina has benefited from increased employment opportunities. Using employment data for employees covered by unemployment insurance, we can identify several important changes that have occurred in South Carolina.[5]

From 1978 to 1985, South Carolina experienced a net increase in private sector employment of 134,143 jobs. However, 96,844 of those jobs (or 72.2%) were in the metropolitan counties. Horry, Beaufort, and Sumter counties together had an increase of 26,857 private sector jobs (20.0% of the total). That leaves only 7.8% of the increase (10,442 jobs) in private sector employment for the other 31 nonmetropolitan counties. The nonmetropolitan counties in the upstate lost the most private sector employment and most of that loss occurred in the manufacturing sector. However, these counties did gain service sector jobs. Even the 10 upstate counties which experienced a net loss in private employment gained slightly more than 2,000 service sector jobs. (This may be attributable in part to some definitional problems in the data (McKenzie and Smith, 1986). For instance, subcontracting some

Table 1

Selected Employment Change in the S.C. Regions, 1978-1985.

Region	Number of Counties	All Private Sector Total Change # of Jobs	Manufacturing Total Change # of Jobs	Services Total Change # of Jobs
Nonmetro	34			
Upstate	18			
Gainer	8	8065	−2636	3177
Loser	10	−5308	−8324	2054
Downstate	13			
Gainer	9	8850	235	1974
Loser	4	−1165	−301	−157
Other	3			
Gainer	3	26857	−1402	8385
Metro	12			
Gainer	11	97015	−3258	39537
Loser	1	−171	−3148	1198

Manufacturing includes SIC codes 20 through 29.
Services includes SIC codes 80 through 89.

Source: Calculated by author, for First Quarter Change, ES 202 employment insurance files.

259

"manufacturing activities" that were internal to the firm (e.g., data processing) to outside service firms would show up as an increase in service jobs and a decrease in manufacturing jobs.) The upswing in service sector employment in the upstate may be a sign that these counties are in transition where service sector jobs are substituted for those that were held in manufacturing.

Nine downstate nonmetropolitan counties gained employment from 1978 to 1985 and were the only nonmetro counties to add manufacturing jobs on a net gain basis. However, the manufacturing employment gains were small (a total of 235 jobs). Their service sector gains were nearly six times as large as the manufacturing growth. The four downstate counties that lost employment were unfortunate in that they lost both manufacturing and service sector jobs and thus appear to have stagnated throughout this period.

The growth of the service sector of the economy (both statewide and nationally) has sparked a concern that the service sector jobs which are replacing the manufacturing jobs are low wage jobs with little advancement prospects. It is likely that the metropolitan areas will generate a wide range of service sector jobs — high and low wage jobs — that will be filled by those with the requisite skills. However, in the nonmetropolitan counties, it may be a matter of exchanging a low wage manufacturing job for a low wage service job with the need to commute longer distances from the remote places. This scenario is most probable for individuals who do not invest in training or education that will enable them to compete for higher paying occupations.

Per Capita Income. South Carolina has grown faster than the national average in terms of per capita income for much of the last two decades. And while income growth has not been strong enough to enable South Carolina to reach national levels of per capita income, progress has been encouraging since the 1960's. For rural South Carolina, the period since 1965 has been mixed in terms of its relative growth compared to urban areas of the state. From 1965 to about 1974, nonmetropolitan areas of the state grew faster in terms of per capita income (which might be used as a measure of well-being) than the metropolitan areas. In other words, the rural areas were catching up to the urban levels of per capita income. Indeed, if compared with national trends over the same period, rural South Carolina out-performed the national average. However, since the middle 1970's this process of per capita income convergence has stalled and urban areas are again outpacing the more rural parts of the state. The nonmetropolitan downstate region made the sharpest gains from 1965 to 1974 but also lost the most ground since then and remains about 28% below the metropolitan per capita income levels. The nonmetropolitan upstate region, as well as Beaufort, Horry, and Sumter counties, have per capita income levels above the downstate level, and have slightly increased their per capita income advantage since the middle 1970's.

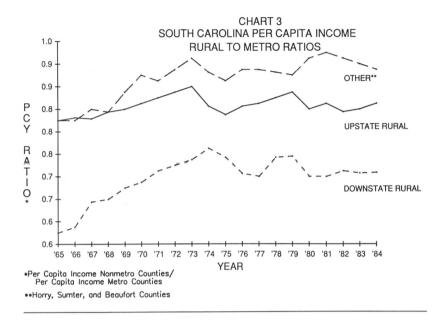

CHART 3
SOUTH CAROLINA PER CAPITA INCOME
RURAL TO METRO RATIOS

•Per Capita Income Nonmetro Counties/
Per Capita Income Metro Counties

••Horry, Sumter, and Beaufort Counties

Population and Real Income. As further evidence of the lagging rural economy, consider the rates of growth of population and real income in Table 2. Population growth over the entire 20 year period has favored metropolitan areas. The only exception has been Beaufort, Sumter and Horry counties (the nonmetropolitan "other" region) which consistently outpaced the urban counties in both population growth and real income growth. The one bright spot for the nonmetropolitan upstate and downstate regions during that 20 year period was the growth rates for real per capita income and total real income during the 1965 to 1973 period. During the same period, however, the upstate rural region experienced almost no population growth and the rural downstate region lost population. In sum, the two aggregate indicators of economic vitality — population and income, as well as per capita income, have been strongest in the metropolitan counties and Beaufort, Horry and Sumter counties.

Why is Rural South Carolina Lagging

After reviewing the economic characteristics of rural South Carolina and the economic trends in the state over the last 20 years, we can now consider the factors which have caused rural South Carolina to lag behind the urban areas of the state. Four forces have contributed to the slow down in rural areas of the state: international factors, the shift to a service economy, deregulation, and agricultural changes.

261

Table 2
Growth Rates Over Recent Business Cycles

| | Nonmetro Region: | | | | | |
	Upstate	Downstate	Other*	All	Metro	State
		– – – – Annual Average Percentage Change – – –				
Real Per Capita Income						
1965-1969	5.4%	7.8	6.7%	6.3%	4.8%	5.5%
1969-1973	4.5	5.5	4.7	4.8	3.4	4.0
1973-1979	0.8	0.7	0.9	0.8	0.9	0.9
1979-1984	0.9	0.8	1.1	0.9	1.1	1.1
Population						
1965-1969	0.0%	– 1.2%	0.6%	– 0.3%	1.6%	0.8%
1969-1973	0.1	– 0.9	0.4	– 0.2	1.5	0.8
1973-1979	1.2	1.7	3.2	1.7	2.3	2.1
1979-1984	1.0	0.9	1.8	1.1	2.0	1.6
Total Real Income						
1965-1969	5.4%	6.4%	7.3%	6.1%	6.5%	6.3%
1969-1973	5.5	6.7	7.1	6.1	5.9	6.0
1973-1979	1.9	2.3	3.2	2.3	3.0	2.7
1979-1984	1.5	1.5	4.1	2.1	2.6	2.4

Source: Calculated by authors using data tapes from Bureau of Economic Analysis, U.S. Dept. of Commerce. CPI deflator used with 1967 = 100 for the income series.

*Sumter, Beaufort, and Horry Counties

International Factors. International forces have diminished farm export demand and low wage manufacturing employment. In terms of manufacturing employment, many of the manufacturing operations in rural South Carolina utilize low cost labor performing routinized jobs. Such jobs have been moving to the lowest labor cost locations on an international scale (South America, the Carribean, and Asia) for the last decade. Probably most important to rural South Carolina is the stiff foreign competition in textile product markets. Rural textile manufacturing plants that are low wage, low skill and labor intensive operations are especially sensitive to this international force. In addition, new textile production facilities may tend to concentrate in the metropolitan areas of the state and rely more heavily on technology than labor. All of these changes are likely to mean increased rural unemployment.

Shift To Services. The service industry is the most rapidly growing sector of the U.S. economy (*The Economist,* 1986), but many rural communities are ill-suited to benefit from this shift to services. Recent studies indicate that the types of service employment that have increased most rapidly are business services, computer and data processing services, and temporary help services. Firms that provide these services prosper in metropolitan areas where potential clients are concentrated. They are not likely to locate in rural areas where clients are fewer and much more dispersed.

While some of the discussion of the United States as a service based economy may be an overstatement based on misinterpretation of employment statistics,[6] there is evidence that new service activity in South Carolina has favored metropolitan locations in the 1980's. However, not all nonmetropolitan counties have been left behind in the service sector. Both the retirement and government counties (Beaufort, Horry, and Sumter) show faster rates of growth in the service sector than the metropolitan areas.

Deregulation. Deregulation of financial markets have been associated with higher costs of doing business in rural areas. When the interest rate that banks could pay on deposits was regulated, the cost of funds to rural banks was lower than the cost to urban banks. Many rural banks had large deposits with no or very low interest costs. In turn, the rate charged to rural borrowers was also lower than in most urban areas. But with the lifting of interest rate ceilings under the Depository Institutions and Monetary Control Act of 1980, nearly all rural banks had to pay more to attract deposits. Thus the cost of funds to borrowers also rose in rural areas. While the efficiency aspect of banking deregulation is important, it most likely has some short-run adverse effects on the cost of funds to borrowers in rural areas.

Transportation deregulation also increased the cost of doing business in rural areas. After deregulation, rural areas experienced a reduced availability of bus services and higher prices of air and other transportation services. From an efficiency perspective, transportation deregulation has no doubt enhanced the ability of this sector to provide lower cost services in highly competitive markets. At the same time, lifting regulatory control eliminated the subsidies that were, in effect, provided to rural areas.

Agricultural Change. The financial stress on the family farm in the 1980's has been a strong blow to rural communities that were built up to service a large number of medium sized farms. As farms grow in size, there is a tendency for the operators to bypass small communities and to seek out better prices for equipment, fuel, fertilizer, and other supplies. Thus, it is not likely that rural South Carolina counties will establish a rapidly growing economy based on farm production alone.

There is also an important link between farming activity and manufacturing activity in many rural areas. Off-farm employment opportunities in rural South Carolina enable many farmers to continue farming. Many would be forced out of farming if their net farm income was the sole source of household income. However, the slow growth of the manufacturing sector in most rural areas may diminish these growth opportunities in the near future.

What Factors Are Important For Rural Growth?

Local policy has little control over international forces, national growth patterns, or the price of equipment, supplies, and fuel needed by agriculture and manufacturing. However, other factors are influenced by state and local policy. From 1978 to 1985, there were 20 nonmetropolitan counties that gained employment and 14 nonmetropolitan counties that lost employment. All but one of the metropolitan counties grew. What are the differences in growth factors between gaining and losing counties in South Carolina?

First, if high school and college education is used as an indicator of the quality of the labor force in a county, the gaining counties generally had a superior quality labor force. Therefore, at least on the surface, labor quality does seem to matter. Of course, it is not possible to positively assert that labor quality was an agent causing employment growth since many other factors may be involved. However, the labor quality indicators are for 1980, near the beginning of the 1978 to 1985 employment change period. Thus, it is reasonable to hypothesize that the higher quality labor at the start of this period may have been an attraction to new employment growth.

As a second factor that might be able to distinguish between gaining and losing counties, relative labor costs tell a mixed story. It might be expected that low wage counties would tend to grow faster than high wage areas because of labor costs to employers. However, the metropolitan counties

Table 3
Selected Characteristics of Growing and Declining Counties, 1978-1985

	[a]Labor Quality		[b]Labor Cost relative to U.S. average:			[c]Tax pc	Other indicators of county attractiveness			
	%Hs Grad	%Col Grad	All Prv	Man-uf	Sr-vc		[d]Adj to Met	[e]On IH	[f]Cost Index	[g]Aggl-om
Nonmetro										
Upstate										
Gain	.25	.20	.81	.75	.73	115	5/8	5/8	.66	28
Lose	.24	.18	.77	.67	.69	82	7/10	3/10	.55	15
Downstate										
Gain	.26	.19	.71	.69	.63	88	7/9	6/9	.54	13
Lose	.24	.20	.78	.69	.63	92	1/4	1/4	.47	13
Other										
Gain	.31	.31	.67	.59	.72	121	1/3	1/3	1.19	43
Metro										
Gain	.29	.29	.86	.82	.81	132	10/11	10/11	1.12	86
Lose	.25	.22	.82	.74	.88	109	1/1	1/1	.76	65

Variable Designations:
[a] Hs Grad — Percent of high school only graduates in labor force.
Col Grad — Percent of College graduates in the labor force.

^{b} All Prv — $\dfrac{\text{Mean county wage in all private jobs}}{\text{Mean U.S. wage in all private jobs}}$

Manuf — $\dfrac{\text{Mean county wage in manufacturing (SIC Division)}}{\text{Mean U.S. wage in manufacturing}}$

Srvc — $\dfrac{\text{Mean county wage in services (SIC Division)}}{\text{Mean U.S. wage in services}}$

^{c} Tax Pc — Local taxes per person in county group county.

^{d} Adj to Met — Counties adjacent to metro county/ # of counties in group.

^{e} On IH — Counties located on interstate highway/counties in group.

^{f} Cost Index — $\dfrac{\text{Median rent in county area}}{\text{Median rent in U.S.}}$

^{g} Agglom — Number of employees per square mile.

Sources:

^{a} Calculated by authors using U.S. Bureau of the Census. *County and City Data Book*, 1983. U.S. Printing Office, Washington, DC 20402.

^{b} Calculated by authors using Bureau of Labor Statistics, U.S. Dept. of Labor, ES202 files on computer tape.

^{c} U.S Dept. of Agriculture, Economic Research Service.

^{d} Federal Reserve Bank, Philadelphia. Unpublished data.

^{e} Calculated from data from the Bureau of Labor Statistics and the U.S. Bureau of the Census, *City and County Data Book* and U.S. Dept. of Agriculture.

tended to have the highest wage rates and the greatest employment growth. This may reflect several facets of the local labor market. First, demand for labor may be growing faster than supply of labor at all wage rates in the metropolitan counties. Secondly, metropolitan counties have an industry mix that is more concentrated in high skill occupations than nonmetropolitan counties.

In contrast, the stagnant nonmetropolitan downstate counties that lost employment tended to have higher wages than the downstate gainers. Moreover, the "other nonmetropolitan" counties of Beaufort, Horry, and Sumter had the fastest rates of growth of all nonmetropolitan counties (e.g., Beaufort up 66% and Horry up 44% from 1978 to 1985) and the lowest relative wages of any region. The relative low wages of these three counties is most pronounced in the manufacturing sector where average wages were 59% of the national average. Thus the low wages in Beaufort, Horry, and Sumter counties is not merely an artifact of cheap labor in the service sectors of tourist related coastal activities. Recall from Table 1 that these three counties also lost manufacturing employment during 1978-1985. Apparently, even the very low wages in this region were not sufficient to stimulate manufacturing employment growth.

When evaluating labor costs across the state, it is important to remember that wages are a limited indicator of labor costs, since labor productivity can be equally important in establishing labor costs. For example, a person who earns $10 per hour and produces 20 units per hour is cheaper labor than a person earning $5 per hour but only producing five units per hour. Only if labor productivity is equal across the state is the relative wage comparison reasonable. In any event, low rural wage rates by themselves did not attract employers away from metropolitan areas of the state to the rural areas during the 1978-1985 period.

A third factor impacting gaining and losing counties in the state is location. Growth was more likely to occur in those counties located on an interstate highway and those counties adjacent to a metropolitan county.

A fourth factor often discussed in regard to economic growth is taxes. Per capita taxes tended to be highest in metropolitan and nonmetropolitan growth counties. Thus, low taxes by themselves do not appear to attract new private sector employment within the state. Quality of public services provided and the relative unimportance of property taxes to service based firms may be important considerations in this context.

State Policy Implications

Rural leaders are faced with an outlook for the traditional rural economic base that suggests that the transition to a new economic structure will be difficult.

While many of the forces behind economic change are beyond state and local control, there are important policy tools available to promote rural economic development. The two most important policy questions are:

1. How to improve the levels of education and skills of the labor force, and
2. How to improve the capacity of communities for long term planning, financing, and implementation of economic development programs.

The Human Capital Base in South Carolina. South Carolina needs a three-pronged effort to improve the human capital base in the state. The first part of that effort is to improve the basic literacy and quality of high school graduates through additional course offerings and standards for graduation. The state government has already taken positive steps in this direction. The ball is now in the court of the local school districts. The local school districts have quickly learned how to respond to the current set of state incentives for additional funding. For example, programs for the gifted and talented have been expanded as schools recognize the funding benefits of having more students in such programs. However, the local districts need to recognize that the state must serve statewide interests and that there will never be enough state funding to provide for the high quality curriculum expansion into mathematics, physical and social sciences that an excellent school system should provide.

State leaders should make it clear to local business and government officials that local revenue efforts are now needed to supplement the basic Education Improvement Act (EIA) program. One important step in this direction is to provide greater autonomy to local school districts to raise revenues and improve the quality of local school districts.

The second part of the effort for human capital enhancement should build on the experience and success of the post-secondary, vocational-technical training institutions in the state. For example, the Piedmont Technical School's program in robotics was cited in a report of the Southern Growth Policies Board as one of the region's exemplary technical training programs (Southern Growth Policies Board, 1986: 1). Unfortunately, there are only a handful of similar programs in South Carolina. More are needed. State leaders can play an important role in directing new training activities into regions of the state that are in greatest need for human capital retooling. However, a successful program at the technical schools will require a mastery of the fundamentals at the high school level. Some areas may require substantial boosts in the fundamentals before the technical training programs will be successful. Still, these programs draw a regional clientele and thus can be strategically placed in the state to draw on a qualified pool of trainees, while the fundamentals are emphasized in those parts of the region with this deficiency.

Careful attention to regional planning will help to use limited training funds most effectively. In particular, rural areas that have been hard pressed by manufacturing job losses and the depressed farm economy may be excellent candidates for new training programs by the technical schools. The Clemson University Extension Service might be used as a conduit for off-campus professional development programs and as a technical resource for education and training of Technical school staff.

Research and development at research universities is the third component of human capital enhancement. This effort rests on the notion that there is a significant spin-off between quality research at the university level and the ability of a state to prosper and adjust to economic change. Certainly, research and development activities are attracted to places with high quality university research. Moreover, the university environment may foster innovation in production technology and local entrepreneurship. Research funding in South Carolina has been insufficient to generate a large university-based research and development industry to date. It is apparent that industry leaders of the future will be looking more and more at "business climate" factors such as number of patents issued by state residents, scientific research papers per faculty member, university/business cooperative research agreements, venture capital for innovative technology, and others. These features of the university system take years to build, but have great potential for improving the competitive position of the state as a place where jobs are created rather than borrowed from high wage states before moving to even cheaper labor areas of the world. The jobs generated by spinoffs from high quality university research would most likely impact the metropolitan counties and rural counties adjacent to metropolitan areas first. However, we expect the long term impact of a research and development industry to be statewide.

Building Community Growth Capacity. In rural areas of the state, the problems faced by communities are severe. Limited tax bases and small numbers of development staff make these communities hard pressed to foster economic development. However, these places will need to maintain a quality public infrastructure if they are to prosper in the future. While new development increasingly may go toward the metropolitan counties and the larger urban places within rural regions, strategic planning by communities can help to assure their attractiveness as a place to live. Rural development policy may entail promoting rural regional growth centers. These are urban-industrial complexes in nonmetropolitan counties with good growth prospects based on the relative advantages of each rural region. This kind of rural development policy would target development efforts in these larger urban

269

areas within each rural region and encourage commuter access to these jobs, rather than promoting growth in each rural community. Rural places with good transportation access to growth centers can prosper as commuter towns and may eventually become growth centers. However, there is a real danger that the more remote, as well as the less assertive towns, will experience more socioeconomic stress as new jobs are created in the urban centers. Those least able to seek out employment in the growth centers may begin to concentrate in the declining places. Rural pockets of economic distress may become more prevalent. These places need special attention of state leaders and should be involved in a regional plan that promotes their economic vitality. While the tools to accomplish infrastructure expansion and improve management skills are well known, they will have to be used strategically to make the best use of the limited funds which will be available for economic development over the next decade in rural South Carolina.

Specifically, state leaders should consider a rural economic development strategy which identifies rural regions with growth centers that are capable of attracting and creating new economic activity. The State Development Board has recognized this problem and instituted a pilot study in the Marlboro county area. It plans to undertake a similar effort in the downstate. This is an important step by the Board and has potential as other agencies with expertise and interests in regional development make similar and hopefully coordinated efforts.

Infrastructure and technical assistance plans should be developed and implemented within each of these regions. These plans would identify areas where infrastructure and human capital investment would have the greatest payoffs in terms of economic development. We have identified two bands of nonmetropolitan counties — upstate and downstate — that require strategic planning for long term development. The precise location of state subsidies within each of these regions is likely to be dominated by the relative bargaining power of political subdivisions within each region. Our point is to have state leaders take a comprehensive view of the impact that they can have in promoting long term development in the state.

In planning for statewide economic development, it should be recognized that the metropolitan areas are in a relatively strong growth position. For these counties, state aid should accommodate development from the private sector. That is, sufficient support for infrastructure maintenance and human capital training is needed to maintain the attractiveness of these counties. However, most of the funding for these concerns in the metropolitan counties should be from the relatively large tax base that exists at the local level.

State planning and subsidies should be directed to rural areas that are lagging the metropolitan counties. The use of state funds to induce (as opposed to accommodate) private development in rural counties should be targeted to those places in the rural regions or even to communities in metropolitan counties that have significant private sector development potential. Commuter zones can be identified and the ability of growth centers to sustain the economic vitality of commuter towns examined. Pilot studies and actions are needed to test the efficacy of government-private cooperation in spreading development to the rural areas of the state. One such study might focus on how downstate counties can build on the rapid growth in Beaufort county. Orangeburg, as a growth center for a rural region for Calhoun, Barnwell, Bamberg and Allendale, could be evaluated.

The types of planning and development efforts described here will require time and resources. However, it appears that many rural areas are unlikely to grow under current and expected market trends without some type of rural development effort. A wait-and-see attitude for rural South Carolina will likely result in a widening of the economic gap and increased socioeconomic stress in the state.

Notes

[1] A Standard Metropolitan Statistical Area comprises one or more counties around a central city or urbanized area with 50,000 or more inhabitants. Contiguous counties are included if they have social and economic links with the area's population nucleus.

[2] The determination of urban-rural residence is made after census results have been tabulated. Geographic areas are classified as urban or rural according to population size and/or density at the time of the census. Urban population is defined as all persons residing in areas determined to be urbanized areas or in places of 2,500 or more outside urbanized areas. Rural population is that population not classified as urban. There can be both urban and rural territory within metro as well as nonmetro areas.

[3] Domination means, in this context, the basic economic sector most important to the county in generating personal income in that county. These county designations were first developed by the Economic Research Service of the U.S. Department of Agriculture and have been modified by the author. While the number of counties nationwide that are dominated by a farm or manufacturing base is about the same (600 or so each), the manufacturing based counties have about three times as many people and generate about three times the income of the farm counties. Furthermore, retirement and government based counties comprise about one-third the number of farm counties yet generate about the same level of personal income as the more numerous farm counties. Finally, an important national trend for rural America is the rapid growth of these retirement and government based counties. Over the 1980's, these counties are the only ones that have been able to keep pace with the metropolitan areas of the country. For details, see Henry M., M. Drabenstott and L. Gibson . "A Changing Rural America." *Economic Review,* Federal Reserve Bank of Kansas City. July/August, 1986.

[4] Once a person quits seeking employment for a given time period, he (she) is no longer considered to be in the labor force. Still, these discouraged potential labor force entrants may continue to reside in the state and can be considered the hidden unemployed. Such potential workers are most likely in areas of persistent high unemployment where new job offerings are rare and workers have become disguntled with the labor market option available. Unfortunately, the persistent high unemployment rate counties are the nonmetro counties in South Carolina. Accordingly, official unemployment statistics may underestimate the actual number of potential

workers without employment in nonmetro South Carolina.
[5]These data are from the Bureau of Labor Statistics, U.S. Dept. of Labor, ES-202 unemployment insurance files. Agricultural firms with fewer than 10 employees and most railroad employees are excluded. (See Bureau of Labor Statistics, U.S. Dept. of Labor "Employment and Wages Covered by Unemployment Insurance." *Handbook of Methods*, Vol. 1, Chapter 5.)
[6]McKenzie (1986) argues that this shift to a service economy is more apparent than real.

References

Bergman, E. et al. (1985). *Shadows in the Sunbelt.* Southern Growth Policies Board.

Bureau of Labor Statistics, U.S. Department of Labor (1988). "Employment and Wages Covered by Unemployment Insurance," chapter 5 in *Handbook of Methods,* Volume 1.

The Economist (1986). May 17: 75.

Henry, M., M Drabenstott and L. Gibson (1986). "A Changing Rural America." *Economic Review* (July/August). Federal Reserve Bank of Kansas City.

Malecki, E. (1986). "Entrepreneurship and Regional Development: A Preliminary Assessment of the Issues." Paper given at the North American Regional Science Association meeting, Columbus, Ohio, November 16.

McKenzie, R. and S. Smith (1986). "The Good News About U.S. Production Jobs." St. Louis, MO: Center for the Study of American Business, Washington University, Formal Publication No. 72, February.

South Carolina Budget and Control Board (1986). *South Carolina Economic Report.*

Southern Growth Policies Board (1986). "The Education of the Renaissance Technician." *Foresight* 4, 2 (Fall): 1.

15

Growth And Development In South Carolina

Harold B. Birch

"Now, here, you see, it takes all the running you can do, to keep in the
same place. If you want to get somewhere else, you have to run at least
twice as fast as that!"

The Red Queen to Alice in Lewis Carroll's
Through the Looking Glass

Introduction

South Carolina is changing. Even though the state's traditional "engines for
economic growth" in the first half of the 20th Century (textiles and
agriculture) are faltering, an increasingly diversified manufacturing community, a burgeoning timber industry, an expanding tourist business, and the
localized importance of defense spending offer opportunities for continued
growth of the state's economy.

Yet, as Lewis Carroll's "Red Queen" suggests, the state must work harder
if it is to make up for its historically low per capita income vis-a-vis the other
49 states. Still, hard evidence of the positive impact that economic changes
are having can be seen in increases in the state's population.[1] In-migration
from other regions of the country and a reversal of a longstanding trend of
out-migration provide tangible evidence that we are, indeed, experiencing
improved economic conditions compared to other sections of the country. In
the past 15 years population increases have exceeded those of the country as
a whole. Thus, the state's population is expected to increase 22% by the year
2000. As this increase occurs, the demographic make up of the state's
population shifts perceptibly on race and age between regions (Clements,
1987: 3).

Changing metropolitan skylines give visual proof of the vitality of the core

*Harold B. Birch is a faculty member in the Department of Government and International Studies
at the University of South Carolina.*

cities in some seven major urban areas in South Carolina. These areas are designated in the census data as "Metropolitan Statistical Areas" (MSAs), and the growth of satellite cities and affluent suburbs around the major core cities in these MSAs reflect the increased incomes and affluence in the state.

However, large numbers of citizens live in the small towns of the state where they continue to rely heavily on traditional sources of income provided by agriculture and the textile industry. Hidden away in the rural areas of the state is an all too numerous underclass that constitutes a rural-labor surplus. An aging and largely black community lives with the hope that a changing economy might somehow provide it with greater income opportunities. A trip to these areas presents a picture of hard-times that is in sharp contrast to the visual impression gained in the major cities.

South Carolina's political leaders now campaign on the basis of their ability to attract industry to the state. With apparent agreement among factions and among political parties as to the wisdom of this goal, the resultant governmental effort is directed towards the development of a network of public and quasi-public activities whose express purpose is working in concert with private interests to attract business and foster commercial and industrial development. Such efforts have apparent widespread bipartisan support, but how well they serve the various regions of the entire state and the various segments of society remains a matter of debate.

At the same time that efforts are underway to forge a stronger partnership between business and government, state and local governments are struggling to control and moderate the effects of growth. It is a precarious balancing act, encouraging growth while responding to citizens' complaints of encroachments on their rights.

In the inevitable clash of interests that arise out of these circumstances, governments attempt to serve the "public interest," even as they struggle to know what that interest is. Always under pressure to arbitrate between private and public interests, governments are beset by even greater pressure during periods of major change and transition such as South Carolina is currently undergoing. Understanding the complex role of government under these circumstances is a challenge.

This chapter takes on that challenge. It addresses the dual and sometimes conflicting roles of government — that of encouraging growth and development while at the same time struggling to shape and control it. Based on this examination, the chapter then provides a summary of major issues related to growth that will require political resolution in the immediate future. We begin by briefly tracing changes in the state's economy and the role that government has played in those changes.

Historic Changes In The State's Economy

There has been a slow evolutionary adjustment in the economy of the state as it has shifted from an agriculturally-based economy to one rooted primarily in manufacturing. Richard Ellson traces the recent details of this evolution in his chapter on "The Changing South Carolina Economy." Woven throughout any narrative of these shifts in the economy are evidences of governmental actions that indirectly or directly encouraged and fostered change. It is upon that facet of the changing economic circumstances that we want to focus.

From Agriculture to Textiles. South Carolina's economy continued from colonial times until the 1930s to be dominated largely by agriculture. As its importance since then has steadily declined, so has family reliance on the farm as a sole source of income. In 1960, for example, the state had 88,000 farms occupying 10 million acres. By 1983 there were only 31,000 farms comprising a total acreage of 5.9 million acres. By 1980 *only* 3% of the state's workforce was employed in agriculture (Clements, 1987: 11).

During the period immediately following the Civil War, northern industrialists saw the advantage in moving their textile industry south to be near the cotton fields and surplus labor. In part, because of state government's far-sighted provisions for inexpensive hydroelectric power, South Carolina by the 1920s had become the nation's top cotton-goods' producer. In the early 1930s when manufacturing at last surpassed agriculture as the top contributor to the state's economy, the textile industry dominated the manufacturing sector. (The term "textile industry" is used here to encompass the apparel industry which is sometimes separated for analytic purposes.) By 1940, the textile industry accounted for 71% of all manufacturing employment in the state (Employment Securities Commission, 1986: VI-25).

During World War II the discovery of a means of creating synthetic fibers attracted both chemical producers and synthetic fabric manufacturers to South Carolina. Their arrival reduced the demand for locally-produced cotton fiber. But, even as dependence on cotton shrank and the locus of cotton farming shifted westward, textile production continued to grow in economic importance in the state through the 1970s.

As a result of competition from foreign imports and development of new types of manufacturing equipment, the textile industry in the 1980s has been either consolidating its manufacturing activities in newer facilities in metropolitan areas or modernizing and reducing the workforces at those plants still operating in the smaller communities. The changes have left the citizens of those small towns and rural areas with a sense of bewilderment and abandonment. In the process, textile's share of the diversifying and growing manufacturing portion of the state's business economy has dropped from 15%

275

in the 1970s to 8% in the 1980s (Employment Securities Commission, 1986: III-15). Still, the industry's successes in modernizing and increasing its efficiency offer the hope that it will regain its former profitability and, in the process, expand its contribution to the state's economy.

Agriculture and textiles have profited by state government encouragement and investment. Even today they each, through their traditional constituencies, exert important influences within state government and selected local governments. The state continues to encourage agriculture as a critical part of its overall economy, and its political leadership persists in pushing for federal imposition of protective tariffs for the textile industry. It is, however, unlikely that either agriculture or textiles will ever again reach their previous share in the overall employment picture.

Tourism. Even as the state grew to rely more and more on textiles, the seeds for the development of a new facet of the economy were being sown by federal and state projects to construct hydroelectric dams. In addition to providing cheap electricity to private consumers and to textile manufacturing plants, the major impoundments of water resulting from the construction of dams in the 1930's and 40's created attractive sites for recreation. By the 1950s people from the southeastern United States had begun to flock to these lakes. Eventually, increased leisure, expanded disposable income, and added accessability made possible by a government-created interstate highway network combined to make these fresh-water lakes and the undeveloped and unspoiled South Carolina coast a magnet for tourists from as far away as the midwestern United States and eastern Canada.

Responding in 1967 to this opportunity, South Carolina created a major state agency: The Department of Parks, Recreation and Tourism (PRT). In their efforts to encourage tourism, PRT, the local Chambers of Commerce, and various private entrepreneurs cooperate in a national and international public relations campaign on behalf of South Carolina's tourist attractions. PRT logically combines this effort with the task of providing recreational opportunities for citizens of the state.[2]

The increasing growth in tourism, particularly in the coastal zone, has had a key impact on the state's employment patterns in the retail sector. And, according to the South Carolina Employment Securities Commission, tourism had, by the mid-80s, become *the* major contributor to the state's business economy (1986: VI-1).

Wood Products/Timber. While tourism is now the state's dominant economic activity, trees are the state's largest cash crop and provide the raw material for its third largest manufacturing activity; wood products. South Carolina now ranks 10th among the 50 states in total production of timber.

Land, much of which had once been marginal farmland, has now been transformed with federal and state government encouragement and assistance into forests which annually furnish over 485 million dollars in raw materials to the manufacturers of various wood products. In 1986, three billion dollars in wood products were produced by the industry in this state. Wood product manufacturers provide 30 thousand manufacturing jobs with a combined payroll of 625 million dollars (South Carolina Forestry Association, 1987: 1).

Today, two-thirds of the state's total acreage is forestland, half of which remains in private ownership. In turn, commercial timber and pulpwood companies, such as Union Camp, Georgia-Pacific, and Westvaco, own and manage about 2,500,000 acres. And, approximately 900,000 acres of land within the state are federally managed, largely by the U.S. Forest Service[3], for timber and other related uses (Southeastern Forest Experiment Station, 1986: 2).

In part, the growing importance of the production of lumber, pulp and paper, and wood products results from the availability of low-cost land, the low taxes on timber lands, the accessability of the terrain for mechanical timber harvesting, the climate and soil characteristics that contribute to the forests' favorable growth rates and the technical assistance and tree planting stocks provided by the federal and state governments.

Defense Spending. South Carolina ranked 43rd in 1986 in defense procurement dollar payments. However, in that year approximately 100 million dollars in major defense manufacturing contracts came to private firms in the state. Those federal dollars were spent on food processing, machine gun manufacturing and military ship and dock repair and construction (Department of Defense Fact Sheet, 1987: 1).

Even though the manufacture of war materials has not played a major role in the state's economy in peacetime, the state has been a major benefactor in terms of federal expenditures on military installations and, as a consequence, ranked 5th in defense personnel dollars. In all, in 1986, 1.8 billion dollars in payrolls were paid in the state to military personnel and civilians employed by the defense establishment. Another 440 million dollars in retirement checks went to the state's retired military community (Department of Defense Fact Sheet, 1987).

Not only do local businesses profit from the spending power of military and civilian employees of nearby military installations, but the six metropolitan areas where they are concentrated (Aiken and North Augusta, Beaufort, Charleston, Columbia, Myrtle Beach, and Sumter) also benefit from the construction work required in their modernization and from the attendant local contracting associated with the provisioning of the personnel at these installations. (See Pomeroy's chapter on South Carolina's Coastal Zone regarding Mendel River's contributions in the Charleston area.) Purchases of supplies, many of them locally procured, amounted to about 5 billion in 1986 (Department of Defense Fact Sheet, 1987).

The net effect of this infusion of defense monies into the state has been to both stimulate the local economies and to buffer them during recessions.

Changes in the Economy and Governmental Involvement. This brief summary of the historic shifts in the economy of South Carolina indicate that state and federal actions have frequently been the foundations upon which various sectors of the economy were advanced. We have mentioned the effects that: (1) the building of hydroelectric dams in the early part of the century had on textile manufacturing and on tourism; (2) the major tree planting efforts of the 1930s had on the wood-product industry; (3) the construction of interstate highways beginning in the 1960s had on tourism; and, (4) the building of military facilities in the post-Korean War era had on the general economic well-being of selected locations.

Having established some notion of the historic role of government in local economic development, it is appropriate to turn our attention to more recent governmental efforts designed to encourage economic change.

Governmental Stimulants to Development

As the foregoing section illustrates, historic actions by the national and state governments have stimulated, sometimes intentionally and sometimes inadvertently, economic development. The federal role in economic development has long been recognized as a legitimate activity, but as Edward M. Bergman says in the introduction to *Local Economies in Transition* (1986: 1), "It is now widely accepted that economic development has taken its place among the principal policy activities carried out at state and urban levels."

Federal government efforts to invest in public works or public infrastructure have historically been used during recessions to provide for employment. But in the 1980s, such investment has become part of a larger strategy used by governments at all levels to stimulate regional growth. At the same time, state and local governments, particularly in the Sunbelt, have adopted efforts to make their region more attractive by upgrading education and providing tax incentives to stimulate development.

Those efforts are capped by aggressive state and local government action in marketing their regions' attributes to would-be investors. In the following section we will examine these actions in South Carolina more closely.

Structural Stimulants to Development. In colonial South Carolina the economy and growth spread from the seaport settlements via the navigable rivers. In the early 19th Century, projects to extend the navigability of rivers became the focus of considerable governmental and private efforts as part of an effort to develop the economy of upcountry South Carolina.

With the advent of steam locomotion, the pattern of governmental and privately-sponsored development persisted in the expectation that it would guide and influence economic growth. The pattern repeated itself in the early days of the automobile when state government emphasized construction of farm-to-market, all-weather roads to provide an economic boost to the farmer.

Federal decisions and funding of the interstate highway system in the 1960s and 70s now reconfirms these historic lessons about the importance of a transportation infrastructure as a guide to growth. Today, the interstate highway system, the single most ambitious public works program in the history of the nation, has dramatically changed patterns of growth and economic development.

Evidence of the effects of the interstates are to be seen nationwide in the development of so-called strip cities. These linear clusters of urban and suburban developments may be best observed in upstate South Carolina in the still-developing patterns of urbanization along the interstate between Charlotte, NC, and Atlanta, GA.[4]

At the state and local level, intrastate development is stimulated by provisions for major connecting roads, airport construction, and seaport development. At the micro-level, governmental decisions over the establishment of sewage systems, construction of water mains and the provisions for electricity also control and direct growth. Zoning, subdivision regulations and provisions of fire and police protection further "fine tune" this growth.

Local government has also come to recognize the importance of particular structural developments that make the area more attractive to the investors. Decisions with respect to such locally financed efforts as civic centers, convention centers, and athletic coliseums, to name but a few, are made both in the name of serving public wants and the long-term impacts on the local economy. For example, the construction of The Koger Center for the Performing Arts in Columbia is being financed by various local governments and the University of South Carolina on the premise that it encourages economic investment in the region and serves the desires of local residents for cultural activities.

Other Public Programs That Shape Development. State and local governments' development efforts are not limited to decisions about transportation infrastructure, services and structural facilities. Two of the less tangible but nevertheless important aspects of economic development strategies here in South Carolina, tax incentives and education, are worthy of mention. A third program of significant importance is the effort to market the state's attributes.

It too will be noted here.

Tax Incentives. Among other attractions, governments may encourage industry to relocate by means of tax incentives which take any of three forms. They can be in the form of low taxes, a tax abatement, or the abolition of taxes for a given period. In addition to the tax incentives, states may provide financial incentives using grants; loans; and interest subsidies, i.e., direct subsidies, loan guarantees, industrial revenue bonds, general revenue bonds and equity and near-equity financing (Phillips, 1987: 5-41).

South Carolina has three tax-related incentives it offers potential investors. They include property tax exemptions, liberalization of the rules on corporate income tax deductions, and two sales tax exemptions. As it now operates, the state provides incentives in the form of a so-called "New Jobs Tax Credit" to an industry for locating in one of the state's 19 "distressed counties." For those industries creating 18 or more jobs in one of these counties, there is a 500 dollar per employee tax credit during the first five years of operation (Walsh and Wheeland, 1981: 2-3).

The cost of services provided by government to such industries during the period of a tax reduction is borne by the taxpaying public. The procedure is justified, however, on the premise that "a rising tide raises all boats" and that taxpayers will ultimately recoup their tax contribution in the economic benefits provided by the new industry. Whether that is always so is a matter of some debate.

Education. In 1981, the Southern Growth Policies Board pointed out in its annual report that "poor students make poor workers" and that "For the South, this relationship between economic productivity and cognitive capacity is truly significant. The quality of life for today's Southern children relates directly to the future quality of the Southern region and to its economic vitality" (Southern Growth Policies Board, 1981: 8).

South Carolinians who push for economic vitality have accepted the Southern Growth Policies Board premise. In 1984, under the leadership of Governor Richard Riley, the state made a concerted effort to rectify its dismal record in public education in the form of the Educational Improvement Act. In large measure the legislation was sold to the political decision makers on its importance to economic development. (See Kearney's and Peterson's Chapter, "Public Education Policy" for a thorough discussion of the Educational Improvement Act.)

The new "high-tech" age, however, demands not only secondary school graduates with traditional academic skills but also workers with technical and job-related educations. The state boasts of its ability to meet industries' needs by providing, at state expense, employee training through the statewide Technical and Comprehensive Education system (TEC). In the 1970s, state Senator John West, an early proponent of the TEC system who later became

Governor, envisioned it as a means of overcoming the functional illiteracy of nearly one-third of the state's citizens and as a magnet for industries looking for a skilled workforce (West, 1987).

Training programs are now undertaken at sixteen permanent TEC campuses located within easy commuting distances of all of the state's citizens. These programs are reputed to have made a difference in numerous corporate decisions to move to the state. Whatever their past influence, their importance was never more apparent than in the recently successful effort to attract Mack Trucks Inc. to Fairfield County.

Among the drawing cards that many states use in attracting industry are those furnished by the presence of major research universities within their boundaries. Universities train new personnel for the high-tech industries, permit professional-level employees to improve existing skills, and provide faculty researchers whose knowledge can be capitalized upon by industry. In addition, they enhance the attractiveness of the industry as an employer by offering the potential employees' families first-class educational and cultural opportunities. Persuasive arguments are being made by the leadership of South Carolina's major universities for much greater state investment in higher education as a strategy for encouraging economic development.

Once tangible and intangible magnets for development are put in place, marketing them to assure the most suitable investors are attracted seems a logical next step for governments.

Beating the Drum for Development. Traditionally, Chambers of Commerce have mounted major efforts to attract business and industry in an effort to expand their own business interests. As pointed out earlier, in more recent years both state and local governments have also taken an increasingly active part in such efforts. In South Carolina, the State Development Board has become the key governmental actor in this process.

But, the new emphasis on economic development may, in fact, represent "old wine in new bottles" in so far as state involvement in economic development is concerned. Created in 1959, the State Development Board can trace its ancestry to the State Planning Board which was formed in 1938 and to the Planning Board's successor, the Department of Research and Planning, which was founded in the closing days of World War II with a mandate to shape the state's economic adjustment to the peacetime economy.

Since its creation, the State Development Board has been involved in a cooperative effort with the state's major utility companies, banks, and the State Chamber of Commerce to encourage growth. Initially, the Development Board was asked to recruit industry and to provide assistance to companies interested in moving to the state. But since the Technical Education Systems' (TEC's) creation in the mid-1970s, it has shared primacy with the Board for these activities.

281

The Development Board has, for its part, now added state-wide economic planning responsibilities to its charter. Further, the state now has a Coordinating Council for what has become a complex network of ten or more state agencies currently charged with various aspects of economic development. This total system has been likened to "a de facto Department of Commerce" by some observers (Phillips, 1987: 5-31).

The public's new-found enthusiasm for the state's involvement in economic development is recognized by Governor Carroll Campbell. His January, 1988, "State of the State" address highlighted the state's efforts in this regard, indicating that they had been rewarded by what he termed "extraordinary success in economic development," a "capital investment for 1987 (that) hit a five-year high," and "foreign investment (that) set an all-time record." In that address the Governor clearly sought to link his vision of progress for the people of the state to continued economic development. Simply put, his argument is that with a larger pie, everybody gets a bigger piece.

There can be little doubt, however, that the powerful business community support for the Board which has developed over the years and the congruence of the interests of the Board with that of the the state's executive leadership have ensured that the State Development Board has a dominant voice in shaping the state's strategy concerning economic development. Until the early 1970s, the Board's basic strategy was one of trying to attract industries from the north and midwest. In turn, those industries were expected to act as engines for economic development. In more recent years the Board has mounted a major effort to attract foreign investors. Today, South Carolina is among the top five states in direct per capita foreign investment, and in 1987, foreign investment in the state amounted to 37.5% of all new capital investments.

But, the whole strategy of attracting outside investors has not been without its doubters. In March of 1987, *The State* newspaper highlighted this argument by citing economist David Birch, Director of the Program on Neighborhood and Regional Change at the Massachusetts Institute of Technology, as presenting evidence that the local entrepreneurs and not big business or foreign investors are, and should be, the primary source of growth.[5] In an extension of this argument, Birch has since claimed to have documented that nationally, fewer and fewer firms are relocating and, by inference, that governments should be encouraging "homegrown" development (1987: 53-54).

As Earle and Merle Black (1987: 23-24) argue, typically, growth in the South has been controlled in such a fashion as to maintain a traditionalistic culture, with careful emphasis on continued control by the established business and economic elites. Perhaps *The State* newspaper merely reflects the concerns of the existing elite, an elite which found voice in a University of South Carolina Business School Research document which set forth a premise that:

> . . . the most stable economic development policy is one that encourages local control through the establishment of companies headquartered within the state, and that the best way to achieve this goal is to seed those potential companies through an enterprise development program — in other words to "grow our own" companies (Phillips, 1987: 5-31).

Naysayers to outside investment do not seem to be winning in what appears to be a "no-holds-barred" effort by the state to recruit outsiders, even though the state has recently created a Business Assistance Office to help local entrepreneurs. In addition, the Governor has proposed legislation intended to attract corporate and regional headquarters of the out-of-state interests. Success in such an effort would not only bring in new capital, but by establishing the "main offices" in the state, it would counter some of the objections to outsiders' control over local enterprises.

Leaders in the state's economic development effort have adopted an eclectic approach. The current Governor seems to have found a theme which strikes a popular chord with most sectors of the state's population. Beating the drum for economic development is high on everyone's political agenda in state and local government.

Encouraging Development. Earlier we examined the historic actions of the private and public sector that wittingly or unwittingly contributed to growth. We have just concluded a closer examination of planned strategies to encourage economic development and pointed out that such efforts now rank high on the agenda of most state and local governments.

However, at the same time they engage in strategies to attract growth, governments are also faced with coping with its negative impacts. We now turn our attention to that aspect of growth and development in South Carolina.

Controlling and Coping with Growth

We have been addressing proactive steps on the part of state government to encourage growth. There is, however, a reactive side to government actions; i. e., a series of regulatory provisions largely prescribed by state laws which provide authority for county and municipal governments' actions. They, in turn, act in a decentralized fashion to cope with, control, or channel the often unintended and negative consequences of development and population growth.

Here we can only briefly sketch the actions of government designed to moderate these "spillovers" from growth. But among the more important aspects of state and local government efforts to cope with these side effects are: (1) the legislative provisions for dealing with the fragmentation of local government, a condition caused by the incremental creation of new units of government in growth areas; (2) the efforts needed to cope with the infringement of new development on neighboring property owner rights; and, (3) the creation of agencies designed to protect the environment that is threatened by unregulated industrial activities and development.

Restructuring Government to Deal With Growth. Annexation and consolidation are two tools employed by local governments to manage an ever-increasing fragmentation of political authority in rapidly growing areas. Small units of local government complicate the process of providing services, limit local governments' ability to practice economies of scale, and limit efforts to deal with problems created in one jurisdiction that have unforeseen spillover effects on neighboring jurisdictions. Annexation of adjacent smaller political units by core cities or consolidation of numerous political units holds out the promise of greater efficiency and avoids the problems of coordination found to arise between small, fragmented, and often overlapping political jurisdictions.

However, according to Kearney (1983: 1) and Lyon (1987), annexation is used relatively infrequently in South Carolina because of the state's conservative annexation laws. According to these sources, the major opponents of change are:

1. The local electric cooperatives which face the potential loss of parts of their service area if they were absorbed by a city.
2. The special-purpose districts which face loss of their tax base or, worse yet, dissolution if their entire service area were to be absorbed by a city.
3. Locally-based citizen groups who are afraid annexation will subject them to higher taxes.
4. Industries that are self-reliant and, hence, have no need of the services provided by the major political jurisdictions.[6]

In view of the formidable opposition to more liberalized provisions for annexation generated by coalitions of these interests, it is easy to understand why the efforts to ease provisions for annexation have repeatedly met such ignoble ends in the South Carolina General Assembly.

In some states urbanized counties merge with the core city to form a single government. No provision for such "consolidation" exists in South Carolina legislation despite the fact that voters have previously approved use of such a procedure in a statewide referendum. But, one alternative is a consolidation of functional services, such as those that deal with recreation, detention facilities, or emergency-preparedness planning. Such efforts do not require a direct citizen vote and are generally permitted under state legislation.

Some efforts at this functional consolidation have met with success. For example, beginning in 1984, Richland County contracted with the city of Columbia to provide fire protection for the County. The County assesses it residents for this and then pays the city for the service. Beaufort and Beaufort County have consolidated personnel departments, recreation activities and the jails. Sumter and Sumter County have consolidated their recreation departments.

Critics of the state's conservative annexation laws and the lack of consolidation authority point to North Carolina's less-restrictive procedures and the consequent growth of its major cities. By capitalizing on these laws, Charlotte, North Carolina, for example, has become a city with a population about equal to that of the population in the entire Columbia area MSA. Charlotte's political power within the state and region is enhanced by its size. Because of its overarching responsibilities in the region, Charlotte is in a better position to coordinate the economic growth within its boundaries and to provide more economically efficient services which, it is argued, encourage even more growth.[7]

Protecting the Property Owner and the Public Interest. Zoning, subdivision regulation, and building codes designed to control and guide growth are based on common law and a 1926 U.S. Supreme Court decision that they are an exercise of the inherent police powers of government in protecting health, safety, or the public welfare (*Euclid v. Ambler,* 1926). Their use is generally welcomed by realtors, homeowners and environmentalists, while some developers and businessmen struggle to overturn existing arrangements. In any event, no matter who the participants, Americans hold very dear their belief in their rights to unrestricted use of private property, and the zoning process is frequently marked by emotional, highly-charged political free-for-alls.[8]

In South Carolina, passage of the *Comprehensive Planning Act of 1967* (sec. 14-350.16 et seq., S.C. Code) provided authority to all municipalities and counties for planning to guide growth and the subsequent creation of a zoning procedure. Prior to passage of that legislation, authority to use zoning was limited to a few major municipalities and urban counties. Until 1984, only eleven counties in South Carolina had completely or partially zoned under the authority provided them by the state.

Zoning involves the designation of permissible uses of land and the subsequent enforcement of those uses. The procedure provides for the orderly adjustment of such designated uses as community needs and circumstances change. Local government officials act in public sessions to consider petitions for zoning changes. At that point they consider the degree to which the zoning changes conform to a master plan. They also entertain public expressions of opposition to specific changes in zoning.

Zoning, used as a means of community control over disruptive growth, is a disjointed effort without some master plan. In the 1976 *County Planning Act* (Sec. 4-27-10 et seq., S.C. Code) the South Carolina General Assembly provided guidelines to counties for the development of and provisions for the update of these comprehensive plans. The comprehensive plans are intended to provide a guide for spatial development and direct the orderly development of transportation networks, sewage and water lines, and commercial utilities. But, legislators in South Carolina have backed away from making it a requirement that zoning conform to the comprehensive plan. And, although courts may on occasion look to the plan in an effort to solve zoning questions that reach their jurisdiction, comprehensive planning in this state serves only as a loose guide to growth and development.

The political decision makers are, nevertheless, under pressures to act on rational planning goals in their zoning decisions. The political process also puts these officials in a position where they may find it difficult to say, "no" to powerful developer interests. In the face of these conflicting tensions, professional planners' best efforts at developing comprehensive plans that will guide growth to the best advantage of the "public interest" are often thwarted. Nonetheless, there is evidence that in areas of South Carolina where development poses clear environmental threats, planners do have a great number of successes in having their specific concerns heard by political decision makers (Birch, 1984: 150-162).

Key State Activities Created to "Protect" The Environment. As a direct result of growth and development, a number of new state agencies were created within the last 20 years to act in protecting the public interest in conservation and environmental matters. These include the Water Resources Commission (WRC), the Land Resources Conservation Commission (LRCC), the Department of Health and Environmental Control (DHEC) and the Coastal Council.

As the name suggests, the Water Resources Commission is responsible for formulating a comprehensive water policy with a view to assuring proper and effective management of the state's water resources. That charter requires that the agency collect data on availability and use of subsurface and ground water, as well as to involve it in matters relating to flooding and preservation of scenic river systems.

The Land Resources Commission traces its lineage to the State Soil and Water Conservation Commission created in the 1930s. Its transformation in the 1970s to The Land Resources Commission can be traced in large measure to an effort by the state to be prepared to capitalize on what appeared to be a major federal grants program intended to encourage state-level comprehensive land-use planning. However, repeated federal efforts in the early 1970s to pass legislation that would have funded state planning and shifted such efforts from the local to the state level failed. A powerful anti-land-use-planning coalition blocked passage of this federal legislation, and the state's LRCC charter expanded only marginally from that of its 1930s-era parent agency. More specifically, the charter expanded to include responsibilities relating to mining and mine reclamation. Still, the agency, in its research agenda, has maintained an interest in the larger issues of land use in the state.

In a consolidation of older public health agencies, DHEC was created in 1976 and given a broad new charter with wide-ranging responsibilities for public health and regulatory programs designed to protect the air and water from dangerous pollutants of both a chemical and radiological nature. (See Kearney's chapter on "Radioactive Waste Policy" relative to the disproportionate role of South Carolina in matters relating to the latter pollutant.) Given its broad charter, it is one of the key agencies that must approve new industrial activities that locate within the state. It has responsibilities for monitoring and controlling the discharge of industrial wastes from existing facilities into either the air or into streams and rivers. The agency also encourages and monitors local governments in their efforts to clean up the environment.

As it is, certain responsibilities are split between these three major state agencies which are concerned with the state's natural resources. For example, WRC is responsible for devising methods to alleviate or circumvent problems related to groundwater, yet DHEC has both a Bureau of Water Supply and a Bureau of Water Pollution Control that must deal with many of the same problems. LRCC has responsibilities for mining and mine reclamation, yet DHEC controls hazardous waste management or water pollution and must, of necessity, deal with the effects of mine tailings that often contaminate ground water. And, if that were not enough, both agencies' interests further overlap with the WRC's interests in ground water.

Some states, such as Georgia and North Carolina, have found it more appropriate to combine the major functions of these three agencies into a single "umbrella" agency. Pressures are mounting among those interested in economic development to rationalize the permitting structure within state government. Such interests are now exerting political pressures on the general assembly to rationalize the structure of these state agencies.

Physical development along the coast is controlled to some degree through the planning and zoning process as used by the local governments of the eight counties adjacent to the ocean. A state agency, The Coastal Council, was created in 1977 by the South Carolina *Coastal Tidelands and Wetlands Act* in response to the explosive development along the coast and to federal encouragement in the form of the *Coastal Zone Management Act*. (See Pomeroy's chapter entitled "South Carolina's Coastal Zone: Finding a Balance Between Man and Nature" for a description of the clash between the dynamic nature of the coast's biological and physical processes and the growing population of the coastal area.)

The Coastal Council provides for the creation and implementation of a comprehensive management program to be used for development in the "critical areas" in those eight coastal counties. The "critical areas" over which the council has jurisdiction consist of: (1) the land seaward from the primary ocean-front dune or the highest advance of the ocean waves; (2) the salt marshes; and, (3) tidelands.[9]

The Coastal Council has established a system of permits to control development on or forward of the primary dunes and to restrict efforts to fill, dredge, or construct dikes in the state-owned salt marshes or tidelands. These actions were taken in hopes of minimizing the erosion of the beaches which are a major attraction of the area. At the same time, restrictions on dike construction and land-fill operations are intended to stop destruction of the tidal areas. These areas serve as a source of the nutrients which are at the head of the food chain that supports the state's off-shore ocean fisheries.

Even as the limitations seem to thwart the efforts of many developers, state government action protects the long-term interests of residents of the area, tourist-related businessmen, fishermen, and seafood industry owners and workers. Because of the impressive growth in the coastal region and the fantastic short-term profits which motivate developers in the region, it is probably the most controversial and dynamic regulatory effort currently being undertaken by South Carolina state government. It has been suggested that even this agency might better and more efficiently perform its regulatory functions if it were part of a consolidated Department of Natural Resources and if the definition of critical areas over which it has jurisdiction were expanded to the landward. Even as this is being written, the General Assembly is seriously considering legislation which would extend jurisdiction of the state in the coastal zone!

Looking to the Long Term. The 1970s were progressive years in which significant provisions for governmental structure and regulatory powers were put in place by the General Assembly to enable the state to cope with and control the negative effects of development. The continued pressures of growth and increasing rate of change only now suggest the wisdom of those efforts. However, economic development and population growth will require added major adjustments before the end of this century. We need to look more closely at issues that will call forth such changes.

Issues Triggered by Continued Growth

Growth will bring both problems and opportunities to the people of South Carolina. State and local governments will be faced with a number of issues, including growth of government and political diversity, strains because of an increasing gap between "haves" and "have-nots" that is regional in nature, increasing threats to the environment and aesthetics, shifts in the demographic make-up of the citizenry with attendant changes in demands for services, financing of new programs and services, and rehabilitation of areas by-passed by economic growth. How governments deal with these issues will help shape the future just as patterns of government action, intermingled with private initiatives, have historically contributed to the state's past growth and development.

Major growth and proliferation of local political units along the coast and around the state's major cities will add to the burdens of state government concerning intergovernmental matters. At the same time, new job opportunities in the public sector for citizens with the appropriate skills and education will be created. The push for privatization of an increasing number of governmental functions in these expanding governmental units will also provide opportunities for the private sector to establish service industries capable of carrying out some of the activities that have traditionally been performed by local government.

Growth and economic diversification in the state will lead to greater political pluralism. A greater variety of interests will put increased pressures on state and local governments to meet differing needs. Faced with increased economic complexity and an increasingly heterogeneous population, government involvement at the state level, in particular, will grow to meet these needs. At the same time, those concerned with economic growth will push for simplification of procedures and organizational structure in government.

The continued economic prosperity and growth of the major cities will pose increased problems of equity within the state as residents in rural communities become relatively more disadvantaged. Political leaders will be challenged to find ways of solving these economic disparities. Pressures on the state to encourage outside investments to help solve these problems are not likely to diminish, notwithstanding concerns by important segments of the community opposed to outside investment and concern over their subsequent loss of influence.

The pressures on government institutions concerned with the environment will increase as technology presents society with a plethora of new processes to be monitored. Kearney addresses the issue of nuclear waste in his chapter, "Radioactive Waste Policy," but that is only one of the conflicts that will intensify as diverse industrial development continues. Illustration of this may be seen by considering the use of commercial chemicals, as in the furor over the use of cyanide for gold mining in Fairfield County. In the 1980s, the American Chemical Society's list of distinctly new chemical compounds has been growing by five thousand a week. The reality of such innovation is that the diverse manufacturing activities attracted to the state will inevitably employ new substances in manufacturing that will present hazardous and toxic effects that are, as yet, unknown.

Lacking basic zoning provisions, many communities are in a poor position to cope with growth when it comes. Even those with zoning ordinances may not be using the procedure to its fullest. Only one of the eleven counties that in 1984 employed county-wide zoning used performance zoning; a procedure that weighs the effects of the proposed change on the environment and establishes the "carrying capacities" of the land. Performance zoning is a more progressive approach that, if adopted, would serve other urbanized and growing counties. At the same time, lack of state authorization to employ contract zoning, a procedure that allows political decision makers to hold land users to their promises, unnecessarily hinders enforcement of existing zoning decisions, although the planning community is increasingly relying on "Planned Development Districts" as a way of assuring that developers build exactly what they have said they planned to build.

Unrestricted growth of the cities, suburbs, and industries threatens to take forest land and prime farmlands near major cities out of production. This phenomenon occurs as developers, in search of cheaper land and lower costs, leapfrog beyond the existing suburban areas and create a patchwork of sprawling developments and new political jurisdictions. The process creates new costs for government services and uses land that might otherwise remain productive forest or farmland. Elsewhere, states have given added authority to local governments to constrain such growth. South Carolinians, in the face of continued growth, may need to consider the wisdom of such action even as it flies in the face of dearly held beliefs in the sanctity of private property rights.

We have established some understanding of the effects of major population increases. We have, however, only mentioned the projected changes in the age composition of that expanding population. But, in-point-of-fact, several authoritative sources predict that by the year 2000, the percentage of the population over 65 and those over 75 will each have grown by several percentage points in the state. At the same time, the age group below 44 years of age will have decreased by 4%. Clements (1987) warns that these circumstances will impact negatively on tax revenues, demands for services, and patterns of consumption. (See Pomeroy's observations in his chapter entitled "South Carolina's Coastal Zone" regarding such demographic shifts in the coastal areas brought on, in part, by an influx of retirees.)

The regional distribution of older citizens within the state is difficult to predict, even as it is apparent that the coast will attract more than its share. Conceivably, an added burden already rests on those counties and small municipalities now suffering from economic stagnation. The young leave these communities for opportunities elsewhere. These rural communities are then left without an adequate source of able workers, and the cycle of poverty perpetuates itself. Imbalances in age groups further raise problems as to the vitality of the community in dealing with its aging population and pose problems in ability of the tax-paying public to provide locally-funded services for the elderly.

The financing of governmental services will increasingly become a problem in the major cities. Citizens in urbanized areas will place even greater demands on the state and local governments. In particular, municipalities surrounded by separate political entities that function as bedroom communities for highly paid executives employed in the central cities will begin to chafe at the cost of services provided those commuters. Some means of resolving the inequities of the situation beyond simply consolidating functions will have to be found if the annexation and consolidation avenues are not opened. Efforts to rejuvenate the inner cities and fight the trend of retailers abandoning them for suburban shopping centers have begun, but the problem is by no means resolved. Shopping centers draw off the retail trade to the suburbs and important tax contributions to the inner city are lost. The consequences are that the inner city, used during office hours, is virtually abandoned at night. Efforts to attract suburbanites to urban high-rise apartments, outsiders to convention centers, and regional residents to sports and cultural events at civic auditoriums help, but citizen dependence on the automobile complicates efforts at rejuvenation. The era of the modern, high-speed mass transit system has not yet overtaken the cities in South Carolina, but eventually, provisions for such systems must be addressed if the inner cities are truly to survive the physical growth of the surrounding communities.

We leave the question of the types of government institutions or the specifics of legislation needed to cope with these problems to others. The private sector will be reacting to them too. The interaction of government and private actions will undoubtedly produce some seemingly unpredictable outcomes. Yet, the public sector, no less than the private sector, must engage in long-range planning if South Carolinians are to improve both their quality of life and their economic well-being.

Conclusion

Even as we examined those circumstances that surround governmental involvement in development and growth, we should have been reminded of the political nature of the entire decision-making process by which such involvement is set in motion. The forces that shape government actions give meaning to Harold Lasswell's (1936) thesis in his famous book on politics entitled *Politics: Who Gets What, When and How.*

Government actions are shaped by groups seeking either assistance or protection for their interests. At their best, choices by government officials serve both those private interests and the interests of the general public. But, in the process, those who cannot or do not represent themselves and their interests are often neglected. As we concern ourselves with economic development, we must also show some concern for the political process that shapes that development. We are, after all, concerned about social justice as well as an improved state economy. As the 1981 Commission on the Future of the South said in its report to the Southern Growth Policies Board, economic development policies are supposed to benefit people, not institutions.

South Carolina does show much evidence of having an increasingly strong economy that serves many private interests, just as it serves the general public interest. In the Red Queen's words, the state is running twice as fast in its efforts to catch up and improve the Palmetto State's relative economic standing among the 50 states. As it does, the population and economic interests will become increasingly more diversified. This will put heavier and heavier demands on government. Therefore, we can expect to see major changes in state and local government structure and procedures in the next twenty years as we struggle both to encourage growth and to control it.

Notes

[1]The population of South Carolina increased by 20.5% between the 1970 and 1980 census. South Carolina, with some 3,121,820 residents in the 1980 census, ranked 26th in population among the 50 states and 40th in total land area. The Bureau of the census estimates that by 1985 this had risen to 3,347,000 or a 7% increase, a rate somewhat in excess of the rate for the country as a whole.

[2]The state currently has about 74,000 acres (0.4% of total state acreage) devoted to state parks and recreation areas and in 1986 drew 9.1 million visitors (Park View, 1987).

[3]In all, the Federal government owns about 6% (1,176,000 acres) of the total acreage in South Carolina. This includes National Forest and military reservations where timber is raised and sold, as well as national wildlife refuges and National Park land where timbering is normally not permitted (S.C. Statistical Abstract, 1986: 226).

[4]This type of development is most pronounced in the Northeast in the corridor between Boston and Washington where the continous urban area has been dubbed "Boswash" by some students of the phenomenon.

[5]A survey conducted in 1985 by the consulting firm of Touche Ross & Co. of 209 mayors of U.S. cities with populations of 30,000 and over revealed that 80% of those mayors believed that small business is more important to a city's overall economic health than is big business.

[6]The effects of this are to be observed in the Spartanburg area where textile plants exist in tiny enclaves not part of the surrounding political jurisdiction.

[7]South Carolina's population grew at twice the rate of North Carolina's between 1970 and 1980. But the Columbia, S.C., population decreased by a very small percentage while the Charlotte, N.C. population grew 30%.

[8]The U.S. Constitution of 1787 established a standard which governs reasonableness and fairness of the exercise of police power. These Constitutional protections assure provisions for due process, equal protection, and protection against unreasonable takings. Court interpretation

of these guarantees have generally established the limits on the practical exercise of these traditional growth controls.

⁹The state is viewed in its statutes as a successor to the Crown in ownership of these lands, except where individuals can trace ownership from a colonial grant or to a valid grant from the state.

References

Bergman, Edward M., ed. (1986). *Local Economies in Transition: Policy Realities and Development Potentials.* Durham, NC: Duke University Press.

Birch, David (1987). "The Q Factor." *INC* 9, 4: 53-54.

Birch, Harold B. (1984). *An Appraisal of Traditional Land Use Control in South Carolina.* Columbia, SC: Unpublished Dissertation, The University of South Carolina.

Black, Earl and Black, Merle (1987) *Politics and Society in the South.* Cambridge, MA: Harvard University Press.

Clements, Jeffrey R. (1987). *Roles and Relationships: South Carolina Government in the Year 2000.* Columbia, SC: The South Carolina Advisory Commission on Intergovernmental Relations (January).

Department of Defense Fact Sheet (1987). "Federal Expenditures in South Carolina."

Environmental Quality: The Ninth Annual Report of The Council on Environmental Quality, (1978). Washington, DC: Government Printing Office.

Kearney, Richard C. (1983). "Municipal Annexation in South Carolina." *Public Affairs Bulletin* (May). Columbia, SC: The Bureau of Governmental Research and Service, University of South Carolina.

Lasswell, Harold (1936). *Politics: Who Gets What, When and How.* New York: McGraw-Hill.

Lyon, Bob (1987). SC Municipal Association, Interview June 12, 1987. 1529 Washington St. Columbia, S.C.

Park View (1987). Division of State Parks, PRT Columbia, S.C.

Phillips, William H. et al (1987). *South Carolina: An Economy in Transition.* Columbia, S.C.: Division of Research, College of Business Administration, University of South Carolina.

South Carolina Employment Security Commission, (1987). "South Carolina Labor Market Review, 1986." Columbia, S.C.

South Carolina Forestry Association (1987). Fact Sheet, "Economic and Tax Data for the Timber Industry in South Carolina." Columbia, S.C.

Southeastern Forest Experiment Station (1986). Fact Sheet, "Forest Resource Statistics for South Carolina." Asheville, N.C.

"South Carolina Statistical Abstract", (1986). Columbia, S.C: South Carolina Budget and Control Board, Division of Research and Statistical Services.

Southern Growth Policies Board (1981). "Southern Growth: Report of the Task Force on the Southern Economy." Dallas, TX: Center for Policy Studies, University of Texas.

The State Newspaper (1987) "Reasons Why Cities Succeed: Fastest Growing Cities in U.S. Also have Highest Taxes." (March): Business Section. Columbia, S.C.

Village of Euclid v. Ambler Realty Co. (1926). 272 U.S. 394.

West, John (1987). Governor of South Carolina 1971-75. Interview, June 25, 1987. Columbia, S.C.: The University of South Carolina.

Walsh, Susan Murphy and Wheeland, Craig M., (1981). "Tax Incentives for Industry in South Carolina". Columbia, SC: *Public Affairs Bulletin* published by The Bureau of Governmental Research and Service, The University of South Carolina.

For Reference

Not to be taken from this room